MANY SUBTLE CHANNELS

many subtle

In Praise of Potential Literature

channels

DANIEL LEVIN BECKER

HARVARD UNIVERSITY PRESS   Cambridge, Massachusetts

London, England   2012

Library of Congress Cataloging-in-Publication Data
Levin Becker, Daniel.
  Many subtle channels : in praise of potential literature /
Daniel Levin Becker.
      p.   cm.
  Includes index.
  ISBN 978-0-674-06577-2 (alk. paper)
  1. Oulipo (Association).   2. Literary form.   3. Levin Becker,
Daniel.   4. Authors, American—21st century—Biography.   I. Title.
  PQ22.O8B35   2012
  840.9'11—dc23   2011044577

For Elaine,
who doesn't entirely buy it
but is willing to listen anyway

CONTENTS

III FUTURE

A NOTE ON FORMATTING

In keeping with French standards of demonymy, the word *oulipian* is capitalized here only when it refers to a person: Georges Perec was an Oulipian, but his output was (for the most part) oulipian. For the sake of consistency, the same applies to *surrealist* and the ever-maddening *'pataphysical*. (The apostrophe is explained in note 8 of the chapter "Imaginary Solutions.")

The proper name of the workshop in question is OuLiPo, but in order to reduce strain on your eyes and my shift key I have rendered it as *Oulipo* after its first mention. (I cut this corner with the security of many years of precedent; for example, nobody writes out "U.S.A. P.A.T.R.I.O.T. Act"—and thank goodness, because the actual acronym is odious.) On the other hand, quasi-affiliated workshops such as the OuBaPo and the OuPhoPo remain formatted as you see them here, for the sake of keeping them distinct.

Most foreign words are italicized, and translated in the text or in a footnote if their meaning is of any consequence. The exception is titles of poems and stories, which appear in roman but between quotation marks. Titles are generally given in English when published English translations exist; they are given in their original language, with translation between parentheses, when not. Translations are mine, unless noted otherwise.

Most split infinitives are intentional.

There are doubtless people to whom the torments of such an order appear hardly more natural than the contortions of disease; but I don't after all know why I should in this connection so much as mention them. For the few persons, at any rate, normal or not, with whom my anecdote is concerned, literature was a game of skill, and skill meant courage, and courage meant honour, and honour meant passion, meant life.

— HENRY JAMES

"The Figure in the Carpet"

I PRESENT

a library burning 2008

B Y THE TIME I ARRIVE at the Montparnasse cemetery to
pay my last respects to François Caradec, on a deco-
rously still Thursday afternoon in late November, roughly
two hundred people have gathered already. There is a fine
mist in the air; collars are up but no umbrellas. Dress is
casual. Most people are wearing black, but look like they
would be anyway.

Caradec, who died at eighty-four a week prior from
respiratory problems, was one of France's first comics ex-
perts, a regular on various radio roundtables, and a biographer of the eccentrics of late nineteenth-century Paris. He
wrote on writers like Raymond Roussel and Alphonse Allais, but also on pseudo-celebs like the noted Moulin Rouge
showgirl Jane Avril and the music critic Henry Gauthier-
Villars, better known as Willy, whose claims to fame include cheating on the novelist Colette and being challenged

to a duel by Erik Satie. Caradec wrote stories and poems, published an international dictionary of gestures catalogued by body part, and had a seemingly endless supply of references, usually complete with yellowed original, to the cruder points in French literary history. His trademarks included an oddly even nasal voice, an abiding love for rancid puns, and a phosphorescent white mustache with matching eyebrows the size and temperament of extremely furry caterpillars. The one time I called on him at his home in the south of Paris, he absently kneaded those eyebrows throughout our entire conversation, and my tape recording picked up nothing but the slow, steady squeal of his rocking chair.

At a microphone beneath a white canopy, half a dozen friends and relatives share memories of Caradec. A woman sings a verse from *La Bohème;* a man reads a scene from one of Caradec's books in which a peevish God sips a Picon-Grenadine while debating metaphysics with a drunkard. A little while later, a mannerly math teacher named Olivier Salon reads a text he has written for the occasion: a short, solemn poem, unrhymed and mostly to the point, equal parts melancholy and playful. *François caresses readers' crania in a deep rose derision,* one line might go in English, *in a fine ironic farce free of disdain.* The poem, Salon explains falteringly, is called a *beau présent:* a kind of ode, read sometimes at weddings and funerals, that contains only the letters in the addressee's name. When he finishes he shrinks back among the mourners assembled in the mist, none of whom appear to find it peculiar that they have just heard a eulogy from which sixteen letters of the alphabet are missing.

The service closes with a recording from the radio of Caradec, unaccompanied, singing a rustic mountain song with a refrain about bicycles, which over the course of seven or eight verses gets pretty dirty. (Only the gravediggers seem surprised.) Then the crowd shuffles out, toward the wake at a nearby bar named after Shakespeare's Falstaff, as Caradec is lowered into the same ground that holds Baudelaire and Beckett and Maupassant and Sartre, a few paces from the windmill at whose foot he used to sit and read during the Nazi occupation of Paris.

—◄○►—

What I want to talk about is, first of all, how it comes to be that a math teacher should read a poem at the funeral of an erudite littérateur. And: how does it come to be that this poem is tender and eloquent and funny despite containing fewer than half of the letters in the Roman alphabet? How does it come to be that a *beau présent* is deemed an appropriate form of eulogy, both by its author and by a crowd of people very likely to be making mental notes about what will be read aloud at their own funerals?

The answer, which is just shorthand for a whole constellation of new questions, is the OuLiPo (an acronym for **Ou**vroir de **Li**ttérature **Po**tentielle, or Workshop for Potential Literature): a sort of literary supper club to which Caradec and Salon belong, a hallowed echo chamber for in-

5

vestigations of poetic form and narrative constraint and the mathematics of wordplay. Since its creation in 1960, the Oulipo has served as the laboratory in which some of modernity's most inventive, challenging, and flat-out baffling textual experiments have been undertaken. Salon's *beau présent* is only the tip of the iceberg: oulipian inquiry has yielded novels without certain vowels, love stories without gender, poems without words, books that never end, books that do nothing but end, books that would technically take longer to read than most geological eras have lasted, books that share the exercise of mourning, books that aim to keep the reader from reading them, books that exist for no particular reason other than to amuse and perplex, books that may not actually exist at all. These works, all of them governed in some way by strict technical constraints or elaborate architectural designs, are attempts to prove the hypothesis that the most arbitrary structural mandates can be the most creatively liberating.

Somewhere in this laboratory, despite their differences in vocation and demeanor and facial grooming, Caradec and Salon both made places for themselves as partners in a novel and shapeshifting experiment, becoming united in a way two members of, say, Rotary International or a softball team would not be. What I want to talk about is how the Oulipo, and the principles it incarnates, can make unlikely pairings—of people, of ideas, of ways of life—seem not only plausible but also promising, not only interesting but also indispensable.

As you might imagine, it's difficult to be precise and literal about what, beyond a small Paris-based collective, the Oulipo *is*. The Oulipo itself prefers to be precise and literal about what it is not: it is not a movement, or an -ism, or a school.[1] It does not have an agenda, aesthetic or political or otherwise. It is not a scientific seminar; it is not invested in wrangling randomness or automatism or chance; it is most definitely not an offshoot of Surrealism. It is concerned with literature in the conditional mood, not the imperative, which is to say it does not purport to tell anyone what literature should or must be. What it does is tell anyone who cares to listen about what literature *could* and *might* be, sometimes by speculation, other times by demonstration.

7

Positive definitions of the group are at least as diverse and at least as odd as its members. Its second president, Noël Arnaud, described it as "a secret laboratory of literary structures." British newspaper *The Independent* described it as "a mysterious if not clandestine organisation that has long been a deliberately oblique part of French culture"; Martin Gardner, in *Scientific American,* as "a whimsical, slightly mad French group." A snooty communist character in Harry Mathews's *My Life in CIA* described it as "a gang of cynical formalists"; Philip Howard, in the London *Times,* as "the French avant-garde coterie famous for its masturbatory and literary experiments"; and Michael Silverblatt, of the literary radio program *Bookworm,*

---

[1] On this point the final word is Caradec's: "The Oulipo is not a school; it's a nursery where we force cylinders into square holes and cubes into round ones while our parents and proctors aren't looking. Does it work? Depends on the day."

as a band of "chessmasters who have lost their boards." In essence, the Oulipo is a little bit of a lot of things: sewing circle and secret society, museum of bibliographic oddities and non-lending library, analytic thinktank and cult of counter-culture. It is a place for *les mordus de littérature* —the incurably afflicted, the bitten—people preoccupied with the structure inherent in language, the calculation inherent in storytelling, and the possibility for mystery and mischief inherent in the smallest textual enterprise. It is a place, as the only official definition has it, for "rats who build the labyrinth from which they plan to escape."

What I want to talk about is, finally, how it is a place for me too, and for people like me. I want to figure out who these "people like me" really are, whether they share the group's cockeyed interest in literature or merely the spirit out of which its explorations arise. I want to talk about this because I am absolutely sure I am not alone in appreciating naturally occurring palindromes, or knowing a shorter sentence with all the letters in the alphabet than *The quick brown fox jumps over the lazy dog,* or suspecting it's no accident that *typewriter* is the longest English word that can be written on the top row of a QWERTY keyboard. I want to talk about my affection and my reservations, how this kinship is comforting and how it is isolating, how the Oulipo is necessary and how it is futile, and how it is somehow necessary in its futility.

In November 2010 the Oulipo turned fifty, an unprecedented age in the typically volatile (especially in France) history of literary collectivity. You can attribute this to good humor and to the absence of authoritarian leadership—not to say of ego altogether—but there's also something crucial in the fluidity, the sheer inexhaustible vagueness, of the workshop's shared pursuit: *potential literature*. Potential literature is both the things that literature could be and the things that could be literature. Potential literature is language; potential literature is life. Nobody's ever been entirely, definitively clear on what potential literature is, and this is to everyone's advantage. When you don't know what you're looking for, as they say, your chances of finding it are excellent.

9

—◄○►—

Take me, for instance. I had no idea what I was looking for when I found the Oulipo. As is the case with most Americans who get bitten, my first encounter was through Georges Perec, whose short story "Le Voyage d'hiver" (The Winter Journey) was on the reading list of a survey course in modern French literature I took during my first semester at college. The professor spoke of the Oulipo as one might speak of the Surrealists or the Dada movement or some legendary badminton match between Marguerite Duras and Jean-Paul Sartre—that is, as a point of some interest along a storied terrain with many points of interest. It was a group, she explained, dedicated to exploring the use of mathematical structures to generate literature. By way of illustration, she namedropped a few works not on our syllabus, including Italo Calvino's *If on a winter's night a traveler* and Vladimir Nabokov's *Pale Fire*.

Both of those books, as it turned out, had already

made impressions on me. *If on a winter's night a traveler* alternates the first chapters of ten different novels with the interstitial story of you, the harried reader, embarking on an increasingly harrowing quest to find the rest of the book you began in the first place. *Pale Fire,* ostensibly a 999-line poem in irregular pentameter, spins its real story through two hundred pages of annotation by an editor who is, you gradually realize, totally insane. Both novels are eminently oulipian, in ways I hope will become clear over the course of this whole discussion, but they are oulipian for different reasons: Calvino, who was a member of the Oulipo, wrote the reader's sections of *Winter's night* according to a sophisticated algorithm governing the introduction and behavior of characters; Nabokov, who was not an Oulipian, uses no explicit mathematical calculations in *Pale Fire* but does interrogate the structures external to the "story"— namely, the preface and endnotes. Both novels are, most importantly, about the need to keep your guard up while reading.

In any case, it wasn't until the professor mentioned that Perec was also the author of *La Disparition* (The Disappearance), a mystery novel of some 300-plus pages completely devoid of the letter E, that it clicked. *That is,* I thought to myself without hyperbole, *one of the five coolest things I have ever heard.*

I am well aware, after a few years of trying to explain to friends and acquaintances what the Oulipo is, that this was only one in a wide spectrum of possible reactions, sitting roughly opposite the blank stare and the breathy, full-stopped *"Huh,"* just before they shade into derisive laughter and outright disgust. (My grandmother once clipped and mailed me a sidebar from the *New York Times Book Review* where Ben Schott refers to Perec's exploit as a "commendably futile literary contortion"—which is quite even-handed, when you think about it.) An important lesson to understand early on about the Oulipo: this sort of thing isn't for everyone.

But in my case the act of writing an E-less mystery novel made alarmingly good sense, and not because I had any particular devotion to the French avant-garde: more because I had been raised on Mad Libs and Scrabble and the alphabet game, had outgrown the daily jumble before I learned to swim, had spent history class doing crossword puzzles, and had occupied idle moments in traffic making the numbers and letters on license plates into mathematically true statements. And because when I was sixteen, for no reason that I knew of, I had made myself a mix tape of songs whose titles and performers' names did not contain the letter E.[2]

Point is, there was a spark that moment in French class, a reassuring revelation that there were other people who clearly thought in some of the same ways I did, who probably also edited graffiti in bathroom stalls or jeopardized romantic relationships by correcting completely inconsequential confusions of *which* and *that*. The involuntary workings of my mind suddenly made a little more sense, thanks to a certain safety in numbers. This was not,

11

---

[2] Tie for most ostentatious inclusion between Xzibit and Tha Dogg Pound.

I later learned, a unique experience. Harry Mathews, for many years the only American-born member of the group, recalls that "being welcomed into the Oulipo made me feel like someone who has been denying a shameful habit only to discover that it is perfectly honorable."[3]

All the same, what hooked me on the Oulipo, after that initial flush of excitement, was my desire to be a writer, coupled with my frequent, frustrated disinclination to actually write. At its inception, the Oulipo's project was for the benefit of would-be writers like me, ones who didn't feel inspired enough of the time, and its message was that we shouldn't be striving to be inspired at all. We should stop waiting to be visited by the muse and just get to work, using the structures that literature borrows from language; we could outsource inspiration to the left brain when the right wasn't in the mood and, if lucky, come up with something pleasing to both sides.

The line, in effect, is this: writers are constrained whether or not they acknowledge it—not just by the strictures of poetic forms like the sonnet or the haiku, but also by the conventions of their chosen genre, the format in which they publish, even the grammar and lexicon of their native (or adopted) language. Embracing a set of carefully chosen rules is meant to focus the mind so narrowly that those obscure pressures and preoccupations fade, revealing paths and passageways that one would never notice with-

---

[3] This from someone who has published what is probably modern literature's most thoughtful treatment of the subject of masturbation.

out the blinders. Gilbert Sorrentino, who taught a course on constrained writing at Stanford for almost twenty years, expressed this idea nicely in its syllabus:

> "Generative Devices" are consciously selected, pre-conceived structures, forms, limitations, constraints, developed by the writer before the act of writing. The writing is then made according to the "laws" set in place by the chosen constraint. Paradoxically, these constraints permit the writer a remarkable free-dom. They also serve to destroy the much-cherished myth of "inspiration," and its idiot brother, "writer's block."

13

Igor Stravinsky offers a more bite-sized account of the same reasoning: "The more constraints one imposes, the more one frees one's self of the chains that shackle the spirit."[4] Shorter still is a comment of Perec's, which has come to epigrammatize the Oulipo as a whole: "I set myself rules in order to be totally free."

Whether or not you buy this logic is your call—al-though try writing a paragraph without using the letter E and see if you don't end up somewhere unexpected—but it would be hard to deny its effect. For every Nabokov who can afford to dispense with structure and rules and humil-ity, there are dozens of potentially great writers with craft issues, subject matter issues, motivation issues: writers who need tools to outwit themselves. Even Calvino and Perec, a brilliant storyteller and a brilliant technician re-

---

[4] Translation by Arthur Knodel and Ingolf Dahl.

spectively, benefited from oulipian discipline, from indulg-
ing their attraction to what Sorrentino described as his own
artistic impetuses: "an obsessive concern with formal structure [. . .] a desire to invent problems that only the invention of new forms can solve, and a joy in making mountains
out of molehills." Rules helped focus them, allowed them to
be architects instead of doodlers. Rules made them better
writers.

The Oulipo has sustained itself for half a century
largely on the logic that rules can make you a better writer
too, offering its explorations and techniques in the hopes
that you'll be able to put them to use. An important part of
my argument, though, is that it can make you a better reader
too, that you can benefit from potential literature whether
or not you even consider yourself literarily inclined. All
it takes is an openness to language as something material,
something manipulable, and something with practically infinite possibility.

And you'd be surprised who treats it that way without even realizing it. Think of pharmaceutical companies
who spend millions of dollars on consultants and focus
groups to ensure that their drugs have sufficiently inspiriting names, or of porn stars who add bizarre misspellings to
make their *noms de flume* sufficiently lascivious.[5] Think of
members of the Los Angeles Bloods who find any reminder
of their rival street gang, the Crips, so objectionable that

---

[5] Like "Sindee Coxx" or "Desirae Pinkfuck."

they routinely change initial C's to B's. Think of those members of Bill Clinton's cabinet who, as a defiant parting gesture, removed the W keys from all the keyboards in the White House, or of the underpaid staffer in the California governor's office who acrostically embedded FUCK YOU[6] in a veto letter from Arnold Schwarzenegger to a San Francisco assemblyman who had publicly urged him to "kiss my gay ass." Think of the *Sesame Street* writers who gave us a parable about King Peter the Persnickety, who, after being pelted with a ping-pong ball and pricked by his pet porcupine, decides to banish from his kingdom all things that begin with the letter P; think of Mike Myers's character in *Wayne's World* when he excitedly recognizes a haiku in what Dana Carvey has just said.[7] Think of anyone who has spent at least five minutes looking for the longest complete sentence in the periodic table of the elements.

15

Maybe you're not like any of those people—again, it would be hard to fault you. Potential literature is not about getting in touch with your inner nerd, or at least not just about that: it's more about giving voice to your inner

---

[6] An acrostic is a text that contains a word or phrase spelled out vertically, usually in the first letter of each line: the first line of Schwarzenegger's veto letter begins with "**F**or some time now," the second with "**u**nnecessary bills," and so on. The governor's office insisted this was a coincidence, reasoning that "the left-hand margin of past veto messages [had] spelled out words such as 'poet' and 'soap.'"

[7] "Does anyone else find this weird? I mean, we're looking down on Wayne's basement, only . . . that's not Wayne's basement. Isn't that weird?"

reader and to your inner author and listening to their dialogue. It's about knowing that you can repeat a word out loud until it loses its meaning but gains a weird and exciting new plasticity. It's about finding ways to let the world entertain you, even when it's not trying.

The fall after I finished college, I set off for Paris with seven books, nine months' worth of research funding, a duffel bag full of clothes that I would soon catch myself considering terribly baggy, and a lot of ill-defined questions about the Oulipo. What I wanted to know had less to do with the workshop's Academic Relevance or Literary Appeal than with why I personally found this stuff so cool, so enchanting and validating and probably crucial to the attainment of a fulfilled life. I wanted to know, by association, what kind of person I was—what kind of temperament united the few dozen people engaged in this . . . *activity*. How did they make a living? Did they have families, social skills, more or less acceptable grooming habits? Were they serious about all this?

Slowly, and with a great deal of reverent stammering, I began to make contact with the right people, and eventually settled into the unofficial capacity of *esclave—* slave—at the Arsenal branch of the French National Library (Bibliothèque Nationale de France, or BNF), cataloguing the Oulipo's archives. Later, after working with Paul Fournel, the group's current president, and Marcel Bénabou, its definitively provisional and provisionally definitive secretary,[8] to compile an anthology of the group's productions, I worked up the nerve to conduct interviews with the local and active Oulipians. I spent a couple of months paying them visits all around Paris with a battered tape recorder in tow, asking them questions about their work and taking notes on everything but their answers.

After my grant ended, I found a job writing textbooks and teaching European businessmen the finer points of English grammar, the better to stay and continue my research. I attended more readings, bought and dogeared more books, and met more fixtures in the oulipian firmament. I got called "David" surprisingly often. I attended two consecutive summer workshops in Bourges, writing and eating and drinking alongside the Oulipians for a week at a time, and followed their tracks to Bobigny and Lille and Geneva for performances and exhibitions. I read their books prominently in public, just in case a stranger happened by to offer some valuable man-on-the-street commentary. (Still no luck.)

Over time, the curiosity became mutual. In the fall of 2008 I was invited to present my work at a private Oulipo meeting, and thus, the week after Caradec's funeral, found myself in a well-appointed living room surrounded by my research subjects and telling them about potential

17

---

[8] Fournel and Bénabou used to share the roles of definitively provisional secretary and provisionally definitive secretary, alternating depending on day of the week; since Noël Arnaud's death and Fournel's ascendance to the presidency, Bénabou has officially occupied both positions.

things I had been imagining: an index of first lines to unwritten poems, a cycle of stories whose themes were determined by their word count, a set of vignettes linking a randomly coupled first and last sentence poached from other
works.[9] The Oulipians listened intently, asked intelligent
questions, and remarked that I had my work cut out for me;
then we moved on to the rest of the agenda, had dinner, and
parted ways. Three months later, after I had left Paris, a
casually ceremonious email from Paul Fournel announced
that I had been elected to the Oulipo. Delight and terror.

I do want to talk about the validation of being welcomed into a group of like-minded people, who have made
a sustainable creative endeavor out of what I always
thought was a vestigial personal peculiarity, and about the
vertigo of having my life's greatest honor be induction into
a group that is regularly referred to in the past tense. But
this book is not meant to be just about me, or about my becoming an Oulipian, or about any of the men and women
who became Oulipians before me. If I do dwell on those
things, it's only because that's the best way I have of telling

---

[9] Whether these ideas would have come to me had I not already
spent two years trying to understand and osmose oulipian techniques
is hard to say: most likely I would have had similar inklings, but not
such precise packages in which to place and present them. Before I
found the Oulipo, my life was no less filled with patterns and games
and collected bits of language—circumstantial haikus, choice two-
word phrases, surrealistic spam subject headings—which is to say
that by the time I did find the Oulipo, the sentences were already
poached, the poems already abandoned after the first line. The greatest fortune of potential literature, for me, was the promise of structures through which those fragments could be contemplated and
developed and made more than the sum of their parts.

you about potential literature itself, in as many of its guises and disguises as I have been able to inventory, and about what it can bring to anyone willing to read along as it happens. The Oulipo subscribes to the idea of potential literature more emphatically than anyone else in the world, but does not own it: we all do. The most important point in this book is that it makes no difference whether you are an official rat or a slightly intrigued onlooker. The potential of literature, the potential of language to *be* literature, is squarely in the public domain, and every bit as much yours as it is mine.

19

—◄○►—

In an essay published in 1937, a couple of decades before he co-founded the Oulipo, Raymond Queneau wrote off the formal permissiveness of the modern novel. "Anyone can push an indeterminate number of apparently real characters along in front of him like a gaggle of geese, across a long moor comprising an indeterminate number of pages or chapters," he declared. "The result, whatever else it may be, will always be a novel."[10]

That memorably peevish epigram has been invoked time and again in defense of the oulipian insistence on structural rigor, as a means of explaining why some of the workshop's most remarkable findings are supported by a bundle of blueprints and diagrams about as long as the books themselves. But Jacques Roubaud, in *La Bibliothèque de Warburg* (The Warburg Library), prefers to spin it an-

---

[10] Warren Motte's translation.

other way: the Oulipo, he theorizes, is in fact a living, wandering, intermittently honking gaggle of characters straight out of a novel Queneau never got around to writing. (As it happens, Queneau did write *The Flight of Icarus,* a novel in dialogue in which a character escapes from the clutches of a hapless author named Hubert Lubert, but the trouble young Icarus causes is ultimately anecdotal compared with the protracted spree of literary mischief that is the Oulipo.)

Roubaud's notion, however fanciful, makes good sense for anyone trying to get a handle on the group and its members, a few of whom even I would characterize in all candor as "apparently real." An Oulipian is neither an entirely individual figure nor an entirely cooperative one, and to sort out where any one fits within the grand scheme of the others tends to require some strenuous reading through a long and at times misleading paper trail. The best way to keep them from running together or drifting apart is to bear in mind the greater principle that unites them, inspires them, pushes them across the moor. Bear with me as I begin with the basics.

The Oulipo has thirty-eight members. Five are women and seven are non-French (no overlap). Not all of them are writers: there are poets and novelists and dramatists and journalists and translators, as you would expect, but also linguists, cyclists, communists, literary theorists, graph theorists, photographers, lexicographers, actors, singers, gamers, historians, diplomats, and, well, you get the idea. Rare is the Oulipian who is not at least three of these things at once.

Of those thirty-eight members, seventeen are dead. Shortly after obituaries for Caradec began to appear in

French newspapers, the Oulipo announced that he was "definitively excused" from attendance at subsequent meetings, owing to the handicap of being deceased. This is the only administrative distinction the group makes between living members and dead ones, and, while evidently tongue-in-cheek, it's not as silly as it may sound. In the rarefied orbit of the Oulipo—more so, even, than in the rest of literature—the dead are far from absent. In part because all but one of the founding members had died by the turn of the millennium or thereabouts, there is much talk nowadays of the early Oulipians, of their ideas and accomplishments and inventions. It also helps that most of the members who achieved renown independently of the Oulipo—Queneau, Perec, Calvino, Marcel Duchamp—have been definitively excused for quite a long time now.

Only about a dozen of the twenty living members[11] are active—meaning they attend the monthly meetings, participate in public readings, contribute material to the group's sporadic chapbook series, and from time to time run workshops to school the uninitiated in constrained-writing techniques. One of the rules in the group's unwritten constitution is that membership is permanent, so one may neither quit[12] nor be kicked out of the Oulipo, although a few members have distanced themselves by geographic isolation or declared estrangement. But here Roubaud's

---

[11] The eleventh member, a sometime secretary named QB, is fictional.

[12] Not even by dying, obviously, although the bylaws do provide a loophole: committing suicide, with the express purpose of leaving the Oulipo, in the presence of a notary.

formulation of the group as a living novel is especially apt: the death of a character is not, typically, without consequence for the rest of the story's fabricated world, and so it goes when a member stops being present in the biological sense. The dictum *Once an Oulipian, always an Oulipian* applies to people and ideas alike.

22

Like any good author, Queneau took pains to people his living novel with diverse and colorful characters. (Here the metaphor begins to smear a little: Queneau had basically autocratic control over the first generation of recruits, starting with Roubaud in 1966, whereas now the approval of a new member must be unanimous. That said, the catholic qualities determining who is inducted haven't shifted much at all.) Even in its earliest days, back when the Oulipo had a purer idea of what it intended to accomplish but nothing particularly exciting to share with the world, the primary affinity among its participants was that they were curious, in both senses of the word. Queneau and co-founder François Le Lionnais, an industrial chemist, were polymaths with discipline-hopping hobbies and queer senses of humor seasoned in the cultural crucible of early twentieth-century Europe. The other members fit no prescription: Jacques Bens was a poet from Marseilles who had trained in the natural sciences, Claude Berge a graph theorist and sculptor with a special interest in the Asmat culture of New Guinea, Paul Braffort a pioneer in artificial intelligence who also found time to set poems to music and croon them in those lavish, chandelier-bedecked *salles* that even people who have never been to Paris would recognize as authentically Parisian.

The same purposeful indiscrimination still operates today. Anyone is fair game for recruitment, regardless of profession or inclination, so long as he or she has something to add to a perpetually evolving conception of literary possibility—the purpose of joining the Oulipo is not to fit the mold but to change it. Before he became a member, Olivier Salon hardly ever put pen to paper in what he would call a creative mode; Valérie Beaudouin, a telecommunications network expert whose graduate thesis presented a remarkable computational tool for analyzing metered verse, still rarely does. What the group is at each discrete moment nonetheless depends on their being part of it, however they choose to manifest that belonging. No single person embodies the workshop perfectly, or ever will: only the entire collective force of the thing can encapsulate the Oulipo. The closer you look, the harder it is to make generalizations; there's always someone whose example somehow both contradicts and proves the same idea about potential literature.

From this angle it's not hard to see the advantage of the fact that no static definition of potential literature exists: it remains an ineffable ideal toward which members are free to work as they see fit, each beholden to his or her own fascinations and bugbears and biases. Every month they come together to report their findings and piggyback off one another's ideas—some things stick, others gestate, others fizzle and dwindle and are finally excused. Some members come at the project from a scientific background, others from the winding mirrored road of literature. Some are inveterate classicists, others hardcore modernists. Some are in it to write books, others so they don't have to. Some see it as a means to an end, others as the end unto itself. To paraphrase Walt Whitman, about whom I don't think the Oulipo cares much: very well then, the Oulipo contradicts itself. It is large, it contains multitudes. As of this writing, it contains thirty-eight of them.

—◄◦►—

One week after the funeral, at the François Mitterrand branch of the BNF, a huge modern thing that most French people over thirty abhor out of disdain either for its stark rectilinear construction or for its namesake, the Oulipo gives a reading in homage to Caradec. The scheduling was easy: the date was already on the list of *jeudis* (Thursdays) *de l'Oulipo,* a series for which the group assembles once a month between October and June to read old and new texts devoted to a given subject. While it's not especially tasteful to surmise that Caradec's death precisely two weeks before a regularly scheduled reading was a matter of courtesy, it does tell you a little bit about what one might call an oulipian conception of the silver lining.[13]

---

[13] Precedent in this case comes from a remark by Caradec himself that, while nobody dared suggest that the April Fool's Day death of Noël Arnaud in 2003 was intentional, one could still agree that he would have been pleased with the date. (Similarly, it's not all that hard to imagine Salon taking some small consolation in the fact that, even though *Caradec* contains only two letters not already present in *François,* one of them is E, which facilitates the task of writing a *beau présent* immensely.)

This evening's original theme is *L.H.O.O.Q.*, the caption to Marcel Duchamp's painting of Mona Lisa with a mustache and goatee. One expects that Caradec would have approved, as much for the mustache as for the title, which in French sounds identical to *Elle a chaud au cul* (roughly, "Her ass is hot"). The 425-seat auditorium is full, and chairs and television screens have been set up in the atrium for the runoff crowd. Nine Oulipians have turned up to participate, including a few seldom present for readings: Anne Garréta, for instance, a novelist who teaches in Brittany for one semester each year and at Duke the other, and Bernard Cerquiglini, a linguist with a stunning résumé that includes TV host and vice president of the Superior Council of the French Language. (You can tell they're not regulars: Garréta has a severe, silent presence, and has been known to go entire readings without removing her sunglasses or for that matter reading anything; Cerquiglini is simply more chic than any other Oulipian by an order of magnitude.)

Garréta and Cerquiglini are flanked by their mainstay counterparts, who more or less constitute the core active membership of the Oulipo: besides Salon, there is Roubaud, a much-venerated poet who still lists his profession on paper as "mathematician (retired)"; Marcel Bénabou, the secretary and de facto coordinator; Michelle Grangaud, an anagram phenom whose bearing is a peculiar combination of meekness and intensity; Jacques Jouet, who writes prolifically in just about every medium imaginable; Hervé Le Tellier, perpetually tardy newspaper columnist and notorious wit; and a Toulousain poet named Frédéric Forte, the youngest and most recently inducted member. A few pseudo-regulars are missing—Paul Fournel, the president, works as a cultural attaché to the French embassy in London, and Ian Monk, the only active English Oulipian, lives in Lille—but to call either one "noticeably absent" is to miss the point of a *jeudi de l'Oulipo,* which is always a bit of a crapshoot from an attendance point of view.[14]

The nine Oulipians, who fit neither in their typical arc on the auditorium stage nor on a single television monitor, read mostly passages from Caradec's bibliography, the selections and order having been worked out upstairs at the wake. Garréta reads a long excerpt from his first proper novel, which came out a week or two before his death; Bénabou reads an anecdote from *La Compagnie des zincs* (The Counter Company) in which Caradec recalls meeting Queneau at a bar in which there happened to be two dwarfs, who did not appear to know each other.[15] Salon reads his *beau présent,* as well as the introduction to Caradec's biography of a late nineteenth-century Moulin Rouge performer named Le Pétomane, whose vocation is best described as "fartist." A video is shown of Caradec, looking like a shaggy Shih Tzu in a short-sleeved pink dress shirt, pointing out various art-deco features of the Place Paul Verlaine. Salon relates an anecdote about visiting Caradec in the hospital,

---

[14] At one reading, I had just settled into my seat when the woman in front of me stage-whispered to her companions that she hoped Ian Monk wouldn't be reading that night. (He was.) Monk loves this story, though I'm pretty sure I never told it to him directly.

[15] A third dwarf entered the bar just as Caradec and Queneau were leaving.

including an eerily convincing impression of what the latter sounded like while intubated, which is touching not only for its sentiment but also for its echoes of an anecdote related by Le Lionnais about a discussion with Queneau, four days before Queneau died, about the poetic potential of the word *antepenultimate.*

Normally during *jeudis* the group reads in front of a projection of what is called the *galaxie oulipienne,* an astral map of the members' faces spiraling out from the center in rough chronological order of their recruitment. Viewed from afar, the image suggests that the readers on stage are being benevolently dwarfed by their predecessors, by the accumulated gravitas of the group's history. It also makes it easier to envision the workshop as both a collective pursuit and a constellation of disparate points and ideas and texts, between which a stunning number of lines are potentially traceable. Tonight the backdrop is a series of photographs of Caradec at various ages and in various outfits (here an ascot, there a shiny black jacket that, at least to me, screams "roller disco"), the mustache the only constant. Weirdly, the effect is not much different.

27

◄○►

For all his erudition and literary pedigree, Caradec played a fairly small supporting role in Queneau's unwritten novel: besides the enchanting facial topiary and the occasional contentious comment or memorable maxim, he offered little in the way of plot advancement. For one thing, although he fit the bill of an Oulipian impeccably, he didn't officially become one until 1983, more than twenty years after the workshop was created, owing to a rather volatile relationship with one of the founders, a cactus enthusiast who went by the name of Latis. More importantly, Caradec was not an inventor of new poetic or literary forms, nor did he show much interest in exploring those proposed by others. He was a whiz with the homophones and spoonerisms favored by his biographical subjects, for instance, but displayed a playful contempt for the anagram.[16] Arguably the most Caradecquian weapon in the oulipian arsenal is the false spoonerism, a short aphoristic text that looks as though it might be a homophone or spoonerism but is in fact just an arbitrary mess of words—an illustration of what Oulipians call "the Canada Dry principle."[17]

---

[16] Homophones—also homonyms—are words with different spellings and meanings but identical pronunciations, like *would* and *wood*. They were of particular interest to the humorist Alphonse Allais, who traded in homophonic translations of entire phrases, through which his own name, for instance, could become "All fonts allay" or, why not, "Alf wants a lay" (the latter is also arguably monovocalic, on which more anon). A spoonerism (*contrepèterie* in French) is a felicitous reversal of the leading consonants of two more or less adjacent words, usually with ribald results—e.g., the woebegone Reverend Spooner's "cunning array of stunts." Anagrams are words or phrases with the same letters arranged differently: *subtle, sublet, bustle, bluest.*

[17] The term comes from an old French ad campaign intimating that the color, name, and bottle of the namesake ginger ale would lead you to believe that it's alcoholic, when in fact it isn't. A contemporary, non-oulipian Canada Dry analogue is Amir Blumenfeld's "falindromes," which look like they should be palindromes but aren't: "So cats taste staccato tacos?"

Caradec had known Queneau and Le Lionnais from the resurgent post–World War II literary circuit. He admired Queneau's work and got him to preface some of his early texts; he also worked with Le Lionnais to inventory the sources of what they called literature's "third sector," or "environmental literature"—the incidental texts of everyday life, literature where it was least expected: "bank stubs, calendars, tattoos, record sleeves, job applications, ecclesiastical texts, phylacteries, testaments, and so on."[18] Caradec explained to me once that Louis-Ferdinand Céline, author of *Journey to the End of the Night,* also wrote the indication inserts for pharmaceutical products. "That's still a work by Céline," he said.

For Caradec, who was weaned on the literary experimentalism of the late nineteenth century, literature's potential lay in its history, both technically and creatively. He was more interested in where the idea of the Oulipo had

29

---

[18] The conventional breakdown is that the first "sector" is literary literature and the second is prefixed genre-literature: mystery novels, science fiction, self-help, chick-lit, novelizations of action movies, etc. The boundaries between the two are obviously porous, but the point of the third sector is that, unlike the first two, it's not intended to be literary, or even to be literature: think of the sectors as degrees of separation from the dream of being anthologized one day in a series of handsome leatherbound volumes.

Peripherally, the third sector is one of eighteen "challenges in contemporary literature" bewailed in 2009 by Bruce Sterling in *Wired:* "barriers to publication entry have crashed, enabling [a] huge torrent of subliterary and/or nonliterary textual expression." Of course, to paraphrase the famous misstatement about the Chinese, the Oulipians have the same word for challenge and opportunity.

come from than in where the flesh-and-blood workshop was going; to meetings he would customarily bring a poem or epigraph or pamphlet from that era, showcasing one or another of the tricks that kept the workshop atwitter. (The other primary source of historical curios, which go under the *érudition* section of the monthly agenda, is Bénabou, whose offerings are generally derived from Greco-Roman antiquity.)

Although it's not what first comes to mind, this historical consciousness is central to the Oulipo's self-conception. The early years in particular were devoted mostly to articulating a lineage in which the group's explorations could be inscribed, and to finding in the woodwork what Le Lionnais called "anticipatory plagiarists"—authors operating in an oulipian mode before there was such a thing as the Oulipo. There's no scarcity of such authors, from Stéphane Mallarmé and Raymond Roussel and Lewis Carroll, whose elaborations on technique and form gave modern experimental literature its sense of self, to hardcore nerds like Ernest Vincent Wright, whose E-less novel *Gadsby* preceded Perec's *Disparition* by a few decades, or Joseph-Henri Flacon, who rewrote the entire 1804 French Civil Code in rhyming verse because the original was too dry for his liking.

These were the characters who appealed most to Caradec, biographer at heart that he was. ("I've done only one thing in my life," he told an interviewer once: "read.") He may as well have been present at the lunch in 1961 where the question was broached as to whether the Oulipo was in favor of literary madmen; he would surely have responded less cryptically than Queneau, who weighed in with the characteristically Confucian remark that all literature is voluntary literature. But it didn't pan out that way: by the time Caradec became an Oulipian by title, not just by affinity, the workshop was most preoccupied with creating new texts governed by formal rules and involute mechanisms, not with following the breadcrumb trail back into history.

—◄○►—

In the Oulipo's first manifesto, a mock-serious treatise written in 1962 and published in 1973, Le Lionnais divides the workshop's fundamental activities into analytical and synthetic branches: "*anoulipism* is devoted to discovery, *synthoulipism* to invention."[19] If most of the group's acclaim comes from the latter, that's only because it makes for far more arresting literary gestures. The lipogram,[20] for instance, a text written without one or more letters—*La Disparition* is a particularly illustrious example, but the *beau présent* is also a more complex variant—is a stunt liable to make people pause for a moment, whether they end up rolling their eyes or trying it themselves. A demonstration of redundancy in Mallarmé's sonnets, or an inquiry into certain structural features common to subpar murder mysteries, will likely attract a smaller crowd.

So be it; spectacle always sells better than field-

---

[19] Warren Motte's translation.

[20] The name does not come from "Oulipo," tidy though that might be (nor from the field of liposuction, which would also make some sense), but from the Greek word *leipein,* meaning "to leave out."

work. The twin modes of discovery and invention continue to go hand in hand in the oulipian laboratory, even if one hogs the spotlight and the other dotes eagerly behind the scenes. There isn't a single member of the group who wouldn't insist, rightly, that one branch cannot exist functionally without the other. But an essential point about the Oulipo is that *anoulipo* and *synthoulipo* come from the same place, emanate from the same kind of consciousness. "From the one to the other," Le Lionnais wrote, "there exist many subtle channels."

The branches began to diverge soon after the workshop expanded past the circle of founders. Georges Perec became a member in 1967, and Italo Calvino and Harry Mathews joined in 1973. These three in particular were good readers but truly gifted writers, and they came to the Oulipo with designs on creation, not speculation. The first iconically *synthoulipian* moment is of course *La Disparition,* which came out in 1969—not Perec's best work by a long shot, nor even his most monumental, but the first example you'll usually hear of an oulipian work because it's the simplest to explain. (I usually let the E-lessness sink in for a second before telling my interlocutor that Perec wrote a sequel of sorts, *Les Revenentes* (The Specters), that didn't contain A, I, O, U, or Y. This has never once made anyone revise his or her first impression.)

From then on, at the expense of the first decade's erudite historiography, the workshop began to be about writing first and asking questions later; for its most eager participants, it became desirable above all to write the text you conceived, rather than just suppose what it might be like if you or someone else ever wrote it. Oulipians began to couple off and collaborate on collective writing projects, intra- and extramurally. Under Le Lionnais, the foundational policy on the matter had been to prize the theory as most important, and the resultant text as a non-essential bonus. Spoken by these new voices, the word *potential* began to obsolesce.

Indeed, for many second- and third-generation Oulipians, Perec in particular, the workshop's most enticing offering was a way to *exhaust* potential—an outlet for restless creative energy, a lexicon of techniques and rules that could not only inspire writing projects but also make them cleverer, richer, weirder—in short, liberate them. The new recruits were well aware of the importance of the tradition within which they were acting; Perec compiled a comprehensive historical survey of the lipogram the same year *La Disparition* came out, while Calvino continued to publish essays and deliver lectures on what he held to be timeless literary virtues. But the Oulipo's central orientation had begun to resemble that of a writers' workshop, not an academic colloquium, and the literature in question had started to look distinctly kinetic.

What's changed since those years is not so much the workshop's relationship to the past as its relationship to *its* past. No *jeudi*, memorial or otherwise, goes by without at least a few texts by someone no longer alive; no variation on a previously elaborated technique fails to give credit where it's due. (At worst, the would-be inventor doesn't realize that his or her invention has already been explored—usually by Perec—and is quickly brought down to earth.) But with fifty years of internal experimental data at hand, the analytical and synthetic models are more intertwined than ever. Classic oulipian hits and dusties generate new discoveries, which generate new texts, which generate new ways to read the old ones, and so on in infinite regress. The Oulipo has become a writing group in a way its founders didn't intend, but it also moves forward by remaining a reading group in exactly the way they did.

reading out loud 2007

THE OULIPO DIDN'T START reading publicly until the early 1970s, before which its activities were steeped in a cautious, low-level clandestinity. Its first sorties were mostly tied to festivals and colloquia: a conference at Reid Hall, the Parisian branch of Columbia University; the Europalia festival in Brussels; a "Pompidoulipo" at the Centre Pompidou; the Festival de la Chartreuse in Villeneuve-lès-Avignon. The Paris *jeudi* readings began in 1996, at the 100-seat Halle Saint-Pierre in Montmartre; afterward, they migrated to a 250-place auditorium at Jussieu, a University of Paris campus near the Panthéon, then to the far more capacious Forum des Images in the massive underground shopping complex at Les Halles, and finally, in 2005, to the slightly smaller but more suitably prestigious *grand auditorium* at the BNF.

Readings are a natural and sustaining part of the

Oulipo's public life for a number of reasons. For one, they give the audience a reason to care, to buy a book afterwards, to put a face to the name on the spine, to rub elbows with other elegantly disheveled *mordus*. Conversely, while readings allow the Oulipians to be approached by their admirers, they have also become a significant means of evolution for the group's collective corpus. The BNF, which is fairly intimate despite its seating capacity, is a place where new material can be tested before a sympathetic audience and where old material can be repurposed and given new valence—a place, for the most part, where oulipian texts attain the life they were meant to lead.

The *jeudis* for the past several years have been organized by theme. Each reading in the 2006–2007 season, for instance, was devoted to a color, beginning with *Infrarouge* and ending with *Ultraviolet*.[1] For the occasional writer like Salon, someone whose daily life is not centered on literature, a monthly reading is a great impetus to compose, with a sufficiently pliable prompt to yield quality results. (Salon's offerings, pun-besotted shaggy-dog stories that are at once savant and howlingly corny, are invariably

---

[1] At least according to the schedule: the *Infrarouge* reading in October 2006 turned out to be an homage to the Romanian-born Oulipian Oskar Pastior, who had died about a week prior in Berlin, just before he was to be awarded the prestigious Georg-Büchner-Preis for literary achievement. The *jeudi* timing wasn't as felicitous as it was for Caradec, although Bénabou pointed out that Pastior's expiration among the books and papers he had spread out in order to prepare his acceptance speech was "a nice death for an Oulipian."

among the most crowd-pleasing texts of the evening.) For younger members who have not yet published much, the theme of an upcoming *jeudi* can provide the concrete hook for a new idea: Forte found that the reading on *le bleu du ciel,* or blue of the sky, lent itself well to a form he had recently created, a series of ninety-nine pseudo-randomly ordered observations that collectively depict a single topic. (Likewise, after my induction, I used a reading on the theme of *les premiers outrages*—first indignities—as an excuse to develop my half-baked theory that the Tower of Babel episode in the book of Genesis was the first oulipian event in history.) Meanwhile, more seasoned and prolific authors like Jouet can reach into their own back catalogues and find something relevant to the evening's theme; others—such as Bénabou, whose bibliography is concentrated mostly on metaliterary issues—can just as easily trot out a beloved or obscure text by a deceased Oulipian, or a particularly apropos one from someone outside the clan: French poet Tristan Corbière, British screenwriter Richard Curtis, Roman rhetorician Quintilian, and so on.

37

All this gives an effect not unlike that of the spiral of Oulipian heads projected behind the stage: it suggests that there is no end to the connections that are possible between disparate minds focusing on one thing, the sheer volume of stuff that can be brought together under the aegis of even a couple of humdrum ideas. Like the *galaxie,* the themes seem to signify this both in practice—what's been written already—and in theory—what could be written, given a theme and some time and a handful of techniques. Each reading is, in this respect, a small and casual affirmation of potential literature's potential applicability to the real world.

Yet today's *jeudis* aren't as exciting as they must have been a decade ago. Some are joyous occasions of sublimely mischievous wit, with all the giddy energy of a talent show on the last night of summer camp; others can verge on the tedious, especially when few readers have shown up or the theme is a little threadbare. The element of risk, though, the blush of unpredictability, the on-the-spot feeling of proof through creation, is typically absent. As a rule, the BNF audience is collectively well versed and complicit in oulipian trickery: not many of the few hundred listeners have to be told what a *beau présent* is, or need explicit indication that a poem is written without such-and-such a vowel or in antonymic relationship to such-and-such a poem by Victor Hugo. (Based on no empirical data whatsoever, I would guess that less than a quarter of the crowd at any given *jeudi,* save exceptional ones like the tribute to Caradec, is there for the first time.) There is a certain creative leeway that comes from this; attending a really good BNF reading feels thrillingly similar to spying on one of the group's private monthly meetings. But sometimes the result is the kind of esoteric self-reference that one ideally needs to be an oulipophile already in order to appreciate.

Fortunately, it's become commonplace for members of the workshop to go "troubadouring around the world," as Fournel puts it, calling at French or francophile culture centers from Argentina and Austria and Australia to Berlin and Bombay and Burkina Faso to Tel Aviv and Tokyo and Tunis, as emissaries of potential literature. (Roubaud, even in his late seventies, is particularly well traveled; if he's missing from a *jeudi,* it's usually because he's off reading in Tokyo or Rio or Oklahoma or something.) And predictably enough, the most interesting readings happen when the Oulipo forays out of its comfort zone and into uncharted, unconvinced territory. The gospel never fails to delight the adepts, but it's so much more powerful when there are potential converts in the audience.

—◦—

On a chilly night in December 2007, four Oulipians are waiting to give one such reading in Bobigny, a northeastern suburb of Paris. Their performance is part of a series called *A quoi jouons-nous?* (What are we playing at?), organized by the regional government at various libraries throughout the towns north of Paris. The Bibliothèque Elsa-Triolet, not far from a metro stop named after Raymond Queneau, is slightly forbidding and futuristic, but inside it's warm and welcoming. Thirty or forty people, most of whom turn out to be either librarians or the small children of same, are milling about, playing various games with magnets and dice; as soon as I enter, a white-haired man holding an empty snifter obliges me to play "Japanese billiards," which turns out to bear a suspicious resemblance to shuffleboard. There are cubes of cheese, wine from a box, a few shelves of oulipian books laid out for the perusing. On one wall are anagrams made from the names of well-known authors (Boris Vian is *bison ravi,* or delighted bison; Gertrude Stein is *stridente grue,* strident crane) and palindromes laid out in enlarged Scrabble tiles (*non à ce canon:* no to this canon). Another is fully devoted to an interactive version of the grafted alexandrine, a technique elaborated several years ago by Marcel Bénabou: one may pick and choose between magnetized hemistiches—six-syllable alexandrine-halves, missing their heads or tails—such as *Poète prends ton luth* (Musset), *ne va point sans soupirs* (La Fontaine); *Oui, c'est Agamemnon* (Racine)[2]—and recouple them at will to make a Frankensonnet.

Bénabou, who is deep in conversation with some friends on a nearby sofa, is for all intents and purposes the elder statesman of the Oulipo. He is neither the oldest living member nor the one of longest standing, but he belongs firmly to the first generation of recruits, which began in the late 1960s, and has remained close to the heart of oulipian activity ever since. As the workshop's secretary, he is the first point of contact for outside parties who have business with the group (publishers, journalists, ravenous packs of librarians), which makes him a gatekeeper of sorts; the collective paper trail (minutes from meetings, correspondence with notable outsiders, photocopies of texts deemed anticipatorily oulipian, the occasional manuscript) also ends up in his care. Even unofficially, though, Bénabou tends to explain, instruct, correct, preside: from behind his owlish eyes and earnest eyebrows he exudes a certain no-nonsense, deference-inviting dignity. He addresses any plurality of

---

[2] The missing parts are *et me donne un baiser, La perte d'un époux,* and *c'est ton roi qui t'éveille.* Obviously.

younger Oulipians as *mes enfants*—my children—with the irony level set permanently at around 40 percent.

Bénabou was born in 1939 in Meknes, Morocco, and moved to Paris in his late teens to study and later teach history. He came to the Oulipo by way of his friendship with Perec, with whom he collaborated in the 1960s on a couple of dictionary-based party tricks. And more than any other currently active member, with the technical exception of Roubaud—who is older than and was recruited a few years prior to Bénabou, but who is decidedly aloof in his relation to the workshop's administrative concerns—he has been around since before things were the way they are now, and makes little secret of his fondness for how they used to be. At readings, he tends to applaud most vigorously when someone reads a text by one of the group's deceased members.

His books—not counting his first, a historiographic survey of Africa's resistance to Romanization—are frustrating. That's meant as a verb, not an adjective: they are active attempts to foil any overtures you might make toward readerly complacency, toward premature self-congratulation, toward thinking you've got things figured out. His books are meant to outwit you. They work as well as they do because they're predicated on an intimate knowledge of the joys and sorrows and risks and pitfalls of reading; they work because the author knows exactly what the reader's next move is going to be, and *that's* the story he's telling.

Bénabou's two best-known works are of a piece: *Why I Have Not Written Any of My Books,* which is about (not) writing, and *Dump This Book While You Still Can!,* which is about (not) reading. Both are fascinatingly anomalous and unclassifiable, equal parts fanciful memoir and literary philosophy and metaphysical raspberry in your general direction. The former is a lyrical, erudite inventory of the techniques at a writer's disposal for procrastinating and prevaricating: choosing a good epigraph or five, polishing the first sentence down to the bone, getting so caught up in the Proustian redolence of a good thick paper stock that an entire summer goes by unnoticed.[3] The latter, which Warren Motte describes as "a perverse whodunit, where the reader is both the victim and the guilty party," is a slow-moving allegory about the enchantment of reading—in the sense that one could be enchanted, to one's enduring inconvenience, by an ill-intentioned sorcerer. (To Bénabou's credit, my experience with *Dump This Book* does bear out a certain occult essence: the French version is presently out of print, and the copy I borrowed from the library in college was recalled several months after I had already returned it; a few years later I found a secondhand copy of the English translation with a glowing red DISCARD stamped across its lower pages.)

The first time I read Bénabou, I got a few dozen

---

[3] The title is also a nod to Italo Calvino's "How I Wrote One of My Books," an explication of the algorithms behind the reader chapters of *If on a winter's night a traveler*. Calvino's title was itself a play on a posthumous magician's-secrets-revealed essay called "How I Wrote Certain of My Books," by Raymond Roussel, one of the Oulipo's godfathers. According to Warren Motte, Bénabou's proposed and rejected title for his third book, which was published in 1995 as *Jacob, Menahem and Mimoun: A Family Epic*, was "One Always Writes the Same Book."

pages in before remarking, with indelible finality, *What a curmudgeon.* That impression lingered until I met him, whereupon I wondered instantly how I could possibly have thought anything of the kind. Only eventually, and with a gathering comprehension of what it means to be an Oulipian, did I come to the counterintuitive but undeniable conclusion that an author can be kindly and courtly and urbane and still voluntarily, as one of my college professors once put it, a pain in the ass.

—◄o►—

Meanwhile, hovering and hobnobbing around the perimeter of the library is Frédéric Forte. There is an invisible acute accent that you pronounce at the end of *Forte,* making it sound like the way the English word for "strong suit" is commonly said, even though that's actually wrong and the English word should be pronounced as though there were no E in the first place, such that the third and eighth words in "building pillow forts is one of my fortes" should be phonetically identical, which is the opposite of how poor Frédéric's name is meant to sound but not look and it's all very confusing and tiresome.[4] Suffice it to say that Forte, like Bénabou, and in fact like most Oulipians, is compelled

---

[4] To make matters slightly more complicated, there is a renowned French basketball coach who is also named Frédéric Forte (also pronounced Forté), and whose nickname is "the Brain." Instinct compels me to include some indication as to how to differentiate references to the two Fortes from this point forward, but I have no present intention of mentioning the basketball coach again.

surprisingly often to correct the spelling or pronunciation of his name.

Forte was born in 1973—the same year, he likes to point out, as the Oulipo's first mainstream publication, *La littérature potentielle.* He lived and worked in Toulouse until moving to Paris in 2007, thanks to which he speaks French with a breathless southern twang for which the other Oulipians are especially fond of chiding him. He has never committed to a career, sticking instead to low-impact jobs in bookstores and record shops, in the mode of someone who treasures the time to be creative but would pretty obviously wither without a cultural lifeline. (For the year or so before he officially moved in with his girlfriend, an American poet and translator, he lived in his 17th-arrondissement apartment in name only, unpacking his electric bass and huge Japanese speakers and much huger library but not, as far as I know, his bed.) He is energetic and excitable, and matter-of-factly encyclopedic about the things he likes, the sort of person who not only speaks animatedly about PJ Harvey and John Zorn but also knows the name of every session musician who plays on their records.

When he was little, he told me once, Forte would classify his favorite comic-book heroes in different groups based on characteristics they shared; later on, he did the same with musicians, creating imaginary supergroups with the bassist from one band, the singer from another, and so on. To him, the Oulipo is the ultimate literary fantasy baseball team, uniting as it does most of the writers whose ideas have been meaningful in his own formation. He remembers vividly the first time he saw the word *Oulipo,* at age twelve, upon discovering Queneau's *Exercises in Style,* in which the same mundane anecdote is related in ninety-nine different forms and registers. When he began writing poetry some years later, he never had any doubt that he was doing so in an oulipian fashion.

The way in which this makes his relationship to the workshop different from Bénabou's is important. Forte is a writer for whom the Oulipo has always existed, as a stable part of literary culture rather than an undigested idea that a handful of serious-looking middle-aged men poked and prodded once a month over lunch. At present he is one of only four members in the group to have been born after its inception in 1960.[5] That's a bit of a red herring—plenty of other members came of literary age after the Oulipo had hit its stride—but it's worth pointing out in Forte's case because his approach to poetry presupposes both the importance of structure and the importance of playing around with it, which has freed him to work on proving proofs the founding members would never have even considered. Forte is heavily preoccupied with the idea of form, but he sees no reason that it should be fixed, or firm, or perceptible at all. The potential of uncertainty excites him.

Indeed, very little of his published work is what you would call conventionally constrained, much less conventional at all. The most classifiable is probably 2009's

45

---

[5] The others are Garréta (1962), Beaudouin (1968), and myself (1984). Like the *Ouvroir,* Monk was born in 1960, but technically he's older by a few months.

Une collecte (A Gathering), whose bite-sized poems are also anagrams of short passages from Marcel Mauss's *Manual of Ethnography.* For the most part, though, his poetic projects flirt with fixed forms only for the sake of contorting or perverting or submerging them; some ignore literary precedents and take their cues from musical arrangements or sumo lore or Tom Waits lyrics or crossword clues or adulatory adjectives lifted from Amazon.com customer reviews. His most expansive book to date, *Opéras-Minute,* is a series of quasi-theatrical and visually intricate poems that would take up at least four dimensions were they not constrained to the printed page.[6] (It was based largely on his presentation of some of these, in progress at the time, that the Oulipo inducted him shortly after the book's publication in 2005.)

This divergence is not an accident. As it starts a sixth decade, the workshop has less and less of a stake in preserving what is familiar, and more in opening its doors to the new, unproven, and precarious. The presence of the Oulipo's founding members has already dwindled to near zero; at some not-too-distant point the group will consist of nobody but people who knew what the Oulipo was before they knew they wanted to be writers, people for whom the experiments of the first generation are, for all their bril-

---

[6] For the sake of comparison, most pages in *Opéras-Minute* look a little like those making-of editions where, for instance, Ezra Pound's revisions to *The Waste Land* are computerized with text of different sizes and lots of diagonal slashes and curvy arrows and stuff. The poems are much easier to follow when read aloud, but only when Forte reads them.

liance, received wisdom. (What will those men and women poke and prod over lunch?) Forte's knowledge of potential literature is that of a lifelong fan, but his interpretation of it is libertine, interdisciplinary, legitimately experimental. That's not why he's a good poet, but it's why the Oulipo was wise to recruit—the official verb is *co-opt*—him.

—◄○►—

At the de facto front of the playroom, a small woman has begun to speak about the *A quoi jouons-nous?* series and various goings-on in the Seine–St. Denis region. Next to her, Olivier Salon stands smiling in a vague way and looking charmingly uncomfortable about, among other things, being much taller than she is. From certain angles, Salon—father of two, alpinist, well-liked math teacher, actor of recent minting—has the appearance of a good-natured off-season pirate. From others, particularly when he's wearing his glasses, he looks like a librarian from the twenty-second century. His style is tastefully unpredictable, subtly quirky: during the season of color-themed *jeudis,* he showed up at each in a loud dress shirt corresponding roughly to the color of the evening.

Salon is a positively engaging reader, unabashedly hammy with the smallest hint of self-effacement; he has also been a hit as one of three performers in *Pièces détachées,*[7] a theatrical adaptation of various oulipian texts, which has sold out bookings of various lengths from Paris

---

[7] Literally "spare parts," but *pièce* also means "play," in the theatrical sense.

to Avignon since 2006. (Oddly, or maybe predictably, he projects a certain nervousness in person, at least around people with whom he is not on intimate terms, and his extemporaneous public speaking style can be described only as "faltering," so it's no small mystery why he is always the one to make the announcements at the end of *jeudis*.) Beyond that, he is one of those good-men-to-have-around, somebody who gets things done: he oversaw the layout and printing of the *Bibliothèque Oulipienne* (B.O.) chapbook series until late 2007, when Forte took over, but still deals with the altogether more frustrating business of selling the volumes at readings and distributing them to a few far-flung subscribers.

He will also be the first to remind you that he is not a writer—even with two small books and a handful of B.O. publications under his belt, he will not use the word without a few phrases of qualification. True, he is not much of an inventor of forms—the texts he composes for readings are either exemplary takes on old forms like the *beau présent* or rambling, structurally unimaginative stories built around a core of wordplay—but his modesty reflects something sheepish, almost a little guilty, in his perception of the group's project and the way he fits into it.

Salon became a member of the Oulipo in 2000, after he began corresponding with Jacques Roubaud, who had seen Salon give a lecture on an issue in number theory called the Prouhet-Tarry-Escott problem and invited him to meet the workshop and present more generally his work on sequences in number theory. Bénabou, in a communiqué to then-president Noël Arnaud, described him as "made of the same wood from which Oulipians are cut"—but there was little secret that the group chose to induct Salon largely in the hopes that he would bring new steam to its mathematical side, supply some new ideas of the sort that had yielded the hidden algorithmic reveries of *If on a winter's night a traveler* and Perec's *Life A User's Manual*,[8] which is governed by both an elaborate Eulerian matrix and a graph theory problem based on the way a knight moves around a chessboard.

But for some reason, this just flat out didn't happen. Salon admits, both ruefully and with evident relish, that he was seduced by the things he could do with language, things that stimulated his mathematical way of thinking but were not, contrary to what he had maybe believed at heart about literature, taxing or arduous or highfalutin. If he hasn't reinvigorated the workshop's flagging engagement with mathematics, though, he has further proven how much fun literary strictures can be for the non-pedigreed writer.

49

—◄○►—

While the woman talks, Hervé Le Tellier stands toward the back of the room, facing away from the crowd, puttering on his iPhone. He does not turn around when she gets to the part about how delighted everyone is to receive the Oulipo

---

[8] Perec was insistent that there be no punctuation between "Life" and "A User's Manual," which does nothing to discourage the idea that some Oulipians just like bedeviling innocent fact-checkers.

and so on and so forth, or when she begins to put the wrong first names with the right last names, turning the whole business of introduction into a sort of live variation on Bénabou's (Marcel, not Michel) grafted alexandrine exercise. Salon corrects her with unfailing politesse. Le Tellier, the only one whose name gets by unmangled, snickers gently.

Le Tellier is a tricky one to pin down. The first time I met him he lied to me for no apparent reason: I was in the throes of an essay on the series of sequels to Perec's "Voyage d'hiver," of which Le Tellier's "Voyage d'Hitler" had instigated a flood of others, and mentioned something about how my copy of one episode was missing every other page and wasn't that curious. "Ah yes," he said knowingly, if a little absently, "it's meant to be like that." I smiled knowingly too, content to have been let in on an Oulipo in-joke, and remained thus until the following week I went to the library and found another copy of the same story without any pages missing. (An early lesson about the Oulipo's market share, to paraphrase Kevin Spacey in *The Usual Suspects:* the greatest trick the Oulipo ever played was convincing the world that its typos and misprints were intentional and devious.) This wasn't malicious, just a little naughty in the same spirit evident at the end of his doctoral dissertation, *Esthétique de l'Oulipo* (Aesthetic of the Oulipo), where he justifies himself by quoting François Le Lionnais's non-existent[9] third Oulipian manifesto.

---

[9] Well, okay, that's not entirely true. Notes by Le Lionnais for what was to become the third manifesto do exist, and were unearthed in time to be lovingly transcribed by yours truly and included in 2009's

"Hervé Le Tellier," writes Martine Laval matter-of-factly in the magazine *Télérama,* "is *un brouilleur de pistes*": a misdirector.

But Le Tellier isn't quite the prankster he seems to be, nor is he as mean as very funny people sometimes seem. His books, which run the gamut from quick-and-dirty pastiche to lofty academic discourse, barely conceal a sentimentality both poignant and endearing; in person he has a magnetism that's all brooding humor and sniperlike wit, and you get the sense that for him keeping the room in thrall is second nature, not because it's fun but because it's emotionally necessary. He is forever late, distracted, shabbily put together, despite all of which there is an ineffable seductive quality about him. (He also has this tic where every third blink or so is a veritable flutter of eyelashes, which probably helps a little.)

In his writing, too, he is typically aloof; he favors pithy and diverse forms, like the thousand one-liner answers to the question "What are you thinking?" in *A Thousand Pearls (for a Thousand Pennies),* or the hundred different perspectives on the Mona Lisa, spread over two books. *Enough About Love,* published in 2009, is his first full-fledged novel since *Le Voleur de nostalgie* (The Nostalgia

51

Anthologie de l'Oulipo. But its relative non-existence before then didn't stop anyone from treating it as a *potential* document, which is to say citing it as case-closing evidence for whatever the argument happened to be. Le Tellier explains in *Esthétique* that, since it outlines a number of future strategies for the group, "naturally the Oulipo maintains this text in a certain confidentiality."

Thief), whose gentle formal connivance earned him entry into the workshop in 1992. Every now and then he brings out something to reassert his academic chops—such as *Esthétique*, a long and not entirely indispensable treatise tying the Oulipo's activities to various theories of art and language—but for the most part he excels at isolating the small ideas gleaming in larger structures, sophisticated or not. (Crowd favorite *The Sextine Chapel* is best described as erudite, episodic, combinatorial softcore porn.)

One gets the strong impression that the Oulipo, for Le Tellier, is a way of reining in a lot of little skills and ideas that play well but would otherwise be hard to consolidate into a coherent literary reputation. If Forte is the Oulipian most attentive to modern pop culture, Le Tellier is the one who has best taken to heart its lessons: make it quick, make it memorable, and make it funny. As such, he is probably best qualified to be the public face of the group vis-à-vis the non-literary grind of the media. With Jouet, and formerly Caradec, he is a regular on the radio show *Des Papous dans la tête,* a more wordplay-focused answer to NPR's *Wait Wait . . . Don't Tell Me!;* he writes a daily aphorism about current events for *Le Monde;* he even sends out Facebook invitations for Oulipo readings, with flyers he designs himself, under the event rubric for "listening party."

—◦—

The Bobigny reading takes place down a few flights of stairs and is slow to get started, due to some epic lighting problems and the convivial sluggishness of the audience. For several minutes after Bénabou, Forte, Salon, and Le Tellier have taken their seats at a table facing the tiny stadium-style auditorium, librarians shuffle in and technicians scurry about trying to figure out a way to keep a large halogen lamp from toppling over. The banter that fills this waiting space—friendly ribbing of Salon about the light glinting off his regally bald pate, of Forte about his twanged vowels, etc.—continues well into the decidedly informal reading itself. (Rarely is a reading decidedly formal, or even implicitly formal, although it's been known to happen on occasion, audience and room size permitting.)

The reading kicks off, once it finally begins, with an excellent sampler of the group's techniques: Perec's "35 Variations on a Theme by Marcel Proust," in which the famous first sentence of *A la recherche du temps perdu*—"Longtemps je me suis couché de bonne heure" ("For a long time I used to go to bed early," in C. K. Scott Moncrieff's 1922 translation)—is submitted to a cool, detached gamut of lexical analyses and tweakings. An extra letter is added, or one is removed; the same vowels are preserved but the consonants are changed, or vice versa; each word is replaced with a synonym or an antonym, and so on, with increasingly funny results.[10] The Oulipians take turns reading

53

---

[10] An equally delightful introduction is Harry Mathews's adaptation of the same exercise into English with thirty-five takes on "To be or not to be: that is the question." Its manipulations range from minimal variations ("To pee or not to pee: that is the question") to antonymy ("Nothing *and* something: this was an answer") to a different perspective altogether ("Hamlet, quit stalling!").

the variations, pausing if they deem something worth clarifying: Salon halts Forte before the anagram to explain what an anagram is, while Bénabou says by way of introduction that a lipogram, *as you are no doubt aware,* is a text written without one or more letters. Scattered members of the audience nod furiously at this.

The variations are, as always, a hit. Bénabou then reads Queneau's "La Cimaise et la fraction," a manipulation of a canonical La Fontaine fable ("La Cigale et la fourmi," or The Ant and the Grasshopper) according to the S + 7 technique, invented by founding Oulipian Jean Lescure, where each noun is replaced by the seventh noun following it in a given dictionary.[11] Le Tellier parries with a version of the same poem that he has crossbred with "The Fox and the Crow." Salon reads another *beau présent,* this one about the Eiffel Tower and using only the letters in *la tour Eiffel:* a more favorable vowel spread than Caradec's name but only four consonants, meaning you can tell immediately that something's off, but not necessarily what. Before reading it, he pauses to get the go-ahead from Bénabou to explain that Perec invented the *beau présent.*[12] As a rule, the Oulipo in-

---

[11] *S* stands for *substantif,* or noun. Both the part of speech and the number are naturally adjustable; a general version of the method is presented as M ± n (M for *mot,* or word). An S + 7 of the sentence "Every word has become a banana peel" (which is how Mathews describes S + 7) according to *Webster's New World Dictionary* is "Every worker has become a bandolier peignoir."

[12] Perec didn't actually invent it, per se, but he popularized its ceremonial use, composing several exemplars for friends' weddings. In

sists that its structures and games are in the public domain, but not to the exclusion of recognizing notable proprietary relationships or personal examples. When Forte remarks during a formal explanation that there is no such thing as theft in the Oulipo, Le Tellier replies mock-churlishly that it's all theft.

The next several texts focus on oulipian staples by active but absent members: Forte reads a text in Great Ape, a language elaborated at length by Jacques Jouet based on Edgar Rice Burroughs's discussion of simian vocabulary in the Tarzan books. ("Let us not forget that they are capable of everything, because they are capable of poems," Jouet says of apes in the B.O. volume that serves as a glossary and preliminary poem primer in the language.) A few pieces by Jacques Roubaud follow, including a dialogue in several acts that consists exclusively of film titles—not only the conversation but the stage directions as well.

Next, some *baobabs.* The form, named after a fruit tree native to Africa and Australia, starts with a homophone

---

those cases he called the form an *epithalamium,* which is Greek for a wedding song or poem; *beau présent,* known in English as "beautiful inlaw," is the general, non-occasion-specific form, so named in contrast to the *belle absente* ("beautiful outlaw"), which to all indications Perec did invent, and which is way harder: an ode that contains the same number of lines as the subject's name does letters, in which each line contains every letter in the alphabet *except* one. In the classic example, dedicated to the Oulipo, the first line omits only O, the second line only U, the third only L, and so on. (To be totally precise, Perec's *belles absentes* don't contain K, W, X, Y or Z—the first two practically don't exist in French, and the others are a rare bit of slack that he cut himself.)

—*bas-haut-bas,* or low-high-low—and takes the jig further by using those sounds as often as possible in a text read aloud, ideally with three people: one reading the body text, one booming every instance of the syllable *bas,* and a third chirping every instance of the syllable *haut.* Luc Etienne, an early Oulipian, did the same with the seven solfège syllables *(do, re, mi, fa, so, la, ti);* others have followed suit with *vie* and *mort* (life and death), or with body parts that shall remain unspecified. This evening's text, which is about hunting, revolves around Forte's expertly plosive interpretation of the sound *pan!*

Evidently, the *baobab* is hard to represent any other way than orally, although not for want of trying: Roubaud's namesake text has been reprinted with the *bas* in subscript and the *haut* in superscript, which could theoretically work with any other set of sounds, like *Vous êtes pourris de $_{vie}$ce, pire que les $_{mort}$ses* ("You are all riddled with sin, worse than walruses"). This makes it an early example of an oulipian exercise conceived with a listener, rather than a reader, in mind. On the more visual side, there's the monovocalism, a text that suppresses all vowels but one. Perec was an adept, of course—see the not-very-good but still impressive *Les Revenentes,* which was published shortly after *La Disparition* and billed as the letter E's revenge—but the standard of monovocalic excellence is borne by the non-Oulipian Canadian poet Christian Bök, whose *Eunoia,* published in 2001, features one astonishingly readable "chapter" that expresses what he claims is the distinct personality of each vowel.[13] The monovocalism is more

---

[13] Let's just say you wouldn't bring U home to meet your parents.

striking on the page than in oral performance, where the oddity is easier to ignore, even in Bök's pyrotechnic readings-aloud. This evening the group reads, in turn, a piece in A (Perec's "What a Man!"), one in E (Salon's "Ce fêlé de mec," or The Demented Gent), and one in O (Jouet's "Oh! L'ostrogoth!").

—◄○►—

The plasticity of these forms makes them surprisingly sustainable. Although the lipogram and the monovocalism (which, like the *beau présent,* is a kind of lipogram) are dumb constraints—what could be conceptually simpler than cutting out a letter or two?—they manage to condition the mind to find ways to work them into more sophisticated ideas. So it's natural for the question of theft to loom, particularly at a beginner's event like this, where the majority of forms presented share variations on a common ancestry; but in the Oulipo, and especially in the latter-day Oulipo, each member does not steal a form so much as inherit and put his or her own spin on it. This is what makes the research collaborative, after all, and what makes the workshop function as a continuum.

Le Tellier's sense of humor is uniquely predisposed to this. His *Jocondes,* the riffs on the Mona Lisa, are his answer to Queneau's beloved *Exercises in Style;* his thousand answers to the same question in *A Thousand Pearls* borrow formally from Perec's *Je me souviens* (I Remember), in which each bite-sized reminiscence begins with the same three words. Most recently, his *opossums célèbres* (famous opossums, which merely tacks some extra syllables onto *hommes célèbres,* or famous men) join a series of short vignette collections describing creatures bred from portmanteau words.[14] First Salon and Roubaud collaborated on a menagerie of interspecies lovechildren called *sardinosaures;* then came Paul Fournel's *animaux d'amour* (animals of love, an extension of *maux d'amour,* or pains of love); and finally—for now—Le Tellier rounded it out with his animal-celebrity mashups, such as *le marsupialcapone* (scourge of the Chicago zoo) and *le calamarcelproust* (wandering the seas in search of lost tuna).

These ideas are road-tested at public readings, but the most encouraging approval is internal, in-joke-borne: a reliable gauge of a form's potentiality at this juncture in the Oulipo's evolution is whether or not it inspires riffing from others, whether it can withstand variations and adaptations that fall somewhere between homage and parody. If it doesn't, it won't necessarily die—it just may take a while for anything to become of the germs.

The perfect example of this latter delay is the *morale élémentaire* (elementary morality), a rather specific form Queneau minted in his last book. (The book, not the form, was called *Morale élémentaire;* the form, to which one of the book's three sections is dedicated exclusively, was christened thusly for simplicity's sake.) The form has a very deliberate sense of economy to it: it consists of three sets of three-plus-one *bimots*—a noun modified by an adjective,

---

[14] A portmanteau word, after Lewis Carroll's coinage, is one made from the intermingling and contraction of two others: for instance, smoke + fog = *smog;* motor + hotel = *motel;* spoon + fork = *spork.*

such as *maison rouge*[15]—then a refrain of seven lines of one to five syllables each, and finally one more three-plus-one *bimot* set. For instance:[16]

tri sélectif	bibliothèque démontée rayon vide	carton rempli
scotch appliqué	carton pesé mur nu	rayon poussiéreux
guichet particulier	carton pesé citation indisponible	envoi groupé
	c'est pas démontée me dit-elle tu as juste enlevé les livres on s'est jamais vraiment entendus	
envoi pesant	tri infini rayon vide	bibliothèque brûlée

---

[15] In English the adjective precedes the noun, so *maison rouge* (noun adjective) would be flipped to *red house*. Monk has written a bilingual *morale élémentaire*, using words that work as adjectives in English and nouns in French, and vice versa. *Vague promise,* for instance, means "promised wave" in French.

[16] I wrote this at an Oulipo workshop in the summer of 2008, shortly after packing up my books and shipping them off to Chicago—or trying to, anyway, as the French postal service ended up losing most of them in transit. (Happily, I was unaware of this part when I wrote the *morale élémentaire,* which is angsty enough as it is.)

That is:

selective sort	dismantled library empty shelf	full box
scotch tape	weighed box naked wall	dusty shelf
postal counter	weighed box missing citation	media mail
	it's not dismantled she told me you just took out the books we never really got along	
weighty shipment	infinite sort empty shelf	burned library

Queneau was said to have been thinking about the *I Ching* a lot when he devised the form; he told an interviewer one was supposed to hear a gong sounding between *bimots*.

And for a form that would seem to be quite rigid, the *morale élémentaire* has proven to have its fair share of poetic give. Forte condensed it to the *petite morale élémentaire portative* (a riff on Queneau's *Petite cosmogonie portative,* or little portable cosmogony, a versified tour through the history of human knowledge) by removing a few repetitions. The ALAMO, an oulipian annex focused on computer-midwifed literature, developed a program that shuffles the nouns while keeping the adjectives in place, creating 255 possible alternate poems. Valérie Beaudouin has been working on a double-sided version that airs two contrasting perspectives on an issue, and is exploring ways to display the balance subtly through Microsoft PowerPoint. (Having had to make innumerable slideshows for her work at France Télécom, she describes using the software for poetry as "revenge.") I have tinkered with *morales élémentaires* in prose, as well as *bimots* with ambiguous modifiers.[17] In 2008 a whole volume of essays on and experiments with the form was published, bundled with a CD on which various Oulipians read their work aloud, with the occasional literal gong in the background.

61

Toward the end of tonight's reading in Bobigny, Bénabou speaks for a spell about the *morale élémentaire*, then debuts a game he has created: he will read a series of *bimots* that are all roughly synonymous with a hidden phrase that is also the title of a well-known literary work. (For instance: *dim blaze, wan flame, ashen inferno, sallow burn . . .*)[18] Salon urges the audience to shout out the answer as soon as they know what the famous work in question is. Bénabou objects gently on the grounds that these are, after

---

[17] For instance, *rabid dog catcher,* in which the adjective could conceivably modify either word of the compound noun (in French this also requires that both parts of the noun have the same gender). Of course, this makes the *bimot* not really a *bimot* at all, but my point about the evolution of oulipian forms is that this kind of recklessness vis-à-vis the original rules is not only permitted but absolutely healthy as well.

[18] *Pale Fire!*

all, poems. The debate is for naught; nobody identifies any of the titles correctly.[19] Someone guesses wrong for a word pair that turns out to be Tristan Corbière's *Amours jaunes* (Yellow Loves); Bénabou says no with a certain relish.

—◦—

62

The difference between the *morale élémentaire* and Bénabou's interactive game (later named *éthique simpliste,* or simplistic ethics) is a prime example of the difference between traditional oulipian work and what has come to be known within the group, medium-smirkingly, as Oulipo light. An *éthique simpliste* is an amusing guessing game, short on literary gravitas but meant to delight a crowd all but guaranteed to appreciate it; the same could be said for a *sardinosaure* or an *opossum célèbre* or even Perec's mock-axiomatic Proust variations. As with the *baobab,* it works best when heard by an audience, not read quietly to oneself in front of the fireplace. As the Oulipo found more and more success in its public appearances, it began to shift its energy toward performance, and to tailor more and more of its texts for a listenership rather than a readership. "Brevity, orality, and humor," Bénabou told me once, have become the three staples of the public Oulipo.

The old guard of the workshop has not, histori-

---

[19] Whereas, at the *jeudi* not long after where Bénabou introduces the same game to the BNF crowd, most titles are correctly shouted out by two or three *bimots* in.

cally, been without reservations about this. Caradec, closest in sensibility to the spotlight-wary founders, was one of the more vocal members on this point: he didn't quite openly disapprove, but groused in his own way that the sacrifices the group made in order to keep or increase its audience were turning it from *société de littérature* to *société de spectacle*. The intentionally lively character of the group's performances hardly contradicts this, but it's hard to argue that this is wholly negative, or that the group is abandoning its share in the weighty stuff—what Roubaud calls "Oulipo 'ard"—in favor of simple pleasantry. The concern is one that begins and ends in the public sphere, where the workshop's very presence is the real issue.

To wit, hovering somewhere in the wings is a conviction that literature is not *meant* to be performed. For the older members in the group, the threat that multimedia miscegenation poses to the bookish, dignified aura of the French literary industry is not so ridiculous. Fournel explained to me once that some people—indeed, most people—are interested in the Oulipo as a performing group: they have been coming to readings for years and years but have never read a printed oulipian line. (Perhaps they buy a chapbook as a souvenir to recall the fun of the reading, but the reverse used to be the case: you came to hear someone read because you already knew his written work and wanted to hear it from human lungs.) The real threat is that the group will spread itself ever thinner in response to the literary market's demands for people and not printed matter. "We're asked to travel all over the place," Fournel told me—this just after outlining a hellish itinerary for the next couple of months, including Italy, Hungary, Australia, and Louisiana—"but nobody asks us to send them our books."

Fournel himself is one of the group's most engaging readers, as well as a willing creator of some of its most immediate delights. For one thing, he created the *chicago* (of which Bénabou's *éthique simpliste* is a savant and less universally pleasing spinoff): another guessing game where four sets of words or phrases with similar syntax act as clues for a fifth set that is also the homophonized name of a city.[20] True enough, oulipian work should not be over-performed—this much is demonstrated every so often by some well-meaning local theater troupe—but most public appearances the group makes, or agrees to make, strike a suitable balance between respectability and liveliness, profundity and convicted fatuity. The literary texts and the aural ones are little diminished by their coexistence, at least as far as the audience is concerned.

The other effect of this evolution, of course, is that the Oulipians are starting to become seasoned performers. Salon and Fournel are wonderfully magnetic presences on stage; Bénabou is a lusty, charming reader, albeit with the

---

[20] An English example found in the B.O. volume co-authored by Fournel and Roubaud: *suitcase mom; big box brother; vanity case sister; purse grand-ma.* The solution, as it were, is *Baghdad.* The form takes its name, and presumably took its initial inspiration, from the fact that *Chicago* pronounced in French sounds exactly like *chie cagot,* or "shit *(v.)* hypocrite." (The second word is broadened from the Cagots, a historically despised minority in the Basque country of France and Spain.)

occasionally vexing habit of putting a sentence's worth of accumulated emphasis on the final word, giving whatever text he's reading a rather distracting resemblance to an early-eighties rap song. Forte is animated and easy to follow, despite his accent; Le Tellier, to hear Bénabou tell it, has made great progress, at least in terms of articulating his words—he still lacks what you would call a solid stage presence, but he's cultivated this to the point where his lack of stage presence is actually quite satisfying to watch.

One way to think of the twenty-first-century Oulipo, then, is as a group that makes fewer and fewer demands on its audience: all one has to do is show up with a mind open enough to let the oulipian way of thinking take over for an hour or two, the better to follow the acrobatics and convolutions and jokey references to French literature.[21] Those who catch on are apt to be a bit more sympathetic to the heavier stuff, and those who find it lame or pointless never have to come back.

It seems to work on this December evening, insofar as a roomful of librarians with an abstract inkling of what the Oulipo is constitutes the most likely class of actual people[22] to be won over. Members of the audience nod knowingly when they get it—be *it* the veiled pun or the organizing principle of the text itself—and elbow their seatmates inquisitively when they don't. They guess at the

65

---

[21] Of which, in the interest of compassionate disclosure, I understand maybe 65 percent on a good day.

[22] As opposed to French literature scholars. Or rabid dog catchers, for that matter.

éthiques simplistes and the *chicagos,* bolder and bolder each round, and make their own puns about the lighting problems too. The room simply isn't big enough for any meaningful separation between the audience and the stars, and maybe this is what's becoming increasingly possible through the oulipian embrace of performance. It's a big party where four people are facing the other thirty and doing most of the talking, but where, most importantly, just about everyone is in on the joke without knowing the punchline ahead of time.

Nonetheless, there is little ceremony afterwards, little congratulatory hobnobbing: at the end of the night, the Oulipians are still just performers, not so much friends. Some attendees go back for another glass of box wine or another round of pseudo-billiards before they depart, but they don't make a point of interacting with Bénabou or Forte or Salon or Le Tellier any more than they would with the cast of a particularly good *Tartuffe*. Literature is now a little more fun, but not forever demystified. The Oulipians remain for a while, chatting amiably with the few stragglers who approach them, and soon enough they leave, walk for a few blocks, get on the Métro one station short of Bobigny–Raymond Queneau on the Line 5, and go home.

little demons of subtlety

As I write this in San Francisco, Jacques Jouet is at the Place Stalingrad in Paris, writing a serial novel in thirty-two parts. He has agreed to sit for eight hours a day inside a windowed tent at the southwestern tip of the Bassin de la Villette, typing away in 18-point Times while the text on his computer screen is projected onto a display nearby for anyone who cares to monitor his progress. The novel, *Agatha de Paris*, spins a new adventure for Agatha de Win'theuil, a libertine sexagenarian head of state in a post-republican Paris and a central character in Jouet's multi-volume epic about a truck driver called Mek-Ouyes.[1]

---

[1] Because Jouet is by all accounts an uncommonly dignified man, the obvious homophony of *Mek-Ouyes* and *mes couilles*, which can't be translated any more politely than "my balls," is bewilderingly funny. The titles of the first two novels in the series translate, to the unsuspecting ear, as *The Republic of My Balls* and *My Balls in Love.*

This is going on as part of the first edition of *Paris en toutes lettres,* a citywide literature festival sponsored by various cultural and municipal institutions. Its schedule is keeping the Parisian members of the Oulipo busy: Forte, Bénabou, and Le Tellier are running a series of public constrained-writing workshops. Roubaud is reading and discussing poems about Paris, both his and Queneau's. Two actors are performing a selection of texts from the latter's *Exercises in Style.* Odile Fillion, a journalist and director, is screening *L'Oulipo dans les rues* (Oulipo in the Streets), a series of short, lightly constrained films in which members of the group discuss Parisian streets of interest (such as the one where Caradec waxes philosophical about the Place Paul Verlaine, as shown at the *jeudi* in homage to him). Several Oulipians have signed on to hold a reading one night from 11 P.M. to seven the next morning, with the exaggeratedly modest but pleasingly scheherazadian mandate of keeping the audience awake.

The name of Jouet's spectacle is *Tentative d'épuisement d'un auteur* (Attempt to Exhaust an Author)—a nod to Perec's *Tentative d'épuisement d'un lieu parisien* (translated by Mary Folliet as *Attempt to Exhaust a Parisian Spot,* and later by Marc Lowenthal as *An Attempt at Exhausting a Place in Paris*),[2] the book that resulted from the three days in October 1974 that Perec spent on the Place Saint-Sulpice, just writing down what he saw. For Jouet, who is the only member of the Oulipo to make his living solely as an author,

---

[2] Look out for the eminently potential volume *Tentative d'épuisement de Mek-Ouyes* one day in the distant future.

eight hours a day engaged in the act of writing doesn't seem too tall an order, because one assumes he would be doing more or less the same thing somewhere anyway, even if passersby couldn't stop to watch it happen sentence by sentence.

Besides, if this *tentative* is the most public writing gesture he has ever undertaken, it is neither the first nor the most exhausting of its kind. In the mid-1990s Jouet invented the metro poem (or subway poem), a medium that is exactly what it sounds like but where the formal properties of the poem are heavily influenced by the length and route of one's trip: by definition, a metro poem contains one fewer line than the journey contains stops from beginning to end. After a couple of years of playing with the form, Jouet decided to write the *ne plus ultra* of metro poems by passing through every station in the Parisian Métro in a single trip. This he did in April 1996, over fifteen and a half hours and 490 verses, with the aid of an optimized route drawn up for him by graph theorist and fellow Oulipian Pierre Rosenstiehl. ("At the end of those fifteen and a half hours, I was very tired," Jouet wrote in an essay some time afterward.) Then he did it again, a few months later, taking the same route in reverse. Both poems are included, unostentatiously, in a volume published in 2000 called *Poèmes de métro*.

Jouet, who became a member of the Oulipo in 1983, shortly after Perec's death, has a serious face and a measured, attentive bearing. He sits up straight and often stands or walks with his hands clasped behind his back, looking more trial lawyer than contemplative poet. He seems eternally alert, not just observing but also working, at every moment taking in something that will eventually find its way, with minimal alteration, into a piece of literature. He generates and publishes work in enormous quantity: poems, stories, plays, essays, reviews, and, every few years, a new novel of imposing size and thoughtfulness. Still, more remarkable is the degree to which he seems both committed to and successful at erasing any vestigial distinctions between being alive and making literature. "He writes to pass the time, surely," Warren Motte, the most accomplished of a handful of American Oulipo scholars, has remarked, "but also to feel time passing."

To that end, Jouet has written at least a poem a day since 1992, the first four years' worth of which are collected in a 938-page volume called *Navet, linge, oeil-de-vieux* (Turnip, Napkin, Old-Man's-Eye; the last is a kind of biconcave lens). Many of these are addressed poems, which he wrote and mailed to someone, allowing the content of the poem to be determined in part by what he knew or did not know about its intended recipient. (He once said, at least partly in jest, that instead of aspiring to have many people read a few of his poems, he preferred to write many poems and have each one read, if only at first, by a single person.) This is not the only testament to his willed conflation of poetic composition and everyday life; he has also invented the chronopoem, designed to take exactly as much time to recite as a non-poetic task does to execute, and helped to popularize the *gestomètre,* which inventories and examines the tics and motions of a given routine or period of daily time (taking a walk, peeling an orange, skinning a rabbit, composing a *gestomètre*). Many authors write poems that come from the everyday world, but Jouet's usually return there as well, and seem to travel a very short total distance.

Perhaps as a consequence of this, Jouet is sometimes pegged as the most political author in the Oulipo. His longer prose work, such as the *Mek-Ouyes* series and the larger, cyclical "Republic novel" to which it belongs, deals with concepts of governance and citizenship in a civically existential way. Ditto for early poetic works like *107 âmes* (107 Souls), a sort of nationwide micro-census filtered through a subtle structural and rhyming system. In both cases, though, it's important to note that the political is literary, not the other way around. His social critique is "principally ironic and interrogative in character, rather than prescriptive," Motte writes. "Jouet's example argues that even the bleakest of our daily landscapes—a supermarket, a traffic jam, a dentist's waiting room, for heaven's sake—can be traversed poetically." And when your daily landscape becomes poetic, how do you go about writing poetry if not . . . daily?

The more exceptional thing about Jouet's work is its underlying conception of poetry as a fundamentally communal activity, which manifests itself not only in the authorial self-effacement of *107 âmes* and a later collection of explicitly multi-player poems called *Cantates de proximité* (Local Cantatas), but also in the example he sets by demonstrating structures other people can use wherever they are, whatever they're doing. To call Jouet an exemplary poet is more than a compliment: it explains something important about the way he approaches his métier.

71

There is a rare outward quality in his work, without any sacrifice of interiority—he's simply interested in making the practice of composition accessible, in fostering understanding of and appreciation for it on all sides. You or I could also write one poem for each day's commute to work, or for each tree in a public garden; that Jouet has already done such things seems meant foremost to inspire, not discourage, the rest of us.

This is hardly new: recall that oulipian practice grew up around the idea that any structures and forms the workshop turned up in the course of its brainstorming should be available to any writer who saw fit to use them. What is more noteworthy about Jouet's model is that it brackets out the part where you have to be a writer already, someone invested in generating literature for literature's sake. What Jouet brings to the endeavor, besides an easy lyrical grace and a heroic attention span and really good posture, is an actual sustainable way to realize the aphorism by the early twentieth-century poet Lautréamont, quoted early and often in and around the Oulipo: poetry must be made not by one, but by all.

⬥

This has, in turn, changed what it means to characterize something, whether a text or a gesture or a person, as *oulipian*. If the first major evolutionary step in the workshop's conception of its activity was the one Perec and Calvino and their generation took by turning the focus from pseudo-historical speculation to sleeves-rolled-up writing, the second has been a steady enlargement of the notion of oulipian technique to include not only external form but creative procedure as well. First came thinking about constraint, then the actual production of texts reflecting that constraint, then the actual production of texts whose constraint *is* their production.

The metro poem, for instance: it's a free-verse form with rigid compositional rules. You get on the metro and compose the first line of a poem in your head. When the train makes its first stop, you write the line down. When the train starts again, you begin to compose the second line. No writing while the train is in motion; no composing while it's stopped. If you change to a different metro line, you pause on the platform to write down the line you composed before getting off, then start a new stanza for the next leg of the trip. You write down the last line upon arriving at your destination, and then go wherever it is you were going in the first place.

The metro poem is oulipian mostly in the sense that, if done rigorously, it's surprisingly challenging—straightforward as it sounds, the time strictures make it less like a Surrealist free-association exercise and more like a suicide-aerobics drill for the parts of your mind that usually make observations into ruminations and ruminations into language. It constrains the space around your thoughts, not the letters or words in which you will eventually fit them: you have to work to think thoughts of the right size, to focus on the line at hand without workshopping the previous one or anticipating the next. You have to actively avoid the master craftsman's impulse to map out the whole poem, since that would defeat the momentary experientiality of the thing. "There is no question of correcting one's composition, beyond the time of composing the verse, which means that the time for premeditation is reduced to a minimum," Jouet writes. "No manuscript version." (As a rule, Jouet burns his drafts.)

This should be starting to sound a little fishy. No premeditation? No planning, no tweaking, no trial and error? "Free-verse form with rigid compositional rules"? Doesn't much resemble the careful, empirical Oulipo we got to know in the 1970s, where the 400-page novel was propped up on a 100-page set of blueprints and the success or failure of the text could be evaluated by anyone aware of its foreordained structure. The metro poem is a departure from the classical (so to speak) oulipian mode not least because it is unverifiable: its rules affect only the moment of composition, meaning that, for all we can tell, Jouet wrote his 490-line überpoem in three hours in his bedroom, or at a café on the rue Mouffetard over a Perrier with lemon syrup, instead of on a mind-numbing series of trains under the curious gaze of a revolving cast of passengers. Jouet has since stopped writing metro poems for this reason: once he realized how easily he could fake them, he lost interest.

Essentially, the chief constraint in the metro poem is what you can notate in the ten seconds or so the train is stopped at a station. (I asked Jouet about this once, suspicious that some of his lines were simply too long to transcribe in such an interval, to which he replied coolly that he had a pretty sophisticated shorthand system.) Fixed forms like the sonnet and the sestina were the bread and butter of the early Oulipo; even Jean Lescure's S + 7 technique, which is nothing if not procedural, leaves no real room for the vagaries of process—nothing accidental ever happens on the way from one noun to the seventh that comes after it in a dictionary. Shifting the group's orientation from poetry seminar to writers' workshop didn't change that; the lipogram and the palindrome and the *morale élémentaire,* whether you use them to determine what letters are allowed or what actions a character should take, are still mechanisms you can examine later and evaluate in basically black-and-white terms. Jouet's innovation in the Oulipo has largely been to screw with that binary system, to unfix the forms.

75

     This, too, hearkens back to one of the many theses bandied about in the group's exploratory early years, in this case by the insuperably wise Le Lionnais, who argued that procedures and protocols, not texts, were potential. This makes particular sense in that whatever constraint or rule you embrace can unlock words and angles and ideas that would have been inaccessible otherwise—solutions that wouldn't exist, in effect, without the problem. Jouet has taken it further by making the connection between constraint and protocol more explicit and intuitive, and by extending the range of potentially potential activities to include those so innocuous as to be indistinguishable from everyday life.

◄○►

The word *constraint,* it may as well be said, is not the optimal way to sum up what the Oulipo does. Le Tellier, in *Esthétique de l'Oulipo,* remarks that the term is to be, depending on your translation, taken with a grain of salt or handled with tweezers. It's convenient to speak of "constraint-based literature," as most scholars and reviewers and hapless would-be explainers do, because the most iconic of the group's output truly is beholden to restrictive rules—to write lipograms in E, for instance, Harry Mathews used to actually place an upturned thumbtack on the E key of his typewriter. But the relevance of the word breaks down quickly after that, unless you're willing to take as broad a meaning of it as Mathews does in the *Oulipo Compendium,* where he defines it as "the strict and clearly definable rule, method, procedure, or structure that generates every work that can be properly called oulipian."

That's not the last word about the terminology involved, but it's the most sensible one for our purposes here. The mild scholarly catfighting over the relative universality of the oulipian constraint and how it differs from a convention in the linguistic sense and its "transgressive, nonconsensual nature" vis-à-vis the reader (and so on) tends to get repetitive and abstruse, and is not enough fun to dwell on here; besides, Jouet, who would seem especially entitled to object to nomenclatorial abuses, takes it on faith that *constraint* describes the modus oulipiandi well enough. The encapsulation he offers in the essay "With (and Without) Constraints"[3] is about as complete as the non-theorist needs to be: the constraint is the problem and the text is a solution.

Jouet is no less handy than other Oulipians with

---

[3] Roxanne Lapidus's translation.

the more orthodox, verifiable constraints—in addition to
"Oh! L'ostrogoth!" see "Les sept règles de Perec" (Perec's
Seven Themes), a completely lucid analysis of Perec's aesthetic that also happens to be a monovocalism—just not
floored by them. What concerns him more is the interpretive value of the original problem, the three-way relationship among constraint and writer and reader. The question
of whether an oulipian work should come with an explanation of the rules or structures behind it is the biggest active
debate in the workshop, the one theoretical argument that
can't quite be shrugged off as para-oulipian. After all, a constraint used as a generative device is bound to have an effect on not only the shape but also the content of the resulting text, if the text is any good. On one hand, to conceal its
use from the reader is to deprive him of an integral part of
its meaning. On the other hand, doesn't calling attention to
that artifice potentially corrupt him, close his mind, ensure
that he focuses on the formal peculiarities over the underlying creative soul? "Sometimes," Fournel says, "the constraint is like a clown nose."

77

It makes sense that Jouet should be in favor of
transparency; for him, the valuable thing is where the poem
or story comes from, and the stages of mediation by which
it came into readable being.[4] That process and the polished
final product are not just equally interesting but in fact in-
separable—*artifice,* remember, literally means "the making
of art." Jouet is thus scrupulously accountable to the reader
whenever there's more than meets the eye, and it serves his

---

[4] Not that that's going to stop him from burning his drafts.

work well: one of his most constrained books, a short novel composed of 216 short sections that vary methodically in length, becomes a lot more fascinating when you know that each section is also a potential ending to the same story. A note to that effect is included as a postscript—although the book's title, *Fins* (Ends), might tip you off from the get-go. "The scaffolding is more than a tool," Jouet reasons in "With (and Without) Constraints." "It is a fundamental part of the substance."

The primary spokesperson for the other camp is Mathews, who typically refuses to reveal the Byzantine structures at work in his novels—particularly those he wrote before joining the Oulipo, *The Conversions* and *Tlooth* and *The Sinking of the Odradek Stadium,* which read like movies written by Raymond Roussel and directed by Alfred Hitchcock. The sense of convolution in those novels is thick and ornate; the weirdness of the events and places described is matched only by the well-spoken impassivity of the narrator himself, or herself (it's not always clear which). You never doubt seriously that the author has complete control of the proceedings, but that doesn't mean you understand a whiff of them. Perec, a man who wrote a book where people spontaneously drop dead instead of uttering words that contain the letter E, once described Mathews's narrative world as one "determined by rules from another planet."

For Mathews—who has claimed his ideal reader is someone who finishes one of his novels, throws it out the window of an upper-floor apartment, and is already taking the elevator down to retrieve it by the time it lands—keeping you on your toes and in the dark is just as compassionate a stance as revealing everything is for Jouet. "I find that what most intensifies the reading experience is the *awareness* that a hidden pattern or structure exists," Mathews told an interviewer a few years ago, "without one's exactly knowing what it is." Elsewhere, he makes the same argument more abstractly: "It's obviously much more interesting to be curious about a riddle than to find out the solution."

Historically, Oulipians have erred on Mathews's side, albeit not so staunchly. Queneau, who according to Motte felt that "constraints must not overshadow the finished work, and pretext should never override text," was inclined to treat his methods as genuine use-and-remove scaffolding. He didn't object when Claude Simonnet wrote a book "deciphering" the math behind Queneau's first novel —but then that happened thirty years later, just as Perec's blueprints for his 1978 *Life A User's Manual* weren't published until 1995. The encrypted language of a hyperintelligent dog in Roubaud's *La Princesse Hoppy* went without explication for seventeen years until 2008, when a publisher named Dominique Fagnot cracked the code and won the author's grudging permission to print a new edition. Calvino balked at revealing the algorithmic underpinnings of *If on a winter's night a traveler,* and ended up doing so only for the lucky few francophones who got their hands on the B.O. volume about it. The exegesis has since been translated into English, but Calvino made it plain that it was never to appear in Italian.

These demystifications don't help move any more units, but they prove Mathews right on one score: a reader's certainty that there is something to figure out can ensure

79

the sort of ultra-attentive reading most authors dream of. Cultivating the requisite mystery is a two-way street, though, because a sleuthing reader can miss the forest for the patterns on the bark. "The problem, when you see the constraint," Perec complained once, "is that you see nothing *but* the constraint."

◄○►

"Most writers—poets in especial—prefer having it understood that they compose by a species of fine frenzy—an ecstatic intuition—and would positively shudder at letting the public take a peep behind the scenes, at the elaborate and vacillating crudities of thought." This is Edgar Allan Poe, in an 1846 essay called "The Philosophy of Composition," in which he purports to detail the pseudo-scientific process by which he wrote "The Raven"—"step by step, to its completion, with the precision and rigid consequence of a mathematical problem."[5]

The model of ecstatic intuition is in a sense what the Oulipo was designed to discredit, but the resonance of

---

[5] Posterity is divided as to whether or not he really wrote "The Raven" the way he describes. You want to take him at his word for a while, but eventually he recounts this deductive spree where he decides that the poem should have a refrain and deems the *-or* sound the most dramatic and the word *nevermore* the best suited to it and then concludes that the best way to account for the refrain of *nevermore* is to have it uttered by "a non-reasoning creature capable of speech" ("very naturally, a parrot, in the first instance, suggested itself, but was superseded forthwith by a Raven") and you start to suspect he's having a laugh at your expense.

Poe's exercise only grows as the workshop's antics become more and more familiar. To the question of whether to keep or throw away the scaffolding, we must now add the question of how likely the building underneath is to receive a fair appraisal either way. Jouet is resolute on the point that just because he's a member of the Oulipo doesn't mean everything he writes is oulipian; Mathews takes the same position, frequently referring to *Cigarettes* (of which he will say only that it is based on "a permutation of situations") as his only truly oulipian novel. But try telling this to a reader who's heard of the Oulipo, picks up a book written by an Oulipian without any particular organizing principle, and goes looking for structures that aren't even there.

81

This is something that could be called oulipian reading, which differs from regular reading only in the reader's degree of complicity with the author—regardless of the author's desire for it. Whether or not the constraint is made explicit ahead of time, or ever, the oulipian reader is conditioned to be attentive to formal devices and clever lexical workarounds and things that look like clues—and to register the plot or subject matter, such as it is, on a secondary level. The oulipian reader expects to be duped at every turn; she is convinced, beyond even the author's sworn testimony to the contrary, that nothing is accidental.[6] The oulipian reader would notice that "The Raven" is a lipogram in Z.

---

[6] Being such a reader, I spent two pages of an undergraduate thesis speculating on the potential meaning of the typos I found in certain volumes of the *Bibliothèque Oulipienne,* all of which I'm now pretty sure were just legitimate printing errors.

Those who read an oulipian work without leaving a breadcrumb trail, on the other hand, do so at their own peril. Such was notably the case with René-Marill Albérès of *Les Nouvelles littéraires,* who, reviewing *La Disparition* in May 1969, took Perec to task for his new novel situated in "the murkiest of all recent politico-criminal scandals" and written in "subtly jarring language"—and who has since become the butt of one big ongoing historical joke for completely failing to notice that the book didn't contain the most common vowel in the alphabet:[7]

> *La Disparition* is a raw, violent, and facile fiction. [. . .]
> The mystery remains entire, but the novel is finished;
> that is the contemporary form of "literary" detective
> fiction (as in Robbe-Grillet, though in a different
> style). Perec carries it off perfectly, in a book that is
> captivating and dramatic, but that gives off a strong
> whiff of artifice.[8]

---

[7] By the same token, in *Georges Perec: A Life in Words,* David Bellos reports of Perec's palindrome of 5,000+ words: "At Manchester, in 1989, doctored photocopies and unsigned handwritten versions were given to students and teachers of French who were asked, respectively, to use it for the exercise of *explication de texte* and to mark it as an essay. Perec's palindrome barely made sense to the readers. Some teachers took it for the work of an incompetent student, while others suspected that they had been treated to a surrealist text produced by 'automatic writing.' Those with psychiatric interests identified the author as an adolescent in a dangerously paranoid state; those who had not forgotten the swinging sixties wondered whether it was LSD or marijuana that had generated the disconnected images of the text."

[8] David Bellos's translation.

The Oulipo no longer is in a position—if it ever was—to control the monster it's created, which means that the same defensive reading tactics that taught us to admire a book like *La Disparition* for its technical artistry and compensatory virtuosity more immediately than for its narrative offerings—in essence, to appreciate it on its own terms—now apply to texts that may have no secrets to uncover. (A cynical but not unreasonable interpretation of the Canada Dry principle would be just that: getting the reader to drive herself mad in search of a key, a code-crack, that doesn't exist.) "An Oulipian's name on the cover sends the reader down the path of suspecting a constraint governing the entire work—even or especially when there is none," Jouet explains in an essay called "Rumination des divergences" (Rumination on Divergences) published in the *Bibliothèque Oulipienne*. "The reader, more oulipian than the Oulipian and craftier than the devil, [takes] a clever and quasi-masochistic pleasure in spouting out the farthest-fetched hypotheses." He goes on to recall an interviewer who accused him of not revealing everything going on in *Fins,* declaring triumphantly that she'd discovered that each paragraph contained an adverb.

So the stakes of the debate about revealing constraint include the credibility of the author and maybe the sanity of the reader, too. "In both cases the intention was the same," Leland de la Durantaye explains of the origins of the argument: "telling—or *not* telling—the reader of the existence and nature of a constraint was done—or *not* done—to free the reader from the inessential—*the constraint*—so as to better enjoy, experience, and judge the essential—*the work.*" This might have flown in the workshop's early years, but as its reputation for mischief has solidified, so has readers' disinclination to take any authorial indications at face value.

And once you're convinced that there's something going on behind the scenes, it's really, really hard not to look for it. Perec published a total of two poems—"L'Eternité" (Eternity) and "Poème" (Poem)—that are free of constraint, at least as far as several years' worth of Perec exegetes can tell, and that's essentially all anyone ever has to say about them. But people regularly beg off taking the time to read *La Disparition,* because they know what the trick is: it's a book without the letter E. Which is true—and those people probably do have better things to do if they're not curious to see how the trick pans out—but when you're someone who has spent a totally sociopathic amount of time and effort making that trick successful, it's hardly an ideal reception.

—◄○►—

Henry James deals with all this in a 1896 novella called "The Figure in the Carpet," which pops up every now and then in oulipian discussion. The narrator is an aspiring literary critic who chances to meet an author he venerates, Hugh Vereker. In discussing his work, Vereker alludes mysteriously, but with a hint of long-simmering dissatisfaction, to the unifying *thing* in all of his novels:

> "It stretches, this little trick of mine, from book to book, and every thing else, comparatively, plays over

the surface of it. The order, the form, the texture of my books will perhaps some day constitute for the initiated a complete representation of it. So it's naturally the thing for the critic to look for. It strikes me," my visitor added, smiling, "even as the thing for the critic to find."

This seemed a responsibility indeed. "You call it a little trick?"

"That's only my little modesty. It's really an exquisite scheme."

Naturally the narrator is soon consumed by the pursuit of said scheme, and just as naturally things don't end too happily, especially after a string of inconvenient deaths among everyone who's managed to put a finger on it.[9]

What's powerful about the story is that it does equal justice to the frustration of such a gambit on both sides of the pen: on the reader's end, being absolutely sure that there's some literary McGuffin—on "every page and line and letter," and "stuck into every volume as your foot is stuck into your shoe"—that you simply can't find; on the author's, being exasperated that your readers, even the very best and most devoted among them, simply can't find what you're writing for in the first place. "I live almost to see if it will ever be detected," Vereker admits. "But I needn't worry—it won't!"

It's hard to know, frankly, whether either author or reader would be any happier with the cat out of the bag, no

---

[9] James does not go so far as to suggest that these people die *because* they've put their fingers on the scheme, although that would be pretty badass.

matter who let it out. The reader would lose his essence-permeating quest; the author would lose his air of elegant enigma. (If you had only seen Roubaud's exasperated shrug when Fagnot deciphered the dog code in *La Princesse Hoppy*.) "This is the classic dilemma of the practical joker," writes journalist John Sturrock in a biographical essay about Perec: "whether to play your joke and creep quietly away without revealing yourself, or to wait immodestly on the spot for the acclaim to start." This is as good a reason as any for the lack of formal ruling on the subject within the Oulipo. The mystery remains suspended over Queneau's insistence that the workshop's true concern is only the structure and not the application, only the tools and not the building.

Jouet, more lab-worker than theoretician, would dispense with the Poe in poetry anyway. "There is no such thing as a natural poem," he writes in "With (and Without) Constraints," "but the illusion of one is very real." And even as he goes farther than most in fostering that illusion, he also injects a certain practical honesty into it, not just revealing the methods that led to the work but laying bare the conditions of its existence in order to put you too in the potential position of creator. In the best cases, drawing attention to oulipian constraint—by talking about it or by hiding it—is not a question of exposing the structure so that it can be used again, or even so that it can be admired: it's a question of making you, the reader, aware of your own effort and engagement, of putting you in control, of diminishing the distance between finding and making.

IAN MONK IS AT LUNCH at a Chinese restaurant in Bourges discussing the clinamen with some bearded men. Lucretius, one of the bearded men observes, defined the clinamen as the minute deviation in atomic motion at the source of our productively turbulent universe: that seemingly random swerve which explains why atoms collide with one another, causing nature to create things and keeping us all from being automata. The rest of the table murmurs in assent. It is indeed a good point of origin (even though Lucretius cribbed it from Epicurus) for a term that has, itself, swerved a great deal throughout the history of theory, showing up in the rhetoric of pedagogues like Jacques Derrida and Gilles Deleuze and Harold Bloom with different connotations each time. As far as the Oulipo is concerned, the clinamen is a voluntary breaking of a self-imposed rule. Unsubstantiated rumor has it that a word with the letter E is secreted away somewhere in Perec's *Disparition*—that would be a clinamen, would it not?

Monk, who presides over the discussion patiently but without immediately evident interest, clarifies that for a transgression to be rightly pegged as a clinamen, it must have been possible for the author to achieve his or her goal *without* disobeying the rule. Had Perec simply been unable to think of a lipogrammatic way to say "Sweden," that wouldn't count; only if he could just as easily have used Norway or Finland or "mid-Scandinavia" would the decision—and it has to be a decision—be interesting.[1] The clinamen, in the oulipian sense, is thus a little bit cocky, a show of good-natured disdain for propriety and rectitude and general orderliness, like chipping the nose off the Sphinx just to bewilder posterity.

Good-natured disdain is not unfamiliar to Monk, whom Forte described to me once as *le punk de l'Oulipo*. Monk is as unlikely a public intellectual as one can imagine; his oratory owes more than a little to the anti-style stylings of the post-punk generation, his public bearing and private demeanor convey an equal sense of youthful recklessness, and in good company he drinks, as the French say, like a hole. He was born near London but has lived for several years with his wife and children in a suburb of Lille, in the

---

[1] A better example: the fiendishly detailed blueprints for *Life A User's Manual* required that Chapter 73 contain a floor made of linoleum, but the idea of a linoleum floor irked Perec for some reason, so he named a character in that chapter Lino and called it a day. In defense of this decision (and welcoming any accusations of pretentiousness), Perec liked to quote Paul Klee: "Genius is the error in the system."

north of France, where he works as a literary and industrial translator. His French is impeccable, but he maintains a blunt English accent and one surmises, ultimately, that he derives something important from being a bit of an out-sider—not so much in the group as in the whole country. He is also subject to a larger share of the mispronunciations and misspellings that plague all of the Oulipians besides Olivier Salon and Jacques Jouet,[2] because "Ian" is phoneti-cally unintuitive to the French; his name on the program of one group reading, at an architectural school in Paris, was "Yan Munk." He doesn't seem to care much.

89

Monk's first dalliances with the Oulipo were as a translator of some of Perec's lesser-discussed works, in-cluding *Les Revenentes,* which in his hands became *The Ex-eter Text: Jewels, Secrets, Sex.* (He translated a few pages of *La Disparition* as well, just to see whether it could be done, then got "carried away" and wound up with a com-plete E-less manuscript called *A Vanishing,* which he sub-mitted to the proper authorities only to learn that the rights had been licensed to a Scotsman named Gilbert Adair a few weeks prior. Adair's translation, *A Void,* remains the only English version to have been published.) Monk's induc-

---

[2] That is, both Salon and Jouet have names that are common nouns, the opposite of proper nouns. *Jouet* means toy, *olivier* olive tree, and *salon* living room. (As a noun, *jacques* is roughly the French equiva-lent of *john,* in the sense of "privy.") I bring this up only by way of continuing to illustrate the oulipian conception of the silver lining, in that almost immediately upon learning of Heath Ledger's death in 2008 I began to compile a list of people of historical import whose names also fit this syntactic criterion: River Phoenix, Bob Hope, Carry Nation, etc.

tion into the group came in 1998 after he assisted Harry Mathews in compiling an English primer to the group's work, the *Oulipo Compendium,* by which time he was already an adept poet in the oulipian mode—at least in the kinds of Perecquian forms he was used to translating, or rather transposing into a different language.

His early work in English, now gathered in two volumes called *Family Archaeology* and *Writings for the Oulipo,* is impressively inventive and disciplined; it gives the sense that he is not so much a literary genius as a clever hard worker, one who has taken pains to extend his vocabulary to include all the words and terms useful only in extremely specific circumstances, the way a hardcore Scrabble player might memorize all 100-odd acceptable two-letter words. In French, though, Monk is generally phenomenal. In part because verbal acrobatics do not come as easily in a foreign tongue, and in part because his time in the Oulipo has exposed him to more sophisticated and less obvious models of formal inquiry, he has a far easier time putting abstract rules to sensitive, relevant, conventionally *literary* use. He is better at justifying, and in a sense transcending, the structural contrivances he adopts.

His first major publication in French is a book-length poem called *Plouk Town* (*plouk* translates roughly to "hick"), which narrates the day-to-day frustrations of a small town's worth of rut-bound malcontents[3] and is, for

---

[3] In spite of which, and this testifies either to the book's excellence or to the global obtuseness of elected officials, the city of Lille awarded Monk the Prix Jean Lévy, an annual arts prize with a handsome cash takeaway, a few months after *Plouk Town* was published.

my money, the most significant work the Oulipo has produced since the mid-1990s. It is beholden to some rigorous
formal rules—the numbers of words in each line and of
lines in a stanza and of stanzas in a section are simply but
strictly regulated—and to some more happenstance ones as
well, such as its occasional flirtation with sestina-based
permutations and its total lack of punctuation. But compared to the intensity of the poem, the bitingly colloquial
angst coming from its innumerable nameless speakers, the
structures hardly register. It works so well in part because
Monk is one of the Oulipians who's least afraid to be dirty
or libidinous or gross—his command of crude French ver-
nacular is wonderful, and extroverted with a flair that could
only have originated in a foreigner's consciousness—and in
part because the book is as much about language as it is
about anything else. Since then he has hit his stride with a
vengeance, bringing to his work (including the occasional
dip back into English, such as "Our Why and Our Where
and Our How," which smartly picks apart the limerick
form) a dry intelligence at once indebted to oulipian studies and situated, voluntarily, just outside their purview.

Monk is another technician whose involvement
with the Oulipo has probably made him a better writer, but
he brings to that relationship a non-native perspective that
does justice to both sides. In his case, joining the group
steered him *away* from the cheeky letterplay that brought
him there, replacing it with ideas at once more personal
and higher-concept, more "experimental" in the real sense
of the word rather than the euphemism-for-unnecessarily-
inaccessible sense. (As with Jouet and the metro poem,
Monk says he stopped writing anagrams when he realized

he could use them to say what he intended to—i.e., that the fetters of the constraint were no longer tight enough.) The turning point, maybe, was his move from a dilettante's easy-to-explain version of the Oulipo—*Ah, yes, the people who don't use the letter E*—to a genuine working view of how things like combinatorics and permutation can be both effective and affecting. Not that any of this has diminished his feistiness, or made him any more inclined to tarry on matters of theoretical dogma. "The Oulipo is a reaction," someone in Bourges posits later. "Yes," says Monk, without missing a beat, "like an allergy."

—◁o▷—

This afternoon in Bourges the clinamen is on the table, so to speak, because everyone around it has spent the morning trying his or her hand at writing poems under one oulipian constraint or another, and it's become a truth locally acknowledged that finding an ingenious way to break the rules can be just as satisfying as finding an ingenious way to obey them. This is the fifth summer in a row that the Oulipo has held a weeklong constrained-writing immersion course in Bourges, a commune smack in the center of France, open to anyone who cares to pay a couple hundred euros to learn about sestinas and lipograms from the masters.

Bourges is one of those unassuming minor French towns that have a little bit of local flavor but don't seem to have many impressive features—Perec namedropped it once as an example of a town indistinguishable from any other biggish one in Europe—until suddenly you happen upon a six-century-old cathedral that knocks you flat with Gothic classiness. There is a yearly music festival there, Le Printemps de Bourges, and an art school, in whose facilities most of the oulipian *Récréations* take place. The affair is put on by Les Mille Univers, a small letterpress that prints lovely little books and occasionally larger-run titles, like an expanded and illustrated compendium of Roubaud and Salon's *sardinosaures.* The trappings are simple: a few classrooms, a sunny courtyard where a lot of milling and smoking and pacing and syllable-counting goes on, and a small auditorium that each evening holds a reading by one of the Oulipians and then, at the end of the week, a group recital by all the attendees.

93

This year there are about forty-five participants, more than half of whom are women. Some are weekend warriors who have shown up on a lark; others are self-appointed members of *la famille,* the groupies who constitute the core audience of the *jeudis* and are regulars at the Oulipo's forays outside Paris. Many of us know one another already, but the week is refreshingly cliqueless—too small for anyone to feel estranged, since everyone is there for some variation on the same reason. By the end of the week all the parties involved come to seem familiar, from the off-duty publishers and journalists and teachers to the small Mille Univers team running the show, to the art school groundskeeper, who can be seen in the courtyard in the early evenings walking a baby Rottweiler named Sarko. Facial hair abounds; interesting socks, exotic cigarettes, polka-dotted scarves worn to generally successful effect.

All of us *écrivains potentiels*—potential writers— are divided up the first morning into five groups, which are instructed over the next two days by a revolving cast of Oulipians: Bénabou, Jouet, Le Tellier, Monk, and Forte. (Salon does not make it until a day later; Fournel, though billed to participate, is tied up in London.) Each instructor has more or less the same lesson to get through during each half-day session, so that everybody is up to speed on *beaux présents* and Turkish verses, but each does so at his own speed and with his own emphasis. Bénabou is professorial and quick to correct errors; Jouet takes a sort of Zen approach to conducting the group and perks up only when a mistake opens up a new way of approaching the exercise. Monk is compassionate, but more class prankster than instructor; Le Tellier feigns disinterest but is attentive and oddly masterful; Forte is almost too excited to explain a concept without getting sidetracked by all manner of auxiliary potentialities. I will slowly discover, over the next few years, that what these people are like as workshop leaders is virtually identical to what they're like as writers, as collaborators, as colleagues.

For two days, we learn and try such techniques as the perverb, which splices the beginning of one proverb with the end of another *(A stitch in time gathers no moss),* then write micro-stories illustrating those curious morals. We learn the *textée,* a sort of auto-translated game of telephone whose object is to turn a poem into a set of instructions *(Invite your interlocutor to join you at a time whose ambient conditions call to mind a medical procedure),* then give those instructions to a mentally blindfolded partner who produces something that doesn't resemble the original poem at all.[4] Le Tellier, who leads the workshop when my group learns the *textée,* has everyone write from the same set of instructions, then tells those of us who finish early to begin working on instructions for a second poem to do with a partner—rather beautifully, in my opinion, refusing to account for the possibility that anyone in the room doesn't know at least one poem by heart.

We learn about the sonnet, which according to certain members of the Oulipo couldn't be further from a fixed form, and about the sestina, a centuries-old creature based on six six-line stanzas whose end-words are repeated in a spiral pattern: 1-2-3-4-5-6, then 6-1-5-2-4-3, then 3-6-4-1-2-5, and so on. (Six is not the only number of items that returns to its original order after that number of turns—in mathematics, numbers that can permute this way are called Queneau numbers.) The sestina and its variants are a big

---

[4] The *textée,* a high-concept Mad Lib for poetry buffs, is a variant of the *pictée,* which does the same thing with a painting instead of a poem; the *pictée* takes its name from the *dictée,* or dictation, a French academic tradition in which students have to listen to and transcribe a text filled with phonetic and orthographic traps (such as *Si six scies scient six cigares, six cent six scies scient six cent six cigares,* which is a semantically vacuous statement about saws and cigars but which sounds like the letter C repeated a dozen times with a few other syllables thrown in at random). My example comes from T. S. Eliot's "Let us go then, you and I / When the evening is spread out against the sky / Like a patient etherised upon a table," but the idea is for you to turn it into something like "Join me for dinner, dear one / When the air is undergoing a sex-change operation from dainty dawn to manly mid-morning."

deal in the Oulipo, by virtue of both their antique pedigree and their conceptual versatility; since time is a constraint too, however, we write terinas (1-2-3 / 3-1-2 / 2-3-1) and merely imagine loftier dimensions. We learn about the *parcours obligé* (mandatory path), or *logo-rallye,* in which one word submitted by each member of the group is written on a board, the collected words becoming the milestones in various exercises—a paragraph in which all of them appear in the order they are listed, or a terina using three of them as end-words.

And of course we learn about alphabetical manipulations like tautograms, where each word begins with the same letter; pangrams, which contain all the letters in the alphabet, preferably with as few repeats as possible; and texts where word initials are in alphabetical order. (The rarity of W in French results in a lot of mini-stories that just kind of happen without warning to involve whiskey, wagons, or the Walloons). We learn about the *apéro* constraint, where the letters in each word must alternate between vowels and consonants; the prisoner's constraint, where letters with ascenders and descenders are disallowed;[5] the liberated prisoner's constraint, which allows only letters *with* ascenders and descenders (plus vowels). Most of us already know what anagrams and lipograms and monovo-

---

[5] Ascenders and descenders are the parts of a lowercase letter that extend above or beneath the height of an *x:* the prisoner's constraint thus disallows b, d, f, g, h, j, k, l, p, q, t, and y. (The namesake image is that of a prisoner languishing in a cell writing his memoirs, missives, death threats, etc., limiting himself to the most compact letters in order to conserve ink and paper.) See Monk's "a russian con's economic missive."

calisms and homophones are—imagine agreeing to spend a
week with six Oulipians if you didn't—but we learn about
those too, just in case.

On the blank side of the page, some of these forms
are stimulating; some are annoying, some enchanting, some
just plain difficult. (As a non-native French speaker, I find
most of them harder than everyone else does, but the
French-English dictionary with which I refuse to part gives
me a certain advantage when, for instance, we need to
stockpile a whole lot of adjectives that start with the letter M.) For some exercises you can make do with hard work
or focused imagination—if you have an ear for language and
a reasonably weighty vocabulary (or, again, a dictionary),
you can get into the spirit easily enough. On the other hand,
some seem insurmountably and pointlessly arduous, something like the way most of us feel about standardized tests:
strength training for muscles that we hesitate to imagine
ever using. The cool thing about these workshops, though,
is that one man's piece of cake is another man's ball and
chain; we all excel at totally different things, and part of
making proper use of the Oulipo is recognizing what you're
good at and what you aren't, what you like and what you
don't, what you could brush up on with some practice and
what isn't even worth the effort. Sometimes the spark just
doesn't come, at which times it's actually a little irritating to see what good and fluent poets the workshop leaders are.

But sometimes this beautiful unexpected *eureka*
moment comes, where you take stock of the options available to you and the way forward becomes clear, and you
make your way out of the labyrinth to discover you're no-

97

where near where you thought you were going to end up—and there you are, standing next to a poem that you wouldn't believe you could write if it weren't in your handwriting, surrounded by your false starts and eraser smudges. You've liberated something you didn't know you were holding back, written on a topic you didn't realize was on your mind, or in a tonal register you didn't think you had, or with an alien artistry that amazes you but seems completely natural to the acquaintances all around you. Sometimes that artistry is directly related to the constraint at hand, but just as often it's not—you've just pulled a fast one on yourself and unlocked this weird, encouraging accidental profundity.

This happens to me more than once: while working on an antonymic translation of a Baudelaire poem; after realizing that a word I just learned and that has been rattling around in my head contains only letters that are also in my name; when, in the midst of a lackluster *morale élémentaire,* I decide to fold my frustrations into the poem itself. It's not just me, even if for most people there's less sense of a linguistic challenge to overcome: I see that just-clicked moment repeatedly on faces all around the room, as the other rats-in-training wait eagerly to read out what they've come up with or giggle softly to themselves, chew on their pencils for a second, then resume scribbling with feverish glee.

—◄○►—

On the third morning, each Oulipian announces the theme he will be exploring in greater detail for the rest of the week, leaving the attendees to pick the group that most interests them. Le Tellier will work on forms in collectively authored fiction, Salon on dialogue incorporating oulipian techniques. Forte and Monk plan to tinker with some of the more serious and exotic poetic forms, like the Japanese *tanka* (an extended variant of the haiku) or the Malayan pantoum; Bénabou will run a boot camp for those who don't even know what a haiku is.[6] Jouet will focus on procedural constraints. Each proposal earns a sheepish show of hands, and we all shuffle into our respective groups. I go with Bénabou's boot camp for the day, but, out of impatience masquerading as reportorial conscientiousness, make known my intention to migrate from theme to theme.

The *généraliste* workshop is populated by the attendees whose day-to-day pursuits have the least to do with the Oulipo. (A few among us, as it turns out, genuinely don't know what a haiku is.) Bénabou is in his element, every bit the teacher in a room full of heads to be filled with proper oulipian protocols. After finishing his own exercises—I notice that he moves his eyebrows while he writes—he strolls around the room to check on the progress of ours, sometimes taking a student's pencil in hand to correct errors including but not limited to the spelling of "Bénabou." I get a mild verbal lashing for my failure to grasp the difference between monosyllabic words and two-syllable words that end with a mute E; someone else misunderstands the instructions for a second round of *logo-rallye* and gets a stern reprimand from Bénabou, who nonetheless makes a note of the mistake for follow-up exploration.

---

6 The fools!

The class is as much a history lesson as it is a writing course: when we do *beaux présents,* Bénabou tells us about Perec's writing the first one (for Claude Berge, another Oulipian), and about his reading the first epithalamium at Roubaud's wedding. It is both inspiring and bittersweet to think that Bénabou was there to see the genesis of these forms, these delights, but is now one of only a few to have a firsthand relationship to it. His workshop feels at times like the place where he gets to teach us the Oulipo as he remembers it, before it evolved to attract people like us.

After lunch, talk turns to the alexandrine, the twelve-syllable core of the French sonnet, and to Queneau's proto-oulipian book of 100,000,000,000,000 potential poems powered by the combinatorial presentation of ten metrically identical sonnets. Our collective sluggishness to cotton on to the mathematical implications behind this feat wears on Bénabou's patience; so does our refusal to understand the rules and conventions of French prosody—rules such as where the two halves of an alexandrine are supposed to split, or when an E is pronounced and when it's liaised—despite his impromptu rattling off of a handful of perfect lines. (Any inner smugness I had built up earlier in the day by already being familiar with the elementary constraints is quickly voided by my complete and continuing failure to master these rules.)

At the end of the day, Bénabou tells us we've only glimpsed the tip of the iceberg—a comment that, although true, is harder than it should be to take as encouraging. We have done an honest day's worth of learning and been made into better practitioners of techniques in which we expressed interest, but I come away wondering whether his brusque deskside manner isn't meant, in some way, to dissuade us from too casual an interest in the Oulipo. The message seems to be that there is real, precise work involved—more than can be picked up in a week of *récréation*. And true enough, it's not his place to encourage us to be better writers, or writers at all; his task is only to see that we understand the structures and techniques available to us. It's not hard to imagine Queneau correcting the Oulipo's new recruits with a similar lack of indulgence. Nothing smarts like others taking lightly what you yourself take seriously.

As for me, I take all of this stuff pretty seriously, care a great deal not only about understanding where it comes from but also about doing it right and well: what I feel, though I won't realize it until I have been cast two years later, is that I am *auditioning*. This makes me thinner-skinned than my fellow boot campers, who are here to tickle themselves by writing strange and surprising poems, and who at the end of the week will return to lives totally and wholesomely unrelated to potential literature. One of the least literary people at the workshop later tells me that Bénabou's critiques made her feel completely *nulle*—hopelessly inept—but that she couldn't care less.

—◦—

To hear Fournel tell it, in an article called "Oulipo Workshops: Writing Here and Now" included in a 2001 issue of *Le Magazine Littéraire* devoted to the Oulipo, the group came by its pedagogical gig more by happenstance than by desire. "The technical potential was there, as well as the experience," he writes, pointing out that several Oulipians have teaching backgrounds, "but the desire was middling, and even today certain Oulipians are, frankly, hostile toward courses and workshops." As early as 1962 Queneau declared that, with regard to the group's aims, it was "not a question of conditioning the inspiration of writers—that doesn't concern us."

The first workshop was held in July 1976 at the Chartreuse Notre-Dame-du-val-de-Bénédiction, a Carthusian monastery in Villeneuve-lès-Avignon in the south of France. The notion caught on, and over a few decades demand has grown to the point where, today, Oulipians who show up somewhere to do a reading or take part in a conference are tacitly expected, time and number permitting, to teach a few tricks as well. Bourges is the most intense and prolonged of the group's current regular workshops, but there are repeat command performances in other corners of France: a reading and a class or two each autumn in Lille, for instance, and an unofficially Oulipo-related retreat in Pirou, a small town in Normandy, where the participants prepare a reasonably elaborate theatrical performance. There are sporadic interventions in French public schools, too, on various themes and for various ages. (According to a weird quality curve, very young children make delightfully envelope-pushing poems and stories, while teenagers clam up and can't seem to be bothered to turn in a decent oulipian exercise.)

Like its readings, the Oulipo's workshops vary with the size and sophistication of the audience, but the principle behind them is constant. In line with Queneau's take on the purpose of the group's findings, the stance is more demonstrative than promotional, the workshop leader more motivational speaker than recruitment scout. The Oulipo's intention has never been to mint writers of any kind, Fournel explains; its goal is "to make the participants in its workshops understand that writing is possible here and now, and that, thanks to the benefits of constraint, it is possible to write as one would play." In a country whose educational system stresses grammatical propriety on one hand and lionizes literary genius on the other, he suggests, there is plenty of room for proof that writing—no matter what you use it for—can actually be fun. "Take ten people and ask them to write an unforgettable poem, and you will in all likelihood be met with enduring silence," he says. "Ask them to write a poem without the letter E and there they are at work already, pushed forward by curiosity and challenge."

103

Not a bad testament to the left-field, vaguely antiestablishment fun you can have by bending the grandfathered-in rules of composition, but it doesn't say much for reaching out to the world at large, to people who weren't already looking for a saving grace in literature or in writing. On the other hand, there's an important difference between those two things, and maybe all it takes to view writing as something natural, as something for everyone, is to take literature out of the equation—to keep that part potential, as it were. "No matter how violent his desire to do so, no matter how sophisticated his knowledge of literary history, no matter how intently his publisher wants him to, a writer does not write Literature," Fournel explains. "He writes text. He writes it with a tool called language. The text does not have to bend systematically to the tool. The tool can be questioned; the tool can be transformed; the tool can be broken. The essential thing is the text."

Just as essential, then, is the lesson that text—i.e., what results from the act of writing, before a reader is involved, much less a readership—is its own reward. The spirit of generosity in the oulipian workshop is also, by design, one of indifference to what happens to your piece after you share it: in that moment, at that table, your text has no future, just a here and now. The point is to learn to write for yourself, for that thrill of doing things you didn't know you knew how to do. Perhaps, with great desire and incredible luck, the writing you do for yourself will be published and become Literature—but that's none of the Oulipo's business. So far, nobody seems dissatisfied with that model. "To the best of my judgment, not a single piece of worthwhile literature was produced," Christopher Beha wrote in *The Believer* of a two-day Oulipofest at Princeton University in 2005, "and we all had a blast."

—◦—

The following day I turn up in Forte's workshop—excessive demand has required Monk to jump ship and assume half of Le Tellier's fiction group—where the atmosphere is completely different, not least because Forte is at least a decade younger than almost everyone else in the room. The participants here are the serious ones, the ones who know a *tanka* from a *chôka* and have brought their laptops and are in some non-trivial sense here to work. By the time I arrive, new forms, or at least compelling mashups of old ones, have already been invented: the *tankoum* combines the alternating 5-7-5-7-7 syllable pattern of the *tanka* with the interstanza repetitions of the *pantoum;* a two-handed form whose name I don't know and probably doesn't exist fuses the *tanka* with the early oulipian concept of *tireur à la ligne,* or line stretching—in which you begin with a two-sentence story, then modify it by sticking a new sentence between the original two, and so on, interpolating new sentences between every pair until the story is ready to burst like a goose liver (Warren Motte translates the name accurately, if over-vividly, as "larding"). I make a stab at inventing an irrational pantoum, integrating the pi-based stanza lengths of Jacques Bens's irrational sonnets, but not much comes of it. I am easily out of my depth, this time for reasons I can't chalk up to having a different mother tongue.

105

In contrast to the methods of Bénabou's boot camp, little attention is paid to accuracy or correctness; now and then someone[7] will miscalibrate the echoes of a pantoum or lard a story in the wrong place, but Forte is not here to teach anyone anything—he's here to work, like the rest of us. The room is a miniature version of what I imagine the earliest Oulipo conclaves might have been like: men hunched over pencil and paper, gritting their teeth and scribbling new things that, if successful, they'll show the other men in the

---

[7] Me.

circle and that, if not, they'll scrap before moving on to something else, or going off to have lunch and talk about Lucretius.

—◄o►—

Joining Jouet's group on Friday feels like being taken in by a close-knit hippie community. Its members have been on walks together, used one another as subject matter as well as audience, held in-depth discussions about the successes of each other's poems. Most of the participants (and, to hear some other Oulipians tell it, most of Jouet's readership) are adoring middle-aged women with varying degrees of poetical affliction. Jouet, neither businesslike nor digressive, explains things without lecturing and guides us through thought-provoking spots of oulipian and para-oulipian history. When everyone sets down to writing, he does not make the rounds or look about; he sits and writes, gives it a suitable amount of time, asks if everyone is done, and pantomimes horror when someone inevitably isn't. He ignores the habitual preface of "I didn't get the desired results here" or "This probably isn't that good, but . . ." He says a few constructive words after each reading, almost always limited to how well the piece has respected the given constraint.

Today we begin with partner poems of eleven lines, each line with an imposed opening phrase: *I see, I know, I think, I wonder.* We take our position in pairs of facing chairs in the courtyard and spend eleven minutes making notes about our partners, then repair to our room in the art school to write and read out our poems. These are simple exercises, light on wordplay and technical derring-do: we write about what we have observed. Still, the expected degree of cagey intimacy is surpassed in all of the resulting poems; in some, an otherworldly romance seems on the verge of erupting. My partner makes note of the dictionary I keep at my side at all times, and wonders if I wear the same expression on my face while waiting at the doctor's office; we both end up mentioning the other's beauty marks. When Jouet reads, his partner blushes furiously, but looks positively ecstatic to have a poem about her read by him.

107

In the exercises that follow—which include another portrait, using only the words in some twentieth-century poem supplied to each of us at random by Jouet, then chronopoems that we try to time correctly as we read them aloud—we learn little about techniques or structures. But even when the sparks don't fly, it feels like we're making poetry as an extension of ourselves: sometimes stilted and sometimes perfectly natural, our thoughts slowed down and rarefied and probably in some way overdetermined but still very much our own.

—◄o►—

The whole town of Bourges is invited, and occasionally even shows up, to the evening readings. The point is not so much to remind us who the real Oulipians are as to show us how many ways there are to be oulipian—how many ways to interpret the basic principles, and how many different personal preoccupations, peeves, and proclivities they can accommodate. Bénabou and Salon, for instance, read light, crowd-pleasing ditties that play close to the standard margins of literature, showing more masterly writing abilities than creative formal conceptions. Bénabou, despite his authorial preoccupation with not writing, has an estimable catalogue to his name (one thinks of Victor Mature:[8] "I'm not an actor, and I have sixty-four films to prove it"), and reads some of his punchier texts, including a shaggy-dog tale called "A Sorbet for the Admiral," which requires Forte to ring a bell at each instance of a word borrowed or adapted from Arabic. (A reliable indicator of Oulipo light is that a second "reader" is needed to make certain noises every now and then.) Salon reads a long and increasingly punladen fable about being haunted by a gigantic supernatural beet, and gets other Oulipians to join him for some Abbott and Costello–type dialogues that manage to make brittle semantico-ontological arguments funny.

Forte, on the other hand, reads things that hardly gloss as having a form at all, except in the context of a roomful of people who have spent the whole day thinking about forms: a "flat sonnet," which tosses out the prosody and line breaks from the standard sonnet structure and leaves a pleasingly deadpan, lightly echoing stream of words; the little wide-eyed prose poems from his chapbook *Comment(s),* which he describes as being "to the oulipian constraint what military music is to music." These come across like the work either of someone who hasn't yet mastered

---

[8] See note 2 in this chapter.

the classical art of writing, or, more likely, of someone who mastered it a while ago, got bored with it, and decided to send it through the washing machine a few times just to see what would happen.

Jouet and Monk read in tandem one night, alternating texts; Jouet begins playfully but moves into the sober, reflective, and less captivating poetry he does so well. Monk reads some excerpts from the not-yet-published *Plouk Town,* a lightly mocking tone in his English accent. After Jouet reads the introductory, self-explanatory *poème de métro,* Monk, ever the provocateur, reads a *poème de bistrot:* same principle, except replace subway stops with glasses of wine. The following night, Le Tellier offers a *poème de couteau,* or knife poem, for those occasions when you feel like writing a poem while engaged in the act of stabbing somebody.[9]

Le Tellier also reads the self-portrait of a seducer, a spinoff of the opening story in Paul Fournel's 1988 collection *Les Athlètes dans leur tête* (The Athletes in Their Head)—a tale narrated by a downhill skier who muses on the rigors and pitfalls of the vocation. Le Tellier's version is what you might call a macro-isosyntaxism, or a homosemantic translation: from sentence to sentence it's virtually identical to the original, except that the profession in question and all the corresponding references have been changed. (This will eventually kick off a brief obsession with the form of the *autoportrait,* resulting in a 2009 *jeudi,*

---

[9] No composing while the knife is outside the victim's stomach, no writing while it is inside, etc.

a subsequent B.O. volume, and finally a book—which illustrates not only Le Tellier's talent for pastiche but also the degree to which it drives the Oulipo forward.) He reads Fournel's original first and then his spinoff, in part to make it clear where his text comes from and in part because without the original he would just sound like a lecherous middle-aged man—which some woman from the audience ends up accusing him of being anyway.

—◦—

On Friday night the stage belongs to everyone else, as the groups that have been working on specific ideas for the past three days come together to share their findings. Most of the forms we present to each other are tried and tested and known quantities already, but this is more than made up for by the number and demographic variety of the readers: the takeaway message is that these people, all of them, can be given the same set of structures and will make wildly diverse, typically successful work from them. Besides, after a week of work, we want to be entertained, not inspired. Salon, acting as emcee, is shouted down every time he begs us to save our applause until the end of a group's entire presentation.

And so we hear a snowball dialogue, wherein each successive word grows or shrinks by one letter, and watch an argument at a travel agency where one character speaks in E-lipogram and another in E-monovocalism. We see a group-authored, Icelandic-style metaphysical police novel, in which an undead miscreant named Agar causes general unrest among a handful of singularly bizarre characters. We get an appetizing sampler of the "basic" forms from Bénabou's boot camp, including a combinatorial recoupling of poems whose verses all follow the same rules of meter and rhyme. We hear a poem from an octogenarian about making peace with mortality, and a poem from another octogenarian about doin' it. The Oulipians lurk at the sides like stage mothers while the performers radiate excitement, sheer jittery satisfaction at getting to share their literary mischief. Even Forte's bearded poemsmiths, after a brisk recital of their inventions, bask a little in the celebratory mood of it all.

The atmosphere carries over to the farewell moonlight picnic, where the Oulipians hold court among their recently minted co-conspirators. Tomorrow we participants will return whence we came and resume lives in which the alphabet is unrestricted and the number of syllables in a given utterance is not pivotal for anything at all—but tonight, especially after a lot of Côtes du Rhône, there is a sense of some other kind of potential. Milling and flirting and tippling around the courtyard are a non-trivial number of people newly sensitized to something in the language they speak and hear every day, newly fluent in its inherent and fetchingly non-utilitarian possibilities.

So maybe we'll go home and write for fun a little more often; maybe we'll go to a *jeudi* or two in the fall or check out a Perec novel from the library.[10] (Personally, I will

---

[10] Although not from the BNF, where we will be chased down by angry hounds for trying to remove a book from the premises.

go home, type up my notes, and spend the rest of the weekend drying out to a therapeutic background of American sitcoms.) These workshops, these readings, the whole corpus to which they endlessly refer—all of this has prepared us to do so, on the off chance that we want to. But the emphasis on understanding the structures and forms of oulipian production is more than random education: in showing us how to write, and how to enjoy what others have written, it gives us the tools—tools that, like language, can be questioned and transformed and broken—not to produce or reproduce moments of aesthetic wonderment, but to *recognize* them. It empowers us to find them in poems and stories, of course, but why not also in newspaper clippings and restaurant menus and dactylic rhythms in radio traffic news? It teaches us to make them happen here and now, simply by seeing them and hearing them—and only later, optionally, by creating them ourselves.

II PAST

let there be limit 1960

W HAT FOLLOWS IS AN ACCOUNT of how, over the past fifty years, the Oulipo grew from a hard-to-articulate idea to a hard-to-articulate global phenomenon. Bear in mind that for a good forty-two of those years I was altogether oblivious to the fact that the Oulipo existed, and that, while I've spent much more time than you'd probably ever want to talking shop with members of the group and poring over private archives and considering the ample contradictions in a rather dispersed paper trail, my perspective is nonetheless heavily indebted to books that you too could read, desire permitting.[1] In some places I go into

---

[1] I draw in particular on Jacques Bens's inexhaustive minutes from the first three years of meetings, published in 1980 as *Oulipo 1960–1963*, then in 2005 as *Genèse de l'Oulipo* (Genesis of the Oulipo); on Warren Motte's *Oulipo: A Primer of Potential Literature*, published

more detail about people and ideas and moments; more often, much less. But the next few chapters are, in sum, what I think you should know in order to understand where potential literature comes from, gauge how it's evolved, and, should you want to, guess where it might yet go.

—◦—

The Oulipo was conceived in September 1960 in Cerisy-la-Salle, a small commune in Normandy, at a colloquium devoted to Raymond Queneau's contributions to the French language. Queneau, who was already an acclaimed novelist and poet as well as director of a classics series at the Parisian publishing giant Gallimard, had won public acclaim the previous year with *Zazie in the Métro,* a sprightly yarn that stars a sailor-mouthed little girl visiting her uncle in Paris and that was later made into a film by Louis Malle. In early drafts of the book Zazie does indeed caper in the Métro, but in the published version she never gets to see it, because it's on strike. Queneau knew how to make his work forever timely.

Queneau was born in 1903 in Le Havre, a city on the northwest coast of France, where, by his own account,

in 1986, which compiles cogent translations of many of the group's foundational essays; and on Harry Mathews and Alastair Brotchie's *Oulipo Compendium,* published in 1998, which gives definitions and examples and/or English adaptations of more oulipian and proto-oulipian forms than it is possible to absorb in a single sitting. (All of these books have since been expanded and reprinted.)

he spent most of his youth in the library reading the *La-rousse* encyclopedia. The list he kept of books he read, which accounts for nearly two hundred pages in his collected journals, bespeaks a wide-ranging intellectual sponginess easily borne out in his fiction and poetry. "Queneau had a chronic need to know," John Sturrock writes, "whether about the city he lived in or about the dauntingly numerous other topics that he pursued." When he moved to Paris in his late teens to study at the Sorbonne, having already received degrees in Latin and Greek and in philosophy, he became an expert in the layout of the city's public transit system—a recurring character in his writing, *Zazie* constituting an ironic exception.

In Paris in the 1920s, Queneau fell in with the Surrealists, narrowly avoided becoming André Breton's brother-in-law, and eventually fell out with the Surrealists again, both personally and politically. He began working at Gallimard as a manuscript reader, working his way up over the next twenty years to become director of the *Pléiade* encyclopedia and a member of the Académie Goncourt, an organization that patronizes French literature in more or less constant defiance of the stodgy old Académie Française.[2] He also translated a few novels from English and quietly

---

[2] The Académie Française, est. 1635, is a council that governs on matters pertaining to the purity and propriety of the French language. (The AF is probably the world's most famous such council, and almost certainly the one with the best costumes, but lots of languages have some official regulatory body; English is among the handful that have no such thing.)

amassed an estimable bibliography of poetry, fiction, and essays that did not, until *Zazie,* get paid a whole lot of attention by the general reading public.

His literary career began early on, but, Sturrock argues, manifested itself not as that of a man who knew all along he wanted to write, but as that of one who felt woefully earthbound as a philosopher and turned to writing as a way to express "his old transcendental perplexities." An early preoccupation with *fous littéraires*—literary madmen—did not result in a salable historical study, as Queneau had hoped, so he folded it into a novel, *Children of Clay,* about a writer trying to compile a history of, as Sturrock says, "deluded but determined eccentrics who have struggled vainly in the past to square the circle, trisect an angle, and solve other insoluble puzzles." Yes, this should sound like foreshadowing.

The novelty of *Zazie,* from a linguistic standpoint, is its matter-of-fact use of slang and its inventive transcriptions of barely articulated French utterances. The novel's first word, *Doukipudonktan*—a compression of *D'où qu'ils puent donc tant*[3]—has since come to symbolize the distance, both orthographic and cultural, between textbook French and the language spoken by real live French people. This distance fascinated Queneau, who was precociously well read in linguistics and saw no reason to favor one French over the other; it was dumb and counterproductive, he

---

[3] "So why do they smell so bad?" would be a straightforward version. Barbara Wright renders it in her 1960 translation as *Howcanaystinksotho.*

maintained, to hold what he called *le néofrançais* to the pre-scriptive standards of the Académie. He had toyed with this idea in his early poems, and made it the basis of a handful of essays—including one in which he more than half-seriously equates the syntax of modern French with that of Chinook —but it was *Zazie* that made the issue a *cause célèbre,* and him a seminar-worthy figure, among academics and pub-lishers.

Neo-French and its future weren't much on Que-neau's mind at Cerisy-la-Salle, though. (The Oulipian Jacques Duchateau recalls that Queneau said little during the colloquium, and that during his obligatory closing re-marks he went to a chalkboard and spoke for an hour about fifth-degree equations and the artifice of language and all manner of philosophical whatnot, and never said a blessed thing about *Zazie*.) He had been tinkering with a project in-volving a series of sonnets with interchangeable syntax and end-rhymes, an indulgence of his extramural interest in combinatorial mathematics, but was having trouble sum-moning the patience to continue. It was his friend François Le Lionnais, also present at the colloquium, who urged him to see it through. It was also Le Lionnais who passed along a suggestion from André Blavier, a Belgian editor and pub-lisher, that a research group of sorts be assembled to take stock of various happenings in the past and present of ex-perimental literature.

Le Lionnais, born in Paris in 1901, shared Que-neau's essentially boundless intellectual curiosity but had followed the opposite path professionally, working the sci-entific angle and tending on the side to his fondness for the arts. Trained as a chemical engineer, he worked briefly in the emerging field of automatic telephony and then took over a failing forge in upper Normandy; throughout his early career, he maintained ties to friends from his youth, including poet and painter Max Jacob, painter and sculptor Jean Dubuffet, and various players in the Dada movement. He insinuated himself into other circles through his enduring passion for chess, which is how he met Raymond Roussel and eventual Oulipian Marcel Duchamp.

In the early 1940s Le Lionnais became active in the Marco Polo Network, a French Resistance group whose name has since been taken over, distastefully enough, by an international securities-trading firm. He was arrested, interrogated, and tortured by the SS in 1944, and spent the next four months at a prison in Fresnes, where he passed the time by writing a treatise about chess on the back of a Luftwaffe map.[4] That August he was deported, first to Buchenwald, then to another concentration camp at Dora-Mittelbau, where, for eight more months, he worked on (and occasionally sabotaged) navigation systems for Nazi V-2 missiles. Two years later, after the camp was liberated and Europe returned to relative calm, he wrote an extraordinary memoir, *La Peinture à Dora* (Painting at Dora), about how he survived his stay by mentally reconstructing his fa-

---

[4] He did not, to my knowledge, obey the prisoner's constraint—although Jean Ballard, in his introduction to Le Lionnais's *Great Currents of Mathematical Thought*, recalls "the period when the Frenchmen of the two zones could only correspond by those postcards so strictly rationed by our prudential occupiers" (R. A. Hall's translation).

vorite paintings to an almost inconceivable degree of detail and, despite routine beatings for talking during roll calls, narrating the artworks to a few friends:

> Stone by stone, we built the most marvelous museum in the world. In so doing we managed to extract from each work one detail, occasionally two, infinitely more sonorous, more profound, and more righteous— more *real*—than the wretched reality that mired our bodies, if not our souls. Rubens's *Kermesse* gave us the small jealous girl in the foreground on the left and, on the right, that prodigious passage of human tumult into the melancholy concession of nature. We abstracted the bunch of grapes from Jordaens's *Allegory of Fertility*, the little donkey from Ruisdael's *Buisson*, the heavenly tablecloth from the *Pilgrims of Emmaus*. We stole, hearts beating wildly, into the chamber at the back of *Las Meninas* . . .

The story itself, though not at all oulipian in its composition, testifies to the roving intellect that would in more peaceable times give birth to potential literature. Once separated from his companions, Le Lionnais recounts, he moved on to what sounds quite a lot like an exercise in potential art: transplanting characters and figures from one painting into another. "I would assemble in the same room Antonello da Messina's *Il Condottiere* and the drinker from the *Bon Bock*," he explains, "then vacate the premises on tiptoe, double-lock the door, and observe the reactions through a small secret skylight, as some sadistic doctor monitors his victims."

After the war, Le Lionnais worked in various high-ranking scientific capacities: as head of the Division of

121

Teaching and Diffusion of Sciences at UNESCO; as a scientific advisor to the Musées Nationaux de France; as a member of the science committee of RTF, the national public broadcasting service; as co-editor of a mathematical reference volume published by Presses Universitaires de France; and so on. Throughout the mid-1940s—including his Resistance days—he assembled a series of articles on contemporary mathematical ideas. That collection, published in 1947 as *Great Currents of Mathematical Thought*, put him in contact with Queneau, who contributed an essay on the use of mathematics in scientific classification.

Le Lionnais's life is a topic of reverent mystery within the Oulipo. A few copies of a manuscript called *Un certain disparate*,[5] which gathers together memoirs and a handful of interviews conducted in the 1980s, have circulated in the official and unofficial archives, but, even with the savant commentary it has elicited, the man and his thoroughgoing polymathy seem mythically impossible to fully comprehend, especially for those of us who never knew him. He studied insulation problems in Parisian telephone lines, was a member of the Society for Basic Irreproducible Research and the Association Française des Artistes Prestidigitateurs, helped to organize shelter and repatriation services for his fellow Dora inmates in a nearby town called Seesen just after their liberation, and once spent twenty hours, during the one trip he ever made to

---

[5] Mathews translates this in the *Oulipo Compendium* as "A Certain Fractiousness," explaining that "the notion of *le* (properly *la*) *disparate* [. . .] connotes a refractory, capricious, unreasonable attitude—'the opposite of the quest for unity,' as Le Lionnais says."

Lisbon, in front of Hieronymus Bosch's *Temptation of St. Anthony*. His last work, a compendium entitled *Nombres remarquables* (Remarkable Numbers), is dedicated to "my lifelong friends, delicious and terrifying, the numbers."

—◦—

Le Lionnais's encouragement to a writer's-blocked Queneau at Cerisy would result not only in the Oulipo itself but also in the first truly oulipian work. *Cent mille milliards de poèmes* (One Hundred Thousand Billion Poems) consists of ten sonnets, each containing fourteen lines of identical scansion and rhyme—that is, the first line of each poem is twelve syllables long and ends with the *ease* sound (*chemise, frise, marquise*), so that the first line of the second poem can be substituted into the first poem, and vice versa, ad libitum. Each poem fits on a single page, which is then cut into fourteen strips, one for each line, such that the reader can mix and match between ten different possibilities for each of fourteen lines—yielding 10^{14}, or one hundred trillion, potential poems: a corpus that would take a dedicated reader, by Queneau's estimations, 190,258,751 years to exhaust.[6]

123

Cent mille milliards de poèmes is a strange creature to behold, more flip-flap book than serious poetry vol-

---

[6] Roubaud later remarked that Queneau had underestimated the potentiality of the project, since, without any explicit instructions on what *order* to present the hundred trillion potential poems in, the number of potential presentations of those potential poems is one hundred trillion *factorial,* an even more preposterously large number.

ume, and a precarious delight to handle. (The poems are printed on card stock but the strips are still relatively flimsy, and the rash combinatorialist risks tearing one and reducing the number of possible poems to a paltry 9×10^{13}.) As a thought experiment, however, it's something else altogether: a book that cannot possibly be read in its entirety by any single human being—including its author—and whose significance thus remains, in a strong sense, potential. In his postface to the book, Le Lionnais cites a few precursors in combinatorial literature, but concludes that Queneau's effort stands apart in both its careful construction and its re-imagining of the very concept of a poem. It's easy to call "monumental" something that eclipses in textual quantity the sum of human endeavor since the dawn of writing ("including popular novels, commercial, diplomatic, and private correspondence, drafts thrown into the wastebasket, and graffiti")[7] in just ten pages. Queneau, for his part, concludes his introduction with the Lautréamont dictum his disciples like so much: poetry must be made not by one but by all.

◄○►

The Oulipo was actually born two months after the gathering at Cerisy-la-Salle, in the basement of a restaurant in Paris called Le Vrai Gascon, a few blocks from what is now the Musée d'Orsay. Seven men gathered over a well-watered

---

[7] Warren Motte's translation.

lunch to discuss the possibilities of a systematic study of experimental literature—indeed, the name of the group for this first meeting was not Oulipo but SeLitEx, or *Séminaire de Littérature Expérimentale*. Besides Queneau and Le Lionnais, there was Jacques Bens, a former student of natural sciences who worked with Queneau at Gallimard; Jacques Duchateau, a journalist, film critic, and radio producer for France Culture; Jean Queval, author of a cricket manual and French translations of Defoe, Thackeray, Powys, and others; Jean Lescure, co-president of the colloquium at Cerisy-la-Salle and founder of a semi-clandestine poetry review called *Messages,* which had maintained an intense publication rate during the Occupation; and a sculptor and graph theorist named Claude Berge, the only one who had not been present at the initial powwow at Cerisy.

125

The first meeting's minutes, taken down by Bens, are not revelatory, as the paper trail of momentous things usually isn't. They contain the addresses and telephone numbers (in reverse alphabetical order, apparently just because) of those present, notes on business to work out and people to contact before the next meeting, and so on—but also a preliminary glimmer of stocktaking. Bens boils it down to three questions:

- What should we expect from our explorations?
- Where will they lead us?
- Where do we want to go?

Spend a minute with the fact that the second and third questions are distinct. (*When you don't know what you're looking for.*) For all the baggage heaped on the term *expe-*

rimental literature—which these days tends to presage a game of limbo between accessibility and marketability—it's a funny little word-pair, one that bespeaks a particular state of mind. This was 1960: it would be naïve to think that art hadn't undergone manifold contortions in the name of various avant-gardes, but the rhetoric of structuralism and the bombast of postmodernism weren't household discourses the way they are today. Give or take a few loose canons, the conventional understanding of literature was still that it just sort of happened, caroming forth from the artist's intellect by dint of a lot of inspiration. *Experimental* in the art world was more of an epithet than it is now, more of a catchall bin for the unclassifiable and the weird. That the Oulipo, né SeLitEx, was based on experiment, organized around the principle of testing hypotheses in the pursuit of good solid data, was legitimately radical. When you're an artist, according to the old model, you go where you want to go by taking control, mastering the muse. When you're an experimenter, whether with the human genome or with the Roman alphabet, you don't always end up where you thought you would, or where you initially wanted to go.

—◦—

The first year enlarged the core circle slightly, bringing in friends and colleagues whose absence at meeting one was essentially circumstantial: there was Renaissance scholar and noted Calvinist Albert-Marie Schmidt, who had shared a psychoanalyst with Queneau (though not at the same time). There was Emmanuel Peillet, a writer, photographer, cactus hobbyist, and Belgium-detester who had a veritable Rolodex of pseudonyms but chose to go by "Latis" in the Oulipo. Last, there was a factotum of Latis's named Raymond Muller but whom everyone called Noël Arnaud, who had been active in the French literary resistance and a key player in various art scenes that would later collectively congeal into the Situationist International.

Latis and Arnaud came on the scene largely as liaisons to the Collège de 'Pataphysique, an intentionally inscrutable arts syndicate that counted some of Europe's most illustrious weirdos, including Queneau and Le Lionnais, among its members. (More on this in a moment.) Other associates, many of them Collège mainstays as well, were later designated foreign correspondents: Blavier, who was as fascinated as Queneau was with literary madmen; Australian literary scholar Ross Chambers; and English architect and translator Stanley Chapman. Paul Braffort, a computer scientist back when personal computers didn't yet exist and a friend of Queneau's from the 1940s, was enlisted as a "poet, atomist, and Belgian," despite his repeated protests that he was not Belgian.[8] Devoted 'Pataphysicist Marcel Duchamp was inducted the following year as an American correspondent,[9] after he responded enthusiasti-

---

[8] According to Roubaud, Braffort was also inducted twice because everyone was too drunk to remember inducting him the first time around.

[9] Duchamp had become an American citizen in 1955 and was living in New York when he joined the Oulipo in 1962.

cally to reports of the group's work and claimed to be engaged in similar pursuits. And as early as the third meeting, Le Lionnais declared fictional figures eligible for induction —whence the brief appearance of QB, a single-use character from the woodwork of Rabelais's *Gargantua,* who signed his initials to the minutes for a few months and eventually disappeared without ceremony.

Besides Duchateau, whom I have never met and who no longer participates in oulipian activities, the only living member of the founding circle is Braffort, an obliging and agreeably tortoisey man who confirms my conception of what the first Oulipians were like: learned and wryly self-effacing, slightly contrarian but unlimited in intellectual curiosity. Each of the handful of times he received me in his book-lined shoebox of an apartment in Paris's Marais district, he carried on no fewer than six conversations at once while I tried meekly to keep up: on the long development of artificial intelligence and its impact on alternate-reality games, on Le Lionnais's immediate postwar history and on the two alphabets and dialects of Serbo-Croat, on the consultations he enjoyed with Italo Calvino for a never-completed combinatorial mystery, and on the funny things that happen when you couple 73 and 37.

Braffort remains attentive to oulipian affairs but is no longer very active either; he even went so far as to retire discreetly between 1996 and February 2, 2002—i.e., 02/02/02—during which time he published occasional oulipian texts under the name Walter Henry (an independent scholar whose sole subject of study is the work of Paul

Braffort). He speaks of some of the workshop's more recent developments with a vague air of disapproval, more toward how its approach to the foundational quarries has evolved than toward anyone's aesthetic or intellect—an attitude that would probably have been inevitable among other founders. Talking to Braffort does feel a little like going back to a point in time when the Oulipo was a novelty, when the jitters of uncertainty mingled with a singularity of purpose all the stronger because the purpose wasn't yet defined.

◄o►

After its debut, the group rechristened itself twice. At the second meeting, Schmidt proposed ditching SeLitEx in favor of OLiPo; at the third, Latis suggested adding the U for symmetry's sake. (Roubaud claimed, much later, that he probably wouldn't have consented to join a group called SeLitEx.) "There was a hint of the Masonic Temple in his vision of the *ouvroir*," Arnaud writes of Schmidt's decision to jettison *séminaire,* or seminar (which according to Lescure "conjures up stud farms and artificial insemination") in favor of a word whose connotations include woodshops, nunneries, and sewing circles—"but it pleased him to have the Oulipians regard the group principally as a pleasant spot, warm in winter, cool in summer, abundantly provided with food and drink, where people compete in dexterity in the finest sort of needlework."[10]

---

[10] Warren Motte's translation.

The group eagerly tried the new name on for size. Making a collective pseudonym out of an anagram of Olipo ("Polio," for instance) was discussed; once the U was added, talk turned to commissioning a letterhead, then a logo, then an anthem. (Only a spindly insignia designed by Latis was seen through to completion, and even then it didn't get much mileage.) Ample consideration was given to the possible derivations of "Oulipo," such as whether *oulipien* or *oulipote* (*pote* meaning "buddy") or *oulipoète* was the ideal designation for a member, and whether there was any likelihood of getting a postage stamp printed depicting the Oulipic games. The Roman salutation "Oulè" was adopted as the mandatory group greeting, which rule was promptly never enforced. Queneau reported, to great excitement, that he had glimpsed a map featuring a small French commune near Chartres named Loulipe, or maybe even L'Oulipe. It turned out to have been Loulappe.

Titles were given: Queneau was named the Président-Fondateur and Le Lionnais the Frésident-Pondateur, a spoonerism that means nothing but sounds kind of like it means "layer of fresh teeth." Bens remained the provisional secretary, while QB, despite or perhaps thanks to not existing, leapfrogged him to become the definitively definitive secretary. The other members referred to one another cordially, sometimes with 'pataphysical titles in place of oulipian ones. After the second meeting, the group also elected to dispense with standard (or reverse) alphabetical order and adopt a new one based on the sequence in which letters appear in one of the Collège's foundational texts, the *Testament* of His Magnificence Dr. I. L. Sandomir (who was also, as it turns out, Latis); thenceforth, anything starting with P came first, then O, then U, R, Q, I, V, T, and so on until the alphabet was exhausted.[11]

Amid the administrative silliness that leaps out from Bens's minutes, some serious discussion managed to take place. Since one of the principal ideas that brought the group together was the project of compiling a practical history of experimental literature, energy was devoted early on to surveying and evaluating the available forms and techniques and their relative relevance to the group's still-vague future. Queneau marked up a list of stratagems found in Gabriel Brunet's *Poétique curieuse* (Curious Poetics), from acrostics and anagrams to puns and elaborate rhyme schemes, rating their potential interest. Most were dismissed with a "no"; anagrams and acrostics received a charitable "doubtful." The Oulipotes discussed centos, poems made up of verses from other poems; *anterimes,* in which the rhyme happens at the beginning of the lines rather than at the end; isovocalisms, in which a new text is generated by maintaining the vowels of an old one but changing the consonants between them, and isoconsonantisms, in which vice versa.

131

---

[11] To put this in context, the first words of the treatise are *Pour qui voit lucidement* ("For anyone who sees clearly"). Quasi-interestingly, the *Testament,* like most documents written in French, doesn't contain K or W; those letters were added as an afterthought at the end of the POURQI alphabet.

A few forms, including the lipogram, tautogram, and pangram, were deemed fecund, but most of the Oulipo's work during these first months was intensely analytical, creative almost by afterthought. Queneau demonstrated that Mallarmé's sonnets were sufficiently redundant that one could remove all but the rhyming bit at the end of each line and obtain a "haikuized" version that was not only faithful to the original but also, he argued, more elegant. Le Lionnais followed a similar path in exploring the "borders" of poems, examining only their first and last lines and the first and last words of the lines in between, then looking for points of tangency with other poems and visualizing their intersections in three, perhaps four dimensions. By the same token, he reasoned, one could throw away the borders and concentrate on a poem's innards, which, if repeated enough times, would result in a "systematic peeling of French poetry."

—◄○►—

These demonstrations and reasonings were, at this point, for the benefit of nobody but the Oulipo. The earliest meetings were not exactly clandestine, but the group took care to keep the circle small; Queneau expressed reluctance to expand it beyond ten to a dozen people, which he felt was the ideal size for a research group. The minutes from one meeting begin with open censure of Lescure, whose indiscriminate mention of the group's activities had prompted an anonymous outsider to ask what all this Oulipo business was about and when they were going to have him to lunch.[12] For now, at least, these sessions retained some of the academic character of the Cerisy-la-Salle colloquium: scholars presenting papers and staking theories, discussing the relevance of each historical artifact to the overall theme of the workshop. Not that they didn't enjoy themselves, *à la française,*[13] but the agenda was something to be hewed to, the minutes something for members to study in order to have a worthwhile contribution for the next meeting.

Queneau, who had the highest profile in the group, was also the most sensitive to the potential perils of going public. Before an interview about his *Cent mille milliards de poèmes,* he broached the subject of whether he should talk about the Oulipo. The issue popped up every few months throughout the first year; each time, there was some new reason to stay provisionally mum. Finally, the workshop agreed to stage its formal coming-out in the quarterly-ish

---

[12] In retrospect, this seems like convincing early grounds for the current bylaw dictating that anyone who asks to be a member of the Oulipo thereupon becomes inadmissible for life. (Happily enough I sidestepped this landmine, having learned about the rule long before I met anyone to whom I might have tendered my candidacy—but this really is enforced, and since my co-optation there has already been one groaning invalidation of a reasonably suitable applicant simply because, well, rules are rules, and good luck trying to convince an Oulipian otherwise.)

[13] Bens's minutes frequently lapse into asides castigating one side of the table for hogging the Bordeaux or advising members at future meetings to avoid ordering the mackerel in white wine sauce.

journal *Cahiers du Collège de 'Pataphysique.* It took some months of hedging and grumbling for the right documents to come together, but the dossier, entitled *Exercices de littérature potentielle: Patalégomène à toute poétique future qui voudra bien se présenter en tant que tel,*[14] made its appearance at the end of December 1961.

In true 'pataphysical form, the introduction to the group therein is lofty and lyrical, to the point of deep obnoxiousness ("In order to open the eyes of those Members as yet unaccustomed to the potential sun, they being citizens of the Dark Land of the Obvious Word, the Oulipo applied itself to discovering in these shadows the phosphorescent flashes that filter through," etc.).[15] Nonsense aside, though, Dossier 17, as the issue is quite sensibly abbreviated, does a reasonably comprehensible job of presenting the group and its intent: "It resides more in the ordering of the means than in the intuition of the ends." Schmidt contributed an essay outlining some of the historical precedents of oulipian pursuits, from the proto-oulipian Grands Rhétoriqueurs of the fifteenth century to the Grand Academy at Lagado in *Gulliver's Travels,* in which Swift imagines exactly what a physical "language workshop" would look like.[16] Lescure offered an account of his S + 7 tech-

---

[14] Whatever.

[15] Warren Motte's translation.

[16] See Part III, Chapter 5, in which Gulliver visits a school where students toss around die-sized blocks of wood that contain "all the words of their language, in their several moods, tenses, and declensions, but without any order," recording any and all potential sen-

nique; Duchateau introduced his plans for an intersective novel, which would construct a narrative incorporating the Lionnaisian points of tangency between two Faulkner novels. Rightly, the introduction claims as the group's test subjects not only "the procedures through which expression becomes capable of transmuting itself, solely through its verbal craft, into other more or less numerous expressions," but also "materials unconsciously proposed by previous authors"—that is, the things that make certain great works great, isolated and distilled into formulae for future use.

135

Dossier 17 was slowly but warmly received. Writers and scholars in the 'Pataphysical circuit began to take an interest in the workshop's pursuits, here offering the use of their computational resources, there mailing literary lab reports explicating how they had turned one poem into a different one with only three discrete encryptions. The Oulipo began to invite guests to its meetings to pick their brains in a friendly sort of industrial espionage: Abraham Moles came and talked about his consortium for a more analytical survey of aesthetic criteria for music and other arts; Kazuo Watanabe chatted about translating Rabelais into Japanese; Dimitri Starynkevitch, of IBM, discussed what analyses could be done using microfiche-transcribed poems.

Bens's minutes frame this as an exciting time, not

---

tences. "The professor showed me several volumes in large folio, already collected, of broken sentences, which he intended to piece together, and out of those rich materials, to give the world a complete body of all arts and sciences."

least due to the more or less concurrent development of big efficient calculating machines called computers. Certain tasks with conceivable if outlandish literary merit were becoming possible, as means or as ends unto themselves: compiling concordances, isolating the borders of poems, scanning for metrical qualities, writing poems in programming languages. At one point Braffort mentions a research center in Besançon that has all the tragedies of Racine and Corneille on perforated cards; in Queneau's subsequent questions about whether a computer could classify sonnets by end-rhymes or scan a piece of prose for twelve-syllable units—i.e., involuntary alexandrines—the possibility for mischief nearly jumps off the page.

136

—◄○►—

In 1962, Queneau recorded a series of interviews with radio critic Georges Charbonnier. Among general thoughts on the evolution of language and the state of *le néofrançais,* he gave an overview of the enigmatic research group he had co-founded with Le Lionnais. He summarized the contents of the *Cahiers* dossier, read some S + 7 treatments of the Book of Genesis, and insisted that the workshop's purpose was not to create literature ("There is that risk," he admitted, "but it's not a big deal"). It was, he said, to "furnish future writers with new techniques which can dismiss inspiration from their affectivity."

This definition was hardly spontaneous. Between the appearance of Dossier 17 and Queneau's radio chats, the group had taken the opportunity to think about how to present itself to a public beyond the 'Pataphysics community, which ruminations yielded some memorable stabs at self-encapsulation. *A group which proposes to examine in what manner and by what means, given a scientific theory ultimately concerning language (therefore anthropology), one can introduce aesthetic pleasure (affectivity and fancy) therein:*[17] correct about the circle-squaring aspect of the group's linguistic inquiries, but a little too clinical. *Copernicuses of a future Kepler:* too vague. *Rats who build the labyrinth from which they plan to escape:* pretty evocative, but only once you have some idea of what the whole project is about—which, by design, not much more than a hundred people did.

137

Preparing a self-definition for a slowly growing public allowed, or forced, the Oulipo to begin confronting and hammering out its main theoretical issues—none stickier than the notion of *potential,* which was, after all, the chief criterion of what was deemed worthy of oulipian attention and what moot.[18] For all the accuracy of defining potential as "that which does not yet exist," Charbonnier was right when he pointed out that the group's work skewed toward texts that *did* exist. Queneau responded

---

[17] Warren Motte's translation.

[18] From March 1962:

BERGE: Take, for example, the Tristan Derême character who grades poets according to the length of the streets named after them. That's potential!

BENS: But in that case everything is potential! Even this bottle!

QUENEAU: Quite potential! *(He helps himself.)*

that the word *potential* was to be understood not as an attribute of the word *literature* but as a commentary on its very nature, of the fruit it could bear with the right manipulations. When he had made his illustration of the redundancy of Mallarmé's sonnets, he said, he hadn't felt he was creating literature; he'd felt he was doing a literary experiment. (A boost of empirical credibility: he'd tried the same process on Victor Hugo and it didn't work.) The original sonnets were not the important part—they were mere fruit flies—and neither were the haikus that resulted from stripping them down. The potential was in the stripping-down itself, the demonstration of a method by which language dressed up as literature could be mutated and contorted and crossbred and still be called literature. Of course it was not inconceivable that such a method should generate a new text that could be judged on its own literary merits, but that wasn't the point. Not yet.

Indeed, the most important historical feature of this period is that the Oulipo's twin branches, the analytical and the synthetic, had not meaningfully diverged: making things new and making new things were equally interesting propositions. The inventions presented in Dossier 17, Duchateau's intersective novel and Lescure's S + 7 method, are both based on verifiable experiments, more manipulation than creation. (Lescure defined his role in the latter as that of an operator, not an author.) The same went for a sonnet Queval claimed was an unpublished work by Victor Hugo, which turned out to be composed of twelve-syllable snippets from Hugo's prose work. Even another sonnet that Queval wrote, consisting entirely of infinitive verbs, or a

poem Le Lionnais would later write using only preposi-
tions, balanced creative thrust with data culled from known
syntactic or lexical quantities. These are works based on
preexisting texts only insofar as a phone book or a dictionary or Bescherelle's grammar manual can be considered a
text—but the most inspiring idea to come from this period
is: Why shouldn't it be?

139

imaginary solutions

T HE SPIRIT THAT WOULD possess one to make a poem from a phone book, or a play from a grammar manual, is not uniquely oulipian. It's also a little bit Dada, a little bit Flarf,[1] and a little bit 'pataphysical. And to understand where the Oulipo comes from, it's more than a little bit helpful to understand the Collège de 'Pataphysique—which is a shame, because anyone who claims he or she understands the Collège de 'Pataphysique is probably lying.

Some facts that could constitute a roundabout introduction to 'pataphysics: in Sweden, in 1991, a couple was fined for naming their child Brfxxccxxmnpcccclllmmnprxvclmnckssqlbb11116; his name (pronounced "Albin"), they explained, was to be understood in the spirit of 'pata-

---

[1] Flarf is search engine–generated poetry. There's more to it than that, but nothing we need to talk about here.

physics. The word, including that maddening little apostrophe, comes from a book by Alfred Jarry called *Exploits and Opinions of Dr. Faustroll, Pataphysician: A Neo-Scientific Novel,* written in 1898 but not published until 1911; it is defined therein as "the science of imaginary solutions." Christian Bök, who has written a completely unreadable treatise called *'Pataphysics: The Poetics of an Imaginary Science,* describes the Collège as "a parodic academy of intellectuals, who propose absurd axioms and then use rigorous argument to explicate the logical outcome of these absurdities." Italo Calvino once called it "a kind of academy of intellectual scorn."[2] *Collège* in French does not mean "college"; it means "middle school."

Founded in 1948 to commemorate the fiftieth anniversary of *Faustroll,* the Collège enjoyed a few decades of unparalleled weirdness as it toiled for the advancement of the highbrow and the useless, trading exegeses on Jarry and his work and thriving on meaningless pomp and fancy-sounding titles. Le Lionnais was a regent, Bens a datary (named, respectively, for an incapacitated ruler's interim stand-in and for a mid-level functionary in the Roman Catholic Church); Queneau was a Transcendent Satrap. Latis was Private General Secretary to the Baron Vice-Curator, and Arnaud was Regent of General 'Pataphysics and the Clinic of Rhetoriconosis, as well as Major Conferant of the Order of the Grand Gidouille.[3] The Collège's hi-

---

[2] William Weaver's translation.

[3] And Caradec was Regent of Colombophilia, Toponymous and Celtipetous Regent, Regent of Ethical Alcoholism, and Regent of something called Applied Cephalorgy.

erarchy is a *reductio ad absurdum* of the French passion for the organigram, composed of subcommittee upon subcommission, turtles all the way down. It also has its own calendar—like the French revolutionary calendar, only cruder—in which the thirteenth is always a Friday.[4] Perec, or more likely some forgotten quipster whose byline has been replaced well-meaningly with Perec's, explained once: "If you have a brother and he loves cheese, that's physics. If you have a brother and *therefore* he loves cheese, that's metaphysics. If you *don't* have a brother and he loves cheese, that's pataphysics."

143

By the 1960s, the Collège was a cultural powerhouse throughout Europe. Its members and affiliates included not only writers (Boris Vian, Jacques Prévert, Michel Leiris, Umberto Eco, Julio Cortázar, Eugène Ionesco) but also artists (Joan Miró, M. C. Escher, Max Ernst, Man Ray, Marcel Duchamp, and, at one point, at least in some honorary capacity, the Marx brothers). Its reach was, and still is, surprisingly expansive: there are *patafisico* organizations all over South America; the Beatles even name-dropped it in "Maxwell's Silver Hammer."[5] In matters of taste, beneath the often vulgar excess, it has proved to have its faculties in the right place. For one thing, the Collège's publishing imprint was the first to bring out Ionesco's *Bald Soprano*—a play cobbled together from dialogues found in an English instruction manual—which was rejected ev-

---

[4] One month is *Merdre,* a nonce infinitive form of the French word for "shit," and also the first line of dialogue in Jarry's infamous proto-absurdist play *Ubu roi.* Another month is *Clinamen.* Another is *Haha.*

[5] "Joan was quizzical / Studied 'pataphysical / Science in the home."

erywhere else and is now a revered standard of absurdist theater.

Whether or not there's anything *there* is a hard question to answer, especially because the varying accounts of what the Collège is about tend to be so dense and almost inherently disingenuous. As far as the Oulipo was concerned in its first few years, the partnership was a marriage of no small convenience, providing a readymade outlet for eventual publication and easy access to a network of people who would quite conceivably be interested by the work-

shop's erudite manipulations. (The closest thing the Collège has spawned to an oulipian constraint is the *pataphor,* developed by American writer Pablo Lopez, a metaphor so extended that it voluntarily relinquishes its hold on reality.)

Queneau, whose Surrealist dabblings had left a sour taste in his mouth, based at least partially on André Breton being a dictatorial windbag, came to 'pataphysics through his admiration for the objects of its collective fascination—especially Raymond Roussel, whose approach to writing has amply informed the Oulipo's work. Le Lionnais was equally attracted by shared interests—there wasn't much he wasn't interested in—but also knew many of the influential littérateurs of the time, and thus many 'Pataphysicians, through the French Resistance during World War II. It was thus a combination of personal respect and esteem for the luminaries the Collège was honoring and studying that made for an intuitive relationship between the two groups.

Nonetheless, it was Latis, who had been instrumental in the Collège's creation (at which time he was going by the name J. H. Sainmont, and later Dr. I. L. Sandomir), whose efforts made the connection stick. The Collège's publishing arm had started in semi-active, semi-waggish opposition to Gallimard's *Nouvelle Revue Française* division, of which Queneau was co-director; hindsight makes it look as though Latis brought Arnaud along to buffalo the tepid co-founders into incorporating. Latis was an unabashedly volatile presence in the Oulipo's early history, holding grudges and making demands and threatening to quit the group from time to time before doing so was formally proscribed. It was, recall, at his behest that Caradec didn't become a member until 1983—some nineteen years after he was invited to lunch as guest of honor, and ten after Latis himself had croaked.

The Oulipo was still the Olipo when it was designated a special subset of the Collège's subcommission on Epiphanies and Ithyphanies,[6] itself a subcommission of the Commission of the Unpredictable, of which Queneau was already one of three presidents. The next month it was judged that the Oulipo should be a subcommittee of the *Acrote* (named after the ultimate goal of humanity); a little while later, approval came down from His Magnificence Baron Jean Mollet to make the Oulipo its *own* subcommittee.

Aside from the publication of Dossier 17, the affiliation didn't make a whole lot of difference in the work-

---

[6] *Ithyphallic* refers to a statue depicting a deity with an erect penis. You're getting the picture, right?

shop's actual proceedings. All Oulipians who were not already members of the Collège became dataries, a rule that would continue into the 1970s, but this was a symbolic integration at best. There was Sandomir's POURQI alphabet, and the headgear of early reunions (Le Lionnais in a naval officer's cap, Queneau in a *gidouille*-bedecked top hat),[7] the slightly silly titles, and Le Lionnais's dictum that each year was a century in oulipian time—but the workshop didn't comport itself with the same tongue-in-cheek self-importance. It didn't even devote itself to the same literary forebears, although both were fascinated by Roussel and had a deep interest in the concept of the clinamen. Even in Dossier 17, it was clear enough that potentialities were not the same thing as imaginary solutions.

What's key about the presence of the Collège in the Oulipo's gestation is Latis's assertion, by way of Jarry, that everyone lives 'pataphysics, whether consciously or not: every act, every statement, every criticism can be subsumed under its proto-postmodern, para-metaphysical umbrella.[8] The idea is one of a system that engulfs and ex-

---

[7] The *gidouille* is the spiral emblem of the Collège, named after the helix of energy that begins in Ubu's intestines, issues forth from his navel, and envelops the entire cosmos before returning to his belly.

[8] This supposedly accounts for the apostrophe that sometimes precedes the word and sometimes doesn't: the official Collège regulation is that '*pataphysics* is intentional—that which is practiced—while *pataphysics* is involuntary, that which simply exists. (Jarry himself had nothing to do with this distinction.)

plains, or obfuscates, the entire universe, a micro-science somehow transmitted through language into every nook and cranny of existence. Though it was never expressed in such explicit terms, this was an important idea for the Oulipo to absorb osmotically: (a) that the raw matter of the universe is language; (b) that hypotheses about language can be proven systematically, scientifically, even if the system and the science answer only to their own cryptic logic. Queneau's avowal, at an early meeting, that "we find literary value where there is none" is the 'pataphysical part of the oulipian project speaking.

147

     'Pataphysics also comes from a much darker place than the Oulipo does, though. Beneath its veneer of absurdity is a very cynical and morbid philosophy: like Jarry, it is preoccupied with death coming down from the heavens, Greek-style, to put an end to the comedy of human existence. To call 'pataphysics a postwar renewal of the Surrealist and Dada networks is right on two counts: first because many of the players were the same, and second because the Collège stripped from those earlier counterparts a lightness that, to paraphrase Theodor Adorno, seemed impossible after Auschwitz. The most fascinating text Latis (or in this case Lathis) wrote was a slim pamphlet called *L'Organiste athée* (The Atheist Organist), a novel with seven prefaces, a preface to the prefaces, a postface, a postlude, and no actual novel—the manuscript having been lost during the "global vaudeville of 1939–1945." Le Lionnais's memoir about Dora, though it has none of the Collège's farcical touch, conveys something that could be called 'pataphysical in its staunchly, desperately rational way of coping with the murderous absurdity of the world.[9]

This is not to suggest that the Collège was a post-traumatic support group or that its political engagement was unilateral, but it is to say that there was something deep and serious to it, which had no choice but to inform the Oulipo's sensibilities and its sense of limitless purview. "Everything concerns the Oulipo," Le Lionnais said at one early meeting, "including the Evian Conference and the making of *gibelotte*."[10] In a recent interview Roubaud quoted one of the founders, without specifying which one, as saying that, in the world we live in, we are beholden to all manner of terrible constraints—mental, physical, societal—with death the only way out of the labyrinth. The least we can do is mark off a little section where we get to choose the constraints we are mastered by, where we decide which direction to take.

And yet, Duchateau proposes, Queneau's skepticism was more an open-ended search for meaning, less the 'pataphysical rejection of it. Queneau's description of the

---

[9] In this, 'pataphysics resembled existentialism, which John Sturrock describes in *The Word from Paris* as "an attempt by writers who had lived through the German Occupation to formulate a viable philosophy and a heroic system of values out of a testing wartime experience of rare psychological intensity"—only with the polar opposite of existentialism's self-serious approach to philosophy.

[10] The former was a meeting convened by Franklin D. Roosevelt in 1938 to discuss the widespread flight of Jewish refugees from Nazi persecution; the latter is a kind of rabbit stew native to the north of France.

science as based on "the truth of contradictions and exceptions" leaves more room for hope, sheds more light on his desire to track down the notion of structure in literature, independently of how it was used. It was Queneau the reader, with his "chronic need to know," not Queneau the cynic or even Queneau the writer, who presided over the founding of the Oulipo. As for Le Lionnais, the most entitled of the whole bunch to renounce faith in meaning, the world simply offered too much to delight in, too many questions to answer. "Science, for better or worse, is pursued by men," he wrote in 1966, "and the achievement of its ideals, as in all human activity—be it humble, moderate or great—cannot be attained in a climate completely devoid of emotion."

149

> Why does a pencil, if I lift it a small distance and then release it, fall as far as the table beneath it? And why does it stop there? Is it not amazing that I can communicate my thoughts to you in this essay? What is sound? What is light? What is their precise structure? I have never turned on a light switch in a darkened room without the sudden flood of light releasing in me an undeniable emotion, the impression almost of having witnessed a miracle.[11]

As the Oulipo evolved, its institutional ties to 'pataphysics became increasingly vestigial. Potential literature sharpened into its own approach to reading and writing, while, on its end, the Collège began to lose its mid-century feroc-

---

[11] Translation by George Agoston and Pauline Bentley-Koffler.

ity. In 1975, after some high-ranking deaths, the Collège de 'Pataphysique decided to officially suspend its activities until the millennium. Since its 2000 de-occultation, which was commemorated in a lavish and presumably confusing celebration at the Centre Pompidou in Paris, the Collège continues to operate, with a somewhat diminished and dispersed membership, under the general dominion of an artist with the patently pataphysical name of Thieri Foulc.

The closest thing to a 'pataphysical legacy that remains within the Oulipo circuit is a group, co-founded in 1995 by Hervé Le Tellier, called the Society of Friends of Jean-Baptiste Botul—said Botul being an imaginary Kantian aphorist who had affairs with Simone de Beauvoir and Marie Bonaparte.[12] The society, more of a clique than an organization, sometimes awards prizes (endowed by the Botul Foundation for Botulism) to books mentioning Botul and written by members of the prize jury; its symbol is an anvil, its slogan "The anvil is not the future of anything." In short, it has much of the spirited pomp and nonsense of the Collège de 'Pataphysique, with none of the underpinning philosophical ambitiousness or underhanded cultural urgency—which may be just as well, at least for what it suggests about the climate of the world that created both Botul and the current incarnation of the Oulipo. "If 'pataphysics is the science of imaginary solutions," Paul Braffort wrote

---

[12] It may not have escaped your attention that the frequently open-shirted French public intellectual Bernard-Henri Lévy courted quite a lot of ridicule in 2010 when he earnestly cited Botul's writings in an essay on Kant.

in 2002, "the Oulipo could be the search for real solutions to imaginary problems."[13]

—◁o▷—

The other major infrastructural influence on the Oulipo was a group of anticipatory plagiarists known as the Bourbaki collective: a team of European eggheads who set about rewriting all of mathematics as an ensemble of axioms based on set theory, and who published their work jointly under the pseudonym of Nicolas Bourbaki, citizen of the obscure nation of Poldavia.[14]

151

At a glance, the group, founded in 1934 by a handful of mathematicians from the Ecole Normale Supérieure in Paris—including André Weil and Jean Dieudonné, both of whom would contribute to Le Lionnais's book on mathematical thought—looks a lot like the Oulipo did in its early

---

[13] Which dovetails quite agreeably with Marianne Moore's utopian description of *poetry,* in her poem of that title, as "imaginary gardens with real toads in them."

[14] [*Deep breath.*] The group was named after the French general Charles Denis Bourbaki (1816–1897), whose career was not a particularly glamorous one: even his attempt at a noble suicide backfired, leaving him alive and embarrassed for another sixteen years. Poldavia, meanwhile, which figures in Queneau's early pseudo–detective novel *Pierrot mon ami* (My Friend Pierrot) and then later in Roubaud's *Hortense* novels, goes as least as far back as the 1935 Tintin adventure *The Blue Lotus*. According to Roubaud, Poldavian grammar has six tones and fourteen cases, while the alphabet has fifty-three consonants and eleven vowels. Michèle Audin claims that the laws of Gödel's incompleteness theorem do not apply in Poldavia.

years. It likewise came together through a set of ideas about a diverse and fundamental human endeavor, likewise met regularly, likewise adopted weird bylaws (members were summarily forced to resign when they turned fifty) and occasionally propagated misinformation. It also, like the Oulipo, published its collective findings, but as textbooks rather than chapbooks, wherein lies an important difference: the Bourbakians wanted to replace the reigning mathematical models; the Oulipo, from its inception, was leery of claiming it was reinventing literature or language, and took care to emphasize the challenge-by-choice nature of the structures it was hawking. "The Oulipo's plan, which 'translates' Bourbaki's objectives and method into the domain of the arts of language, is no less serious and ambitious," Roubaud explains, "but it is non-sectarian and not convinced of the validity of its proceedings to the exclusion of all other approaches."[15]

Roubaud also proposes an analogous relationship between the groups' methods—"a structure in Bourbaki's conception of mathematics is capable of producing an infinity of theorems, by deductions from its axioms. A constraint is the oulipian equivalent of a bourbakist structure" —and between the goals behind them, namely a fastening of the practice of mathematics and literature, respectively, to "a sound and rigorous basis" that could be derived over and over again from first principles. This ultimately comes across as a little too neat a comparison, but that's fifty years'

---

[15] Harry Mathews's translation.

hindsight talking. For Queneau and Le Lionnais, both of whom were supremely interested in the work Bourbaki was doing, this model was more than just a constructive counterpoint to that of the Surrealists.

As was the case with 'pataphysics, part of the Oulipo-Bourbaki affinity came from admiration for a mutual progenitor, the German mathematician David Hilbert, who wore a weird hat all the time and whose grasp on reality was literally on another level. The axiomatic method, which Hilbert had elaborated by way of a modern treatment of Euclidean geometry, was both the initial inspiration for the Bourbaki program and a source of great appeal to Queneau, who didn't believe deep down that mathematics was any more real, outside the human mind, than language. One of Queneau's last works applies the principles of Hilbert's *Foundations of Mathematics* to language, replacing the words *points, lines,* and *planes* in each axiom and theorem with *words, sentences,* and *paragraphs:* for instance, "I.6. If two words in a sentence belong to a paragraph, then all the words in that sentence belong to that paragraph." Or, more provocative, Theorem 7: "Between two words in a sentence, there exists an infinity of others."

—◦—

As with the Collège again, the Bourbakist influence has waned somewhat within oulipian activity, but remains apropos in explaining what it means to say that the Oulipo is invested in generating literature from mathematical structures. That's not immediately evident: hardcore leftbrainers like Le Lionnais and Claude Berge are no longer around, and even Valérie Beaudouin and Pierre Rosenstiehl rarely participate in the composition process. To most visible evidence, the Oulipo is involved with the kind of constraints we tend to associate with the puzzles page of the Sunday newspaper, not with honest-to-Gödel mathematics.

Bourbaki is a helpful way to understand that the Oulipo's real connection to math as a discipline is a question of approach: an Oulipian constructs a poem or a novel the way a mathematician proves a theorem—carefully, methodically, embracing a set of rules. The "structures" at issue are not so much arithmetic or algorithmic as they are precise and rigorous—*calculation* would be just as good a term as *mathematical structures,* or what Christian Bök calls "an array of rules for exploring an array of rules," but neither one connotes the same work ethic, the same imaginative balance of empiricism and abstraction, that guides the oulipian model from conception through composition.

Not that there isn't some respectable math still bandied about in the corpus: Le Tellier's longer books, particularly *The Sextine Chapel* and *Le Voleur de nostalgie,* are organized by combinatorial contrivances that one would need a pen and a couple of pages to explain; ditto for some of the forms with which Roubaud continues to experiment, such as the *joséphine,* a variation on the sestina in which certain lines progressively appear or disappear according to a given pattern working within the larger spiral. Nonetheless, and especially in a group-wide aggregate, these structures tend to come through as what Fournel calls "traces of the mathematician in the work of the poet."

They're not usually the sorts of questions the workshop can undertake together: they're too individually meaningful to explain, or too complicated to make into a productive literary collaboration.

Fournel wondered aloud to me once whether the group had been naïve about the possibility of keeping math and literature on equal footings, whether the mathematical input it sought out was too strong, too upper-level, for a truly sustainable text adaptation. "The last mathematical person we recruited was Olivier Salon," he said, "and in the half hour that followed he turned into an actor and a writer and abandoned the capacity of mathematician. If Le Tellier and Roubaud are discussing math at a meeting, sure, Olivier Salon will discuss math with them, but he's never taken the floor as a mathematician and proposed that we work on such-and-such a problem."

The Oulipo has since co-opted Michèle Audin, who teaches at the Institute for Advanced Mathematical Research in Strasbourg and at the French National Center for Scientific Research.[16] In spite of her work in symplectic geometry and differential manifolds and Hamiltonian mechanics and other stuff I can't even begin to think about claiming to understand, she has just the sort of mathemati-

---

[16] Her father, Maurice Audin, also a mathematician, was active in the cause for Algerian independence, which led to his torture and death, at age twenty-five, at the hands of French colonial forces. The French government has never officially acknowledged his death, despite efforts on the part of Michèle and her mother; in 2009, Michèle declined the French national Légion d'Honneur, the highest honorific in the country, for that reason.

cal mind the workshop craves: slightly literary and slightly mischievous, too, attracted to math as much for its characters as for its ideas. In addition to various papers and reference texts—one is called simply *Spinning Tops*—she has published a biography of the pioneering Russian mathematician and feminist Sofia Kovalevskaya; a book about the algebraic topologist Jacques Feldbau, whose career and life were cut short by the Vichy régime; and shorter histories of other kindred figures. She has also written "La vérité sur la Poldévie" (The Truth about Poldavia), a tell-all essay about Nicolas Bourbaki's origins, and *Carrés imparfaits* (Imperfect Squares), which rounds up a handful of mathematical errors in literary works and teases them out in a sestina-shaped series of personal anecdotes.

I have no idea how Audin's involvement in the Oulipo will play out—in a sense, who will influence whom, and how—but it's exciting to think of someone writing about mathematics in a literary voice, rather than the other way around. (An apt example is Ludmila Duchêne and Agnès Leblanc's *Rationnel mon Q*,[17] whose publication Audin helped to midwife: a masterly series of demonstrations of the irrationality of the square root of 2, modeled after Queneau's *Exercises in Style*.) If the meaning of the word *mathematics* in the contemporary Oulipo is more temperamen-

---

[17] Literally, *Rational My Ass. Q*, which stands for the set of all rational numbers, is pronounced like *cul* (the L is silent), just as in Duchamp's *L.H.O.O.Q.* There is also a distinct echo of Queneau's Zazie, who, for example, is told not to act like a snob and responds, brusquely, *"Snob mon cul!"*

tal than literal, the oulipian side of Audin's work to date is pleasingly Bourbakian in the same way: inventive and somewhat arch, grounded in a familiar domain but willing to bring in the unexpected and the foreign, just in case there's something new and fascinating to be learned.

the rat in laboratory 1966–1973

THE TWO OULIPO MEETINGS I have attended so far, nos. 577 and 589—the former as a trial member and the latter as a geographically estranged one—were nothing like the madcap bull sessions I used to enjoy imagining: no contests to see who could go longest without uttering a masculine noun, no heated debates about the merits of the cedilla versus those of the umlaut, no weird occult rituals (at least none that I'm going to tell you about). No trace of decadence or bohemian angst either, just easy evenings among longtime friends, calm and convivial discussions of the newest available variations on old sympathies and old disagreements.

I suspect it took a while for the meetings to be this way. The early ones recorded in Bens's *Genèse de l'Oulipo*, though not especially well organized—by comparison, current meetings' adherence to agenda and protocol is downright Deuteronomic—were more formal and less intimate, and the minutes don't capture the Thanksgiving-dinner overtones of affection and bickering that made me feel, from the moment I arrived, as if I were surrounded by family. Perhaps they couldn't, just as perhaps someone a few decades hence, reading minutes from the present era, would manage only to distill us to the same sort of types as those that recur throughout *Genèse*—the ornery one, the mischievous wit, the quiet sage.

But what Bens's minutes especially failed to prepare me for was the feeling of flux in an Oulipo meeting, the collective conception of the group's own potentiality. In those early years, even when guests of honor came to discuss the oulipian tangencies in their work, the primary mandate was to learn about the tangencies, not to evaluate the guest: the work in progress was the idea of potential literature, not the workshop around it. True to the group's original name, the early minutes read like notes from an ongoing seminar, with generally impolite commentary from various participants, rather than accounts of the mechanics of a working research group. The idea of potential literature is still on the docket these days, of course, but the present structure of the workshop is such that keeping abreast of the people who explore it, as well as deputizing new ones to do so, is of equal if not greater concern.

By the time it became clear that expansion was inevitable if the Oulipo was to continue, a handful of rules had been established. Some would erode over time, such as Queneau's classification of various kinds of potentialities (*austere potentialities* included matrix analysis and attempts to defy mathematical laws, while the variable-length alexandrine[1] was a *patapotentiality*) and the designation of Oulipians as active members, associate members, or correspondents, with attendant voting privileges—but the one that has survived, formally or by common sense, is the dictum limiting the number of active members to twelve at all times. "We have to be able to fit around a dinner table" is the usual explanation. Even after just two meetings, I see what Queneau meant.

Expansion first became an issue in 1966, after the passing of Albert-Marie Schmidt, when Le Lionnais raised the issue of "bringing the Oulipo up to strength whenever a vacancy occurs, or letting it gradually die a natural death."[2] The question brought to a head some discontent that Oulipians had voiced with the group's lack of momentum, despite such publications as Bens's *41 Sonnets irrationnels* (41 Irrational Sonnets)—variations that maintained the

---

[1] The classical alexandrine is by definition a twelve-syllable line with a *césure* (caesura, or pause) after the sixth syllable. As theorized by Roubaud in a 1984 B.O. piece, the *alexandrin de longueur variable,* or ALVA, gives some leeway to the prosodic form depending on whether or not one pronounces mute E's (for instance, Racine's "Oui, prince, je languis, je brûle pour Thésée"—"Ah yes, for Theseus / I languish and I long," in Robert Bruce Boswell's translation—will have the traditional twelve syllables if you stick a good old French schwa at the end of *prince* and *brûle,* ten if you don't, or even eight if you elide the E's in both *je*'s). At the time of the above classification, though, the only example of an ALVA was Jean Queval's "Le train traverse la nuit" ("The train moves across the night"), which has seven syllables at best—whence, presumably, the *pata* prefix.

[2] Iain White's translation.

classical sonnet's fourteen lines but, instead of arranging them in the standard stanza distribution (4-4-3-3 in French, or 4-4-4-2 in English), used the first digits of pi (3-1-4-1-5)—and Jacques Duchateau's *Zinga 8,* a distant derivation of his intersective-novel project that takes place in the fifty-first century. Blavier had complained that the workshop wasn't suitably rigorous, having turned up only "a few mainly mechanical procedures" in its half-decade of work; Queneau had remarked, by way of agreement, that the most significant and innovative oulipian energy had begun to come from outside the Oulipo.

It was in this spirit that Queneau brought up the case of a young mathematician named Jacques Roubaud, whose first collection of poems was to be published by Gallimard in 1967. The book was called $\in$ (the mathematical symbol, used in set theory, signifying "is an element of") and consisted of sonnets transmogrified partly according to the rules of the Japanese tile game *go.* Queneau avowed that $\in$ had been written without any prior knowledge of the Oulipo's activities. It was decided: Roubaud would be invited to a meeting not just as a guest but as a trial member.

$\in$ is a complicated work, to be sure—certain poems are prefixed by white dots and others by black dots, in keeping with the deceptively simple rules of *go,* and the first pages of the book offer four different ways to read it. Even from a distance it's easy to see why it appealed to the Oulipo: it's combinatorial, inventive, and challenging; you have to either work really hard to read the contents as sonnets or just take Roubaud's word for it. At the same time, it pays tribute to a venerable literary form and cautiously, respectfully expands it. It is a series of poems, but also a work on the *potential* of the sonnet.

Roubaud's book was not the first demonstration that people outside the Oulipo were toying with oulipian ideas: a French writer named Marc Saporta had already released a "book" called *Composition No. 1,* a box of unbound pages to be read in any order the reader pleases,[3] while British author B. S. Johnson would publish *The Unfortunates,* a memoir of twenty-seven chapters unordered except for the first and last, a few years later. But ∈ was inspiriting because, while it obeyed the group's desire to remain anchored in literary tradition, it also captured its unspoken restlessness to start *making* things. Queneau saw in Roubaud not only someone whose techniques could be useful—as was the case with most of the group's early guests—but also someone whose ideas, supervised or not, could lend some new momentum to oulipian explorations.

Predictably enough, the audition went well—although Roubaud recalls that several months went by before he had any idea what his auditioners were on about.

---

[3] John Barth seems to zing this more or less directly, in his 1967 essay "The Literature of Exhaustion," by alluding to certain works that are "lively to read about, and make for interesting conversation in fiction-writing classes, for example, where we discuss Somebody-or-other's unbound, unpaginated, randomly assembled novel-in-a-box and the desirability of printing *Finnegans Wake* on a very long roller-towel."

("At the time," he is fond of pointing out, "lots of Oulipians were great drinkers.") Roubaud was the Oulipo's "first investment in the future, and he was charged implicitly with the task of carrying the group's work forward in new ways," explains David Bellos in his biography *Georges Perec: A Life in Words*. "He was, in a sense, a natural Oulipian—not only a mathematician and a poet before he had ever heard of the group, but a mathematician-poet, writing in the intersection of games, formal languages, and words." In the years since, Roubaud has proved to be all that and more; indeed, he has been more active than anyone after Queneau and Le Lionnais in theorizing how the group does and might operate, what it's meant to be and what it's not. For the latter generations, Mathews describes him as "pretty much the Pope."

Roubaud is a large, solid man, a bit aloof in his demeanor, both mischief and wisdom carved into the folds of his face. He collaborates widely in all manner of disciplines, yet his own relationship to writing seems fundamentally solitary. He gets up before dawn each day to write—an email I have from him, in response to my invitation to meet for an interview, says that afternoons are best, and is time-stamped 3:11 A.M.—and does so without looking back or, in certain cases, correcting mistakes. He is early for everything, and generally the first to slip away after a *jeudi*, toting a cloth shopping bag that says, in English, "BIG SHOPPER." Some of this is my observation; some of it is based on his own accounts; some of it is lore. He says he likes to compose poetry while he walks through Paris in his big steel-toed Pataugas boots, as Wallace Stevens did on his way to the insurance office in Hartford. He is a confirmed anglo-phile. He adores root beer.

His critical reception has been charmed, to put it mildly, since he published $\in$—of which Claude Roy wrote in *Le Monde* that all he wanted to do that day was run to the nearest telegraph counter and cable everyone he loved with the message "POETRY NOT DEAD. STOP. JACQUES ROUBAUD IS BORN."[4] Since then, Roubaud has lived up to that almost cripplingly effusive praise as consistently as anyone could; it is not uncommon, these days, to hear him referred to as the greatest living French poet, even though he prefers to call himself a "composer of mathematics and literature." The bio preceding the by-the-same-author list at the back of his books, which by now takes up multiple pages, says simply "Born in 1932. Mathematician."

Most astounding in Roubaud's work, probably, is the variety of registers in which he is comfortable. He is best known for what might be called his serious poetry— the lineage inaugurated by $\in$ and followed by structurally complex works like *Mono no aware* and *The Plurality of Worlds of Lewis,* the latter spun around the analytic philos-opher David Lewis's proposal that ours is just one of infi-nitely many possible worlds—but he is equally effective in the simple, obliging kind that makes reasonably good sense

---

4 Which, aside from missing the whole point of the word STOP in a telegram, anticipatorily echoes the work of Japanese conceptual art-ist On Kawara, who throughout the 1970s would send telegrams to friends that said "I AM STILL ALIVE." (Roubaud and Kawara later worked together on a book called *Codes.*)

on the surface.[5] (Sometimes it even rhymes.) His collection of Parisian "pedestrian poems," *The Form of a City Changes Faster, Alas, Than the Human Heart,* is formally diverse and breezily appealing; *Some Thing Black,* the precursor to *Plurality,* is a devastatingly guileless account of his grief following the death of his second wife. The *Hortense* cycle (*Our Beautiful Heroine, Hortense Is Abducted,* and *Hortense in Exile*), three novels whose plot is patterned after the sestina, are witty and a little lewd. He does Oulipo light—the *chicago,* the *baobab*—as well as Oulipo 'ard, Oulipo heavy, Oulipo dark.

The centerpiece of Roubaud's oeuvre is a lifelong endeavor called *le Projet* (the Project), which began with a dream he had in 1961 about deciding to write a novel called *The Great Fire of London.* He started to act on his decision in waking life but eventually abandoned the project, and has now spent way more time writing about that abandonment than he did working on the novel. There are seven books that collectively constitute the *Projet,* in that they

---

[5] For instance:

> It took me
> much longer
> to compose
> my poems
>
> than you will spend
> reading them
>
> do you find
> that
> fair?

elaborate, in a pseudo-autobiographical style filled with digressions and interpolations and bifurcations, Roubaud's failure to stick to the initial *Projet*. (Very Roubaldian distinction: the imagined work, which he abandoned in 1978 for reasons he explains in a book called *'the great fire of London'* (lowercase and in single quotes, to differentiate it from the unrealized dream-novel), is the "bigger project"; the actual published work is the "minimal project.") "Everything I speak about is, in a way, linked to the old abandoned project," he told an interviewer in 2008. "And if they're not true, at least the events are told truthfully, as I remember them."

167

This is an important point of unity in Roubaud's work, diverse as it is: the absence of legerdemain, the transparency of thought. Many of his writings proceed as though he were writing an outline or proving a theorem: paragraphs are numbered or parenthetical thoughts are indented successively on the page; in the case of *La Dissolution,* the final volume of the *Projet,* a different color is used for each digression. At meetings and colloquia I have attended with him, he has typically taken notes in at least three colors. The first time I asked him to sign a book for me, he insisted that I choose one pen from about a dozen.

This tends to be his mode for discussing the Oulipo in particular, whether for a beginning audience (such as a speech first given in Catalonia and later reprinted as the introduction to the *Oulipo Compendium*) or for the in-crowd (such as his dissection of the meaning of "oulipian author," or of the group's institutional ties to Bourbaki, or the book-length Socratico-Wittgensteinian dialogue he conducts with himself about language and memory in *Poetry Etcetera: Cleaning House*). This is how he breaks down the makeup of the group:

>   (i) the first sort are composers of literature (prose, poetry, criticism) who are not mathematicians;
>   (ii) the second sort are mathematicians who are not composers of literature; the members of type
>   (iii) are composers of literature *and* mathematicians; those of type
>   (iv) are mathematicians *and* composers of literature.
>   (Types (iii) and (iv) are distinct, "and" being used here to signify a hierarchic sequence: "and" = "and secondarily" or, additively, "and also.")[6]

However much of this feeds on the lore cultivated by essays and interviews and scholarly books, there doesn't seem to be any real hedging or jargonmongering going on. The way he writes is the way he thinks, which, given the diversity of his bibliography, is testament to a great intelligence. He has a knack for cutting through knotty conceptual things and laying them out quite clearly—but only when he wants to. On the nature of oulipian constraint: "Speculating about a constraint's potentiality involves discerning the extent to which it is apt to trigger variations and mutations; the extent to which it will naturally and productively participate in families of constraints; and, finally, the extent to which it

---

[6] Harry Mathews's translation.

might evolve over the course of time."[7] Not as catchy as *rats who build the labyrinth from which they plan to escape,* but surely more useful.

—◄○►—

Lately, Roubaud has been giving free rein to his impulse to toy with history, to slip his fictional or semi-fictional characters into the patchwork of the past. He calls the World War II setting of 2008's *Parc Sauvage* (Wild Park) "a fairy tale corrected by history"; *Eros mélancolique* (Melancholy Eros), a decade-jumping novel written in collaboration with Anne Garréta and published the following year, features cameos from old Roubaud figures such as the heroine of the *Hortense* series. Sometimes he sees fit to work the Oulipo into his historical peregrinations: a recent *Bibliothèque Oulipienne* "essay" finds Le Lionnais in correspondence with the imaginary philosopher Jean-Baptiste Botul on matters of oulipian doctrine. And then there's the project he started almost twenty years ago, when he thought to write a sequel to Perec's "Voyage d'hiver."[8]

169

In Perec's story, published in 1979, a young professor named Vincent Degraël visits a colleague, Denis Borrade, at the latter's family villa near Le Havre, where he comes across a book of poems—*Le Voyage d'hiver*—by an

---

[7] Jean-Jacques Poucel's translation.

[8] English translations of the first ten installments in the series exist (see *Winter Journeys,* published by Atlas Press in 2001), but I refer to them by their French titles here because it would be a pity to miss the continual play on the sound of *d'hiver.*

unknown poet named Hugo Vernier. Degraël initially dismisses the slim volume as a hack-job pastiche of Baudelaire and Rimbaud and Mallarmé and all those boys, until he realizes it *predates* them all: he has unwittingly stumbled upon the mysterious urtext of twentieth-century European poetry. He and Borrade prepare to mount an inquiry into the book's origins and find out why nobody has ever heard of Hugo Vernier, but the Second World War breaks out instead and, once Degraël makes it home after six years, the villa has been destroyed, the book lost, and all traces of Vernier's existence seemingly erased. When Degraël dies thirty years later in a mental hospital, still obsessed with the fruitless quest, he leaves behind a notebook called *Le Voyage d'hiver,* spending eight pages recounting what he has found so far and leaving another 392 blank.

Unlike Le Tellier's lighthearted spinoffs, Roubaud's sequel, *Le Voyage d'hier* (Yesterday's Journey), published in 1992 in the *Bibliothèque Oulipienne,* only complicates the historical dimension of the original. Rather than pick up on the theoretical cues offered by Perec's story— plagiarism by anticipation, literary historiography, the death of the author—Roubaud reads it as a puzzle and begins to tease out its unanswered strands. *Le Voyage d'hier* begins with Borrade's son, Dennis, receiving a copy of Perec's story in the mail. Borrade *père,* who was arrested by the S.S. and sent to Buchenwald and spent many years after the war trying unsuccessfully to expose the traitor who gave up their infantry, visits Dennis and shows him a manuscript of a book called *The Month of May Will Have 53 Days.* (The book Perec was working on when he died was called *53 Days;* the plot centers on the disappearance of a character named Robert Serval—same name as the traitor who sent Borrade to Buchenwald.)

This sort of thing goes on for a while, for about twice as long as Perec's story. It comes to light through various family secrets and lore that the teenage Vernier, in love with the young governess of the poet Théophile Gautier, had his first work stolen by an unscrupulous dandy named Charles Baudelaire, to whom the poor girl had proudly but naïvely showed her fiancé's poems. It also comes to light that Degraël is actually Vernier's son and Borrade's half-brother, and that the whole disappearing-book business is actually due to a printing error—the book, which Roubaud endows with curious resemblances to at least two of Queneau's most important works, was supposed to have been called *Le Voyage d'hier,* not *d'hiver.*

After Roubaud's, slowly but surely a deluge of further sequels emerged to renew the search. What began as a serial detective novel eventually turned into a many-handed creation myth, a multifarious rumination on Hugo Vernier according to each contributor's fascinations and fancies. Le Tellier wrote *Le Voyage d'Hitler* (Hitler's Journey) in 1999, followed by Jouet's *Hinterreise*[9] and Monk's *Voyage d'Hoover* (Hoover's Journey). Roubaud has remained more or less the curator of the tale, adding new episodes now and then in one of a couple of guises; at this point, Perec's original included, there are fourteen chapters in a potentially infinite story.

I'll talk more about the whole series later. What I

---

[9] Another typo, this one for *Winterreise* (Winter's Journey), the famous Schubert song cycle.

want to point out right now is Roubaud's act of reading heavily into someone else's work and declaring it a sort of mission statement for the Oulipo—his subtler version, as it were, of Queneau's kindly authoritarian control through the group's first decade and a half of existence. He's up to something expansive and quietly leaderlike, creating a mythological character who is part Queneau, part Perec, part imaginary, all speculative traction. He's plunked that myth into the middle of oulipian discourse, without asking permission or announcing his intent—it's good to be the Pope. He's done it by doing it, just as he always says about poetry: it says what it says by saying it.

172

Beyond his talent for dense and complicated poetry, light and obliging fiction, erudition and mythology and all that, this is where Roubaud has been most interesting and useful for the group. Because he was not there at the beginning, he has been free to hatch ideas about the workshop—ones that might have seemed sacrilegious had he been more invested in its founding principles—and let them drift into its collective sense of self. The ingenious move in this case was to choose to read Degraël's 392 blank pages as the future of the Oulipo, and to begin filling them in accordingly. Thanks to this, a significant part of the group's project is now to develop its own past by way of what it learns and what it fabricates in the present. That historical continuity, one might say, is Roubaud's greatest fiction of all.

◄○►

In the same spirit, Roubaud has proposed a collective memoir of the group to be assembled by fragments called *mo-*

ments oulipiens (oulipian moments). "I picture such a portrait as a large puzzle in which different *moments oulipiens*
are placed, bit by bit, bringing to light the increasingly
sharp face of the model, Oulipo," he writes in *La Bibliothèque de Warburg*, volume six of the *Projet*. "The ensemble
of them, endlessly expanded, year in and year out, if possible with contributions from all of the Oulipians, organized
according to appropriate constraints, will eventually, in the
not-too-distant future, constitute a collection of texts capable of illustrating the hypothesis expressed by the title of
the first part of this chapter."[10]

173

For now, there are no explicit constraints; there is
only the stipulation that a *moment oulipien* involve or have
been witnessed by at least one member of the group, and
that it be as precise as possible on names and dates ("for the
edification of future generations," specifies the back cover
of the first and so far the only collection of the form, published in 2004). It can be monumental, like the meeting
where Perec read out some early excerpts from *La Disparition* and nobody noticed there were no E's in it, or mundane, like the nth time Paul Braffort misplaced his wallet.
Most examples are funny, some bittersweet even if they're
not meant to be—Fournel's story about Perec's IBM typewriter, which rendered the last word of *Life A User's Manual* and then never worked again, chokes me up every time
I read it—but sure enough, each one does fill in a piece of
the puzzle.

If the *moment oulipien* sounds like a slightly self-
indulgent, anecdotal project from a handful of slightly be-

---

[10] "Oulipo: A Novel."

loved public figures, that's because it is. (The book has not sold particularly well.) But it also has a more interesting figurative function: it's how Roubaud has chosen to set about actually writing the unwritten, collective, and necessarily unfinishable novel that he believes the Oulipo to be. The plot is a little bit staid, maybe, but each recurring character comes across with a set of echoes and contradictions consistent with that unnerving overlap between real life and realist fiction. There's also something wonderfully immersive about getting all your information in a novel from its characters: there is only the world that surrounds and unites them, none of the off-the-page interference that Barthes and Foucault theorized. By blurring the lines separating author and person and character, each *moment oulipien* builds a piecemeal portrait of the group that's exactly as faithful and trustworthy as the reader needs it to be, the story of the left leg as told by the right shoulder.

—◁o▷—

The year after Roubaud joined, the Oulipo invited Georges Perec to a meeting. Perec had won the prestigious Prix Renaudot in 1965 for his debut novel, *Les Choses* (translated most recently by David Bellos as *Things: A Story of the Sixties*), which tells of the creeping disillusionment in the lives of a young French couple almost entirely through matter-of-fact descriptions of products they own.[11] His next book,

---

[11] This technique is used to equally expressive effect—albeit a much less focal one, what with all the dead prostitutes—in Bret Easton Ellis's *American Psycho*.

A Man Asleep, was a commercial flop, but the restless experimentalism of its structure—a sort of macro-cento comprising quotation after uncited quotation—perked up oulipian ears. As it turned out, Perec was good friends with
Roubaud's brother-in-law; he had also been working, in
concert with the cousin of Jean Bénabou, Roubaud's mathematical mentor, on a nerdy little dictionary game called
PALF—*production automatique de la langue française*—
which consisted of replacing each word in a text with its
dictionary definition and repeating the process ad libitum.[12]
The founders asked about this Perec; Roubaud told the
group what he knew. They decided to have Perec for lunch,
so to speak, and in March 1967 he was co-opted as the
workshop's second new member.

175

Given that Perec's is the first or second name most
people identify with the Oulipo, it's hard to exaggerate the
contribution he made to what the group is today. He was a
virtuoso of linguistic jiggery-pokery, but also just a really
good, likable writer, his erudition and vocabulary matched
only by his unappeasable ambition. Still, probably the most
important new thing he brought to the workshop in 1967
was dependence: he was the first writer to *need* the Oulipo.
According to Bellos's biography, his relationship to writing was a passive-aggressive love-hate of the most tempes-
tuous kind, and learning that some of his farther-out ideas

---

[12] Polish-English writer Stefan Themerson had introduced a similar process about twenty-five years earlier, christening it "semantic
poetry," and in so doing gave us such memorable works as Words-
worth's "I wandered lonely as a visible mass of condensed watery
vapour at various heights in the upper atmosphere."

and tendencies could be embraced, even systematized, turned him from a promising writer to an accomplished one. "He had such an extraordinary belief in writing," Mathews told an interviewer in 1987. "He really looked upon it as a kind of salvation."

The adoption was also very probably life-saving personally, not just creatively. Perec never quite knew his parents; they both died in World War II, his father in military service and his mother presumed, although never confirmed, at Auschwitz. He was raised by relatives in various parts of France, but the other associations he cultivated in his early years—as a Jew, as a Marxist, as a politically engaged intellectual—never gave him the sense of belonging he would find in the Oulipo. On a questionnaire circulated internally by Le Lionnais in 1970, in response to the question "Do you think about personal oulipian work?" he wrote, "I do nothing else."

For him, "personal oulipian work" meant more than just work done on his own time. He accepted the oulipian idea of constraint readily, almost piously, but changed its application altogether: he had come ready to roll up his sleeves and write, not theorize. In five years or so after his induction, he had written texts using at least half of the oulipian forms in Queneau's inventory; had he not died of lung cancer at forty-six, he might well have exhausted the entire list. Bernard Magné, who co-runs the Perec archive at the BNF, has written an essay on this singularity within the Oulipo,[13] arguing that it was Perec's will

---

[13] Actually, two essays: "Georges Perec, l'oulibiographe" and "Georges Perec oulibiographe."

to realize what was considered potential, coupled with his use of his work to express (however obliquely) his personal preoccupations, that made him more than what Roubaud calls a "composer of literature"—that made him an honest-to-goodness writer.

His bibliography doesn't argue. No two of his books overlap much past the genre marking: even his twin letter-constrained novels, *La Disparition* and *Les Revenentes,* tell completely different kinds of story—not to mention their mutually exclusive vocabularies.[14] His essays collectively elaborate the *infra-ordinary,* a sensibility based on interrogating the unconsidered in everyday life, and he turned that attention on an estimable variety of topics, from politics and architecture and movies and whiskey to books and thoughts and the contents of his desk. He wrote severely constrained poems and disciplined lists, both of which managed to express a fully fleshed-out spirit despite their respectively gnomic and mundane exteriors. He wrote radio plays, compiled interviews with Jews at Ellis Island, and collaborated with Roubaud and mathematician Pierre Lusson on a treatise extolling the pleasures of *go.* He confronted his early life in *W or the Memory of Childhood,* a tapering rabbit hole of allegory and autobiography that mixes anodyne thoughts about the flimsiness of memory with a disturbing adventure story based on one he made up at age thirteen. He wanted to write more—children's books, science fiction, family lore—but never found the time.

His crowning achievement, for which he won the

177

---

[14] According to Le Tellier, *La Disparition* also contains the widest variety of nouns of any novel in French.

Prix Médicis in 1978, is a sprawling jigsaw-novel called *Life A User's Manual,* a tour of the ten-by-ten grid of a Parisian apartment building with its façade removed: each chapter plumbs the frozen moment and hidden past of a different space, the narration hopping from floor to floor and room to room, and thus story to story, according to the same algorithm that permits the knight to touch every square on a chessboard once and only once (adapted for novelistic use by Claude Berge). Each chapter contains at least forty-two obligatory themes tucked into the woodwork of the story—unattributed citations to Kafka or Queneau or Mann, kinds of activities and materials and emotions and animals, alphabetical and semantic oulipian manipulations—governed by their own combinatory model, based on Euler's Graeco-Latin square. But there's plenty to distract you from the mechanics: the building houses a man named Cinoc, whose job is to remove outmoded words from the dictionary;[15] a trained hamster named Polonius, who needs to play dominoes once a week in order to keep from dissipation; an artist named Valène, who is preparing a vast painting whose many scenes encompass all of the stories in the book. Le Tellier has described the novel as "a sort of Goodwill store for any work on the Oulipo, since if you look carefully you can find absolutely everything there."

The central image of *Life* is the long-term artis-

---

[15] Someone told me once, with a conspiratorial I've-figured-it-all-out smile, that those obsolete words were *les mots vides d'emploi,* or words emptied of use—a canny spooneristic tweaking of the novel's French title, *La Vie mode d'emploi.*

tic project of an idly wealthy Englishman, Percival Bartlebooth, who has spent ten years learning to paint passable
watercolors and another twenty traveling the world with
his valet, Smautf, to paint a total of 500 seascapes. Each
painting, once finished, is packed off to a craftsman named
Gaspard Winckler, who affixes it to a special backing, cuts
it into a jigsaw puzzle, and sends it to Bartlebooth for reas-
sembly. Upon completing each puzzle, Bartlebooth "retex-
turizes" it to fill in the jigsaw seams, removes the backing,
and sends the restored painting off to the place it was made,
where it is dipped in a detergent solution to erase everything except perhaps faint marks where the canvas had
been cut.

179

Aside from the spooky sustainability of the project—everyone involved, from Winckler to Smautf to the inventor of the treatment that makes the paintings sea salt–
soluble, lives somewhere in the building on (the imaginary)
rue Simon-Crubellier—one admires the Zen-by-way-of-
Kafka simplicity of its zero-sum goal, the way it is meant to
end in nothing but 500 extremely costly sheets of blank
watercolor paper. Equally troubling is Bartlebooth's death,
moments before time is suspended for the duration of the
book's 500 pages (not including a veritable bouquet of in-
dexes and appendixes): he is in the middle of his 439th
puzzle, nearly blind, sitting before a hole shaped like an X
and holding in his hand a piece shaped like a W. "Even a
self-annihilating project such as Bartlebooth's cannot be
completed," concluded Paul Auster in his *New York Times*
review of the book when it came out in Bellos's English
translation in 1987, "and when we learn in the epilogue that

Valène's enormous painting (which for all intents and purposes is the book we have just been reading) has come no further than a preliminary sketch, we realize that Perec does not exempt himself from the follies of his characters."

—◄o►—

Perec's dark side nonetheless lies a little bit beneath the surface, and one can spend years on his oeuvre without getting past Perec light, a dizzying utopia of bizarre, futile delights. He laughed off backbreaking lexical strictures, from the *beau présent* and the *belle absente* to the heterogram, a cross between an extreme lipogram and the alphabetical version of a Sudoku puzzle from hell. His *Ulcérations,* for example, contains 400 lines, each of which is an anagram of the titular word, chosen because it's the only French word that contains the eleven most commonly used letters in the alphabet.[16] Those lines don't make much sense in block form, but when you supply spacing and punctuation they read about as coherently as any free-verse poem; here's an example from a later exploit, *La Clôture* (Closure), in which Perec augments each line with a "joker" letter from the underprivileged fifteen, represented here by asterisks:

LO*SCURITENA

UNILA*ORTSEC   *L'obscurité n'a uni la mort.*

---

[16] In English, whose letter frequency is different from that of French, the word would be *threnodials* (laments or dirges). Monk has, predictably enough, established himself as a virtuoso threnodialist.

```
OULERCATINS*        Se couler: ça t'inspire plus? . . .
IRE*LUSCATON
```

Which becomes, in a liberal English approximation:

```
CURTAINSO*LE
A*CLOSEITURN        Curtains of lead close.
NOTSECULAR*I        I turn: not secular miracles . . .
RACLESNOT*IU
```

Most of the time, Perec didn't invent forms so much as take old ones and knock them out of the park: he wrote a palindrome of more than 1,200 words, the world's longest until a computer program eclipsed it. His day job as the archivist at a neuroscience lab taught him the language of the scientific paper, so he wrote a study on the effect of projectile tomatoes on the soprano specimen, complete with hilarious made-up bibliography.[17] He sent out holiday greeting cards with elaborate homophone games—one re-parses the names of jazz musicians and invents stories that wind up producing the same utterances in a roundabout way.[18] In short, there were few verbal feats he couldn't do, much less didn't want to. Roubaud remarked once that one of the fifty things he hoped to accomplish before dying was to find a constraint that would genuinely challenge Perec.

181

---

[17] "Heinz, D. Biological effects of ketchup splatching. *J. Food Cosmet. Ind. 72,* 42–62, 1952."

[18] For instance, a vignette about the poet René Char giving a reading but having memorized his texts in advance can be encapsulated by *Char lit par coeur* ("Char reads by heart"), or Charlie Parker.

It has been suggested at length, by those who knew him best, that Perec embraced constraint to get at what Sturrock calls "willed objectivity"—that is, a way of foregrounding the technical in order to take enough pressure off the personal that it can express itself more or less organically. "The intense difficulty posed by this sort of production . . . palls in comparison to the terror I would feel in writing 'poetry' freely," Perec told an interviewer once.[19] Indeed, there is a certain desperate momentum to his tireless verbal acrobatics—but unlike many other Oulipians, he remains a fundamentally generous writer: never for a moment do you doubt the joy he feels to be writing; never does he leave you out of the joke. I would posit that it is impossible to read a text of Perec's closely (not to say geek out on it, as I did with "Le Voyage d'hiver" in college), without falling a little bit in love with him.

For a while after moving to Paris, I saw Perec everywhere, even though he had died two years before I was born. The unibrowed teenager across the aisle on the Métro, the goofy-eyed drunkard outside the post office, the father pushing a stroller and pulling a dog through the Tuileries: they had this gleam of waggish mischief in their eyes, even if it was clearly I who had put it there, looking for apparitions of the reason I was in that city in the first place. Perec was striking, with bad teeth and a wart on his nose and a face that was passably handsome only from certain angles; he grew an accomplished goatee that Harry Mathews says "made him look like a silly scientist in the

---

[19] Warren Motte's translation.

comics" and kept a wild Jew-fro in his Oulipo years, wore tunics and mugged for the camera, sometimes with a black cat perched on his shoulder. According to Bellos, one of his favorite photographs of himself was one he thought made him look like Kafka.

For a while before leaving Paris, I lived a few blocks away from the rue Georges Perec, a 38-meter, 64-pace stretch of graffiti and stairs where the only street address is number 13. It's a peaceful little streetlet in the middle of the 20th arrondissement (which, as Bénabou points out in a Fillion video about it, is known as the countryside of Paris— ironic, because Perec hated the countryside), tucked away between two other streets you would never know existed unless you had direct business in the neighborhood. I made a point of visiting every so often; some nights I would just totter by, a little drunk, to say hi. It was never along my route, and this always felt curiously appropriate as a tribute.

But Perec is a darling to a lot of people, a sort of benevolent spirit animal—because of his endearing orphan-hood, maybe, or his quixotic relationship to the alphabet, or just for the character he was. A woman I met in the gift shop at the Museum of Jewish Art and History in Paris called him a *chouchou*—a sweetheart—hands clasped over her breast in the Jewish-mother pose of faraway fondness. (I cannot for the life of me remember why we were discussing Perec.)[20] There is another street named after him in Burgundy, and a ferret named after him on YouTube; there

---

[20] She also told me Roubaud was "too mathy" for her.

is even a small celestial body, 2817-Perec, discovered in October 1982. "Named for Georges Perec, who wrote a 300-page novel *La Disparition* without using the letter E," reads the description in the *Dictionary of Minor Planet Names*. "This 'eccentricity' would seem to suit him to studies of minor planets."[21]

—◄o►—

Now the Oulipo embarked upon a period of intense—at least by the standard of the first half-decade—expansion. In 1970, it officially co-opted Marcel Bénabou and a high school math and physics teacher named Luc Périn. Périn, who went by the name Luc Etienne, was a pun specialist and contributor to the satirical newspaper *Le Canard enchaîné,* a more informative precursor of *The Onion.* He was also an active member of the Collège de 'Pataphysique, which had published his *L'Art du contrepet* (The Art of the Spoonerism) in 1957.

Etienne's contributions to the Oulipo suited the mood at the time, which drew from both analytical and synthetic wells. He had compiled a collection of French limericks and written about word games in Lewis Carroll and formal oddities in Edward Lear; he had also invented such forward-thinking constraints as the Möbius-strip poem, which can be read forward or backward with dis-

---

[21] Perec would surely have been tickled to know he beat Kafka to minor-planet namesakehood by three months, Proust by ten, and Flaubert by sixteen years.

tinct and contradictory meanings, and "slenderizing," in which stripping a text of each occurrence of a single letter changes its sense.[22] His love for language was also informed by a love for music—he devised, at various points, a ten-tone octave and a mechanical page-turner for sheet music—which led him to connect the usual homophonic play to more sophisticated uses, for instance a phonetic palindrome that, if recorded, would sound the same played backward or forward: *Jean en luge, Jules en nage.*

At the beginning of the 1970s, a young student named Paul Fournel, who in 1959 had received a copy of *Zazie in the Métro* for his eleventh birthday, wrote a thesis on Queneau and went to ask him for help mounting an exposition on the Oulipo at his university in Nanterre, a western suburb of Paris. Queneau sent Fournel to Boulogne to call on Le Lionnais, who gave Fournel a box containing the detritus of the group's first ten years and told him to try to make some sense of it all.

185

---

[22] "The raging borne in dearth" thus becomes "the aging bone in death" (Mathews, from the *Compendium*). That example also belongs to the subcategory of "asphyxiation," so called because it deprives the text of the letter R, which is pronounced "air" in French. As far as I know, asphyxiation has nothing in particular to do with the eighteenth-century German poet Gottlob Burmann, who, according to the critic Leland de la Durantaye (in an essay called "The Cratylic Impulse: Constraint and Work in the Works and Constraints of OuLiPo," which is actually a lot more readable than its name implies), "so disliked the letter R that not only did he write 130 poems in which the letter did not appear, he also sought to exclude it from his everyday conversation—which, as the story goes, led to his refusing to utter his own name for some seventeen years."

Like me, Fournel's administrative help earned him the title of *esclave de l'Oulipo*. In this capacity he spent about a year doing odd chores such as organizing, with Perec, Le Lionnais's library—which is said to have contained over 3,000 books on chess problems alone.[23] In 1971 Fournel joined the group officially and became the definitively provisional (to Bénabou's provisionally definitive) secretary; the next year, his book-length essay *Clefs pour la littérature potentielle* (Keys for Potential Literature) became the first book to be published about the group. After Noël Arnaud's death in 2003, Fournel became the third president of the Oulipo.

186

Fournel, also a competitive bicyclist and a puppetry specialist, has an impeccably trimmed mustache, an earnestly conspiratorial gleam in his eye, and the gentle bearing of a man who has his shit together. He worked for many years as an editor at various reputable Parisian publishing houses, and has since taken a handful of three-year stints as a diplomatic attaché for the French Ministry of Culture—so far San Francisco, Cairo, and London—between which postings he has done shorter engagements, includ-

---

[23] An interview that Olivier Salon conducted recently with Dominique Miollan, Le Lionnais's secretary from 1977 to 1983, reveals that Le Lionnais didn't actually have as many books as he claimed—a paltry 2,500 on chess problems, for instance. She also recalls that he had three cellars filled with books, each with a different name: *le purgatoire* (purgatory) contained books he might call upon at some later date; *la guillotine* (the guillotine) held books he no longer wanted but that might hold some interest for friends or associates; and *le cimetière* (the cemetery) was for books that "were definitively condemned and could be given out to anyone at all."

ing the directorship of a regional literature center in Languedoc and a year as a visiting professor at Princeton.

His writing style is deceptively simple, a calm and unlyrical approach to things that are no less odd or troubling for it. His work is perhaps the quietest in all the Oulipo, on and off the page: it occurred to me at one point to wonder why I had never read anything of his beyond a curatorial presidential paragraph here or there, and subsequently to wonder whether he had written much of anything at all. As it turns out, he has a long and varied bibliography to his name, including several novels and collections of short stories and poems, some of them oulipian in nature. During his diplomatic stint in Cairo, he got up each morning to send a vignette about daily life in Egypt to a list of friends, a sort of Jouetian exercise; more impressively, *Chamboula,* published in 2007, is an experiment in arborescent narrative, essentially a choose-your-own-adventure story with all the choices removed—beginning with the arrival of a sales catalogue in a peaceable African village and branching out, bifurcation by bifurcation, into a fascinating array of plots, all of the permutations aligned in suggestively impassive sequence.

Nonetheless, Fournel is not the kind of Oulipian whose exploits, light or 'ard, draw a lot of attention. He told me once, with no pretense, that he was not one of the great creators of the Oulipo, that he did not engage with mathematics or invent forms,[24] but that a group like this needed

---

[24] I politely protested that he had invented the *chicago,* to which he responded with a wave of the hand that that was really more Oulipo light.

administrators just as much as it did great literary presences—someone to make the machine run, as he put it.

No question, it has run well; so far, under his presidency, the Oulipo has inducted three new members and arguably grown more popular than ever before, for better or
for worse. The summer after the first season of monthly
oulipian performances at the Théâtre du Rond-Point, a
swanky black-box theater on the Champs-Elysées, he told
me decisively that they would not continue—there was just
no way to keep up those and the *jeudis* without overextend-
ing the group's energies. When the 2009 anthology was
held up in the offices of Gallimard by various individual
rights issues—just imagine thirty-odd different writerly approaches to dealing poorly with personal finance—Fournel
was the one to herd all the cats, from his office in London.
He never seems overwhelmed or peevish, though, just permanently tickled to be part of the ongoing experiment.

—◄○►—

At the beginning of the 1970s, Perec signed on to translate
Harry Mathews's second novel, *Tlooth.* He had greatly admired its predecessor, *The Conversions,* and started a free-
wheeling friendship with Mathews, who was living primarily in Paris. When he asked about the language of one
blue scene late in the book—"She hicked with tick jabs of
her cwung, she dently mouthed me, not thucking so much
as twooving me in and out bemean her lips and aslack her
ung which she wept gainst and sobberingly kep"—he was
let in on a multi-layered spoonerism that convinced him
Mathews was Oulipo material. (In fact, Mathews had flit-

ted across oulipian radar about eight years prior, having come up in conversation as someone who had already experimented with the literary applications of matrix analysis.) The Oulipo invited Mathews to a meeting in 1971 and made him a member in 1973.

The *Village Voice* once described Mathews as "a bearish man with the slightly addled manner of a dadaist Garrison Keillor." *The Believer* said he "has the air of a man with a secret he is fighting to withhold"; the *Paris Review* said that he "speaks with the nearly extinct mid-Atlantic accent that can carry off *rather* and *alas*." My mother thinks he looks like "a gangster" in his photo on the Oulipo website. These are all, in their own way, exactly correct; Mathews is an enigma, with every intention of staying that way. He belongs to a bygone time, probably by all accounts a classier one: New York in the 1930s, Europe in the 1950s. He dines well, to say the least.[25]

Mathews was born wealthy,[26] and his novels suggest the intellect of someone who is very smart and denied

189

---

[25] The *Compendium* contains minutes from the monthly Oulipo meeting of April 1990, attended only by Mathews and a guest of honor, a researcher in applied mathematics. The menu, which includes caviar, foie gras, and at least five different wines, is the longest section.

[26] Some nuance, from Mathews: "My own situation when I came to France is punctually described in the opening chapter of *My Life in CIA*. I was blessed in not being rich, in having enough money to live on but not to gamble or buy a Maserati. When that money petered out (plus what I'd been handsomely paid for writing a couple of movies), I started working, first as a translator then as a teacher (1973–1980). After my parents died, I gradually (it's too long a story) accumulated the small fortune I'd always been suspected of having."

very little: supremely cultured, defiantly capricious, and potentially alienating for want of any good reason not to be. His most tangible affinity with the founding members of the Oulipo is an adoration for Raymond Roussel, from whom he claims to have learned "that, in terms of storytelling, you can find masses of materials in solving absurd problems."

It doesn't appear to bother him at all—quite the contrary—that his books are perceived as difficult, things to be solved at least as much as to be read. I would estimate that I know his novels better for having read *about* them than for having read them. To say that Mathews embodies the oulipian spirit of the hoax might be inaccurate, but the Oulipo borrows a page from his book whenever it behaves inscrutably by choice. That willful misdirection—which he has named *pumectation,* after a misprint of the word *permutation* in an article from *Le Magazine Littéraire*—is never so pronounced, or so elegant, as it is in his oeuvre. The meaning behind the title of *The Sinking of the Odradek Stadium,* an immensely entertaining epistolary novel published around the time he joined the Oulipo, is buried in the book's index. The poem collection *Armenian Papers* is said to comprise transcripts of unearthed manuscripts that may or may not exist. The *Oulipo Compendium* cross-references Le Lionnais's third manifesto a few times, even though there's no entry for it. The end of his 2005 "memoir," *My Life in CIA,* which itself centers around Mathews spending most of the 1970s in France playing along with the misapprehension that he was an American spy, has him overhear, then vigorously confirm, the statement that Harry Mathews has been "terminated with extreme prejudice" long ago.

190

Not to say that he hasn't been a devoted practitioner of oulipian doctrine, most heroically in introducing it to the Anglophone world. The *Oulipo Compendium* is mostly his doing, as is the consistent availability through Dalkey Archive Press, on whose board he sits, of oulipian works in English translation. The novel *The Journalist* enacts Queneau's analytical work on the classical dramatic staple of character x mistaking character y for character z; the reach of "Mathews's Algorithm," a Rubik's Cube permutation of anything from letters to phrases to situations, could easily have earned him an invitation to lunch from the founding members. (One wonders who would have schooled whom on the art of fine dining.)

◄○►

The Oulipo's guest of honor in November 1972 was the Italian novelist Italo Calvino. The meeting, whose minutes are excerpted in the *Compendium,* bears various commentaries that are momentous in retrospect: Perec spoke about the plotting of *Life A User's Manual* for the first time; Le Lionnais introduced his study of *Nombres remarquables;* Queneau discussed his fascination with the idea of false coincidences—things that seem like accidents that aren't. For his part, Calvino presented the scheme behind his *Incendio della casa abominevole* (Burning of the Abominable House), an unfinished work about a house in which twelve crimes have been perpetrated by four "exceptionally perverse characters" in a configuration left ambiguous to the reader. He also agreed heartily with Queneau's intimation that many of the motives in his work were consummately oulipian.

By 1967, when he moved to Paris and garnered the nickname *l'ironique amusé* (the amused ironist), Calvino was the author of a body of work at once allegorically classical and urgently contemporary. His earliest novels and stories are influenced by his engagement in the anti-Fascist resistance and the Communist Party, which was, he later recalled, the least unappealing of the options available to him at the time. Later he worked as an anthologist of Italian folktales for the Milanese publisher Einaudi, gradually filling his own fiction with old-school nobles and neo-realist exploits. Both proved to have ample resonance with present-day affairs: the protagonist of *The Baron in the Trees,* who climbs a tree at age seven and never comes down again, and that of *The Cloven Viscount,* who spends his life in two parts after a run-in with a cannonball, work equally as simple storybook characters and as elaborate political metaphors.

The most oulipian writing of Calvino's career was yet to come when he moved to Paris, although he jumped into it readily—translating Queneau's *Blue Flowers* into Italian in 1967 and, the same year, delivering a lecture called "Cybernetics and Ghosts," which not only namechecks the Oulipo but resoundingly sympathizes with its formalistic approach to literature. "Writers, as they have always been up to now, are already writing machines; or at least they are when things are going well," he explains. "What Romantic terminology called genius or talent or inspiration or intuition is nothing other than finding the right road empirically, following one's nose, taking short cuts." If we were to let a machine make these deductions for us, he proposes, echoing the more or less contemporaneous rhubarb of Roland Barthes, the reader of our literature would be no less empowered; all we would lose is the "anachronistic personage" of the author, "that spoiled child of ignorance—to give place to a more thoughtful person, a person who will know that the author is a machine, and will know how this machine works."[27]

Over the next five years, Calvino's writing began more and more to incorporate Borgesian notions of hidden structure and infinite recombination—a third part of his career that Italian critics in particular refer to, usually huffily, as his Parisian phase. By the time he was elected foreign correspondent to the Oulipo on Valentine's Day in 1973, Calvino had written *T-zero,* a sequel to *Cosmicomics,* a cycle of vexingly brilliant stories so densely thought out that they read at times like lyrical lab notes; *Invisible Cities,* a series of vignettes about imaginary places described by Marco Polo to Genghis Khan over a game of chess, and whose underlying structure is visible only in the table of contents; and *The Castle of Crossed Destinies,* a combinatorial masterwork about a set of travelers who meet at a medieval inn, all having somehow lost the power of speech and able to tell their respective stories only via a deck of tarot cards.

Calvino's involvement with the Oulipo probably didn't change the course of his career, as it did Perec's or Bénabou's, but it influenced his thought at least as much as Barthes and the structuralists had in the late 1960s, and it

193

---

[27] William Weaver's translation.

gave him the chance to brainstorm in good company. Jouet recalls a single meeting at which Calvino mused about the potentiality of rewriting *The Odyssey* so that it obeyed the three unities of classical tragedy—that it must happen over twenty-four hours, in one location, and with one main plot—and of reversing *Hamlet* to prove that it was a fundamentally palindromic story. Calvino consulted with Paul Braffort on the combinatorial aspects of his *Incendio,* and joined him in exploring the computing potential of interactive fiction. This period also fostered *If on a winter's night a traveler,* arguably Calvino's late-period masterpiece, in which an obsessive preoccupation with the act of reading is balanced only by the stylish invention of the errant chapters that you, the reader reading yourself being written, shouldn't even be reading in the first place.

For his part, Calvino talked up the Oulipo as well as he could; the lectures and interviews compiled in *The Uses of Literature* frequently mention the group and its "mathematico-literary research," while his *Six Memos for the Next Millennium,* a series of lectures on specific literary virtues that he wrote to deliver at Harvard in 1985,[28] refers to Perec's *Life A User's Manual* as "the last 'real' event in the history of the novel so far."[29] He oversaw more Italian publications of Queneau's work, including Umberto Eco's

---

[28] Unfortunately, he died of a cerebral hemorrhage before leaving Italy. A silver lining perhaps more Kafkaesque than oulipian: the sixth memo, which he died before writing, was to be on consistency.

[29] Patrick Creagh's translation.

translation of *Exercises in Style* and Sergio Solmi's of *Petite cosmogonie portative;* he also worked with Primo Levi to translate *Le Chant du styrène* (The Styrene Song), the versified narration Queneau had written for a thirteen-minute Alain Resnais film about the production of plastic.

Like Perec, Calvino was great at bringing humanity into what could otherwise be a soulless structural shell game. In different hands, *Life A User's Manual* and *If on a winter's night a traveler* could have been emptily virtuosic, all concept and no singularity to their realization, but both authors were wonderfully adept at letting the reader glimpse their hidden hands. War played a part in both cases, although in different ways—for Perec in the loss of his parents and of connection to his identity, for Calvino in his disillusionment with political structures of repression and coercion. Italian scholar Anna Botta, discussing the way Calvino's novels transcend the intuitive contradiction between solid verifiable input and nebulous personal influence, invokes what Michel Serres refers to as *science chaleureuse*—warm science—and ends up describing an ideal fate for oulipian scaffolding. "Once used to generate a particular narrative," she writes, "the formal constraints of these texts are no longer impersonal protocols freed from any historical or human contingency. Instead, they become a part of the story itself."

195

◄o►

With the exception of Queneau, and technically Duchamp, Calvino is the only member of the Oulipo so far to have joined after his artistic reputation was already durably established. As such, he encountered something his fellow Oulipians never did: criticism for falling in with a bad crowd. The Italian critic Gian Carlo Roscioni opined that "the Calvino who subscribed to the Oulipo is not the real Calvino"; Franco Fortini judged simply that he had been "poisoned by the French production of that Parisian period."[30] Regardless of such condemnations (which, according to Botta, Italian critics make routinely, almost as a matter of professional esteem), it's easy to see why he accepted the invitation to become an Oulipian; the affinity was already there, documented in novels and lectures and interviews, and all he had to do was recognize it formally. In the group, Botta says, he found "confirmation of his belief in the mechanical dynamic of literary composition."

Of course, it doesn't usually work this way. Perec had already won a big prize when he became an Oulipian, Roubaud had garnered hyperbolic critical acclaim, Mathews had amassed a cult following among collegiate potheads, and so on. But in all these cases the workshop still intervened early enough to get its hooks in. Remember that the official verb for the induction of a new member is *co-opt:* in the case of someone young and promising (or old and promising, whatever), there is a very real sense that the Oulipo is taking him or her on in order to absorb a new perspective into its collective outlook and direction. What Perec or Roubaud or Mathews would have become had

---

30 Both translations by Anna Botta.

Queneau not invited them to join an elite club, and in so doing taken the reins of their literary becoming, is anyone's
guess; it's hard, at least in the safety of hindsight, to imagine any of them declining.[31]

But an invitation that guarantees both a lifelong
front-row seat to an evolving conception of literature and
an enduring pigeonhole on its outskirts looks a lot different
when extended as a sort of lifetime achievement award.
Unlike his younger counterparts in the second generation,
Calvino had a large enough wingspan to worry about being
clipped, enough literary identity to be justifiably wary of al-
legiance to someone else's ideas. And just as Calvino would
have been within his rights to demur about tying his legacy
to the Oulipo—a fate he has neatly avoided, in any case—so
could his friend Julio Cortázar be defended on the same
grounds.

Cortázar was an Argentinian novelist, Parisian
gadabout, and low-key member of the Collège de 'Pataphysique who produced some work that looks rather oulipian,
particularly his novel *Hopscotch,* a meandering narrative
set between Buenos Aires and Paris. According to a prefatory notice, *Hopscotch* can be read either straight through,
Chapters 1 through 56, or according to a looping order that

197

---

[31] The Oulipians I have queried on this point all respond with some
variation on the unthinkability of the counterfactual. Still, it's easier
to imagine that, without the Oulipo, Salon would have kept on teaching and Forte would have kept on working in bookstores and composing oulipian poetry. The generation for whom this question was
of real weight was this first round of recruits.

includes 99 more "expendable" chapters (some of which bear on the central story, others of which are expendable for good reason) and leaves the reader finally stuck inconclusively between two. As conceptions of bound printed matter go, with all its potential detours and frustrations, *Hopscotch* would put Cortázar in fine company among the rats.

The circumstances under which he declined the invitation to join their ranks are obscure, so far as I can glean from all the people I've asked about it—not just Oulipians, but also a couple of his former inamoratas—but the workshop spent at least a decade trying to track him down for lunch. (His name is on the to-invite list here and there throughout the 1970s, sometimes accompanied by a peevish *Why hasn't Cortázar come yet;* the year before his death, in 1984, he still hadn't materialized.) Hypotheses abound: he wasn't into collaborative work; he was too engaged in the South American political affairs of the moment; he was a closet romantic and found the Oulipo's systematic approach to literature dehumanizing.

Jouet takes a stab at explaining the whole business in an imaginary letter from Cortázar to the Oulipo, in which he maintains that recourse to oulipian constraint was an occasional experiment, by no means something he was interested in making a regular stratagem. Instead of *Hopscotch*—whose chapter order, according to an interview with Cortázar published in 1985, couldn't have been less calculated—Jouet focuses on a short story, "Clone," in which characters and their actions are modeled after the different instruments in a piece by Bach.[32] He concludes, all the same, that unilateral, methodical application of structure wasn't Cortázar's gourd of maté. Besides, an untethered musing in *Hopscotch* nails the early Oulipo between the eyes: "Truth was probably an Alexandrine or a hendecasyllable; perhaps the rhythms again marking the main stress and scanning the periods of the road. Some more themes for eggheads to write theses about."[33]

After Cortázar, only three people, to my knowledge, have declined an invitation to join the Oulipo: the German poet and translator Eugen Helmle, who translated Perec and Queneau and drafted a lengthy presentation of the *Werkstatt für Potentielle Literatur* in 1968; the French fiction writer Régine Detambel, whose work often bears constraints such as the absence of masculine nouns in *La Modéliste* (The Designer);[34] and the French novelist and video artist Valérie Mréjen, who actually *has* made poems

---

[32] An anticipatory plagiarism of "Clone" is Jacques Bens's *Rendez-vous chez François,* which does more or less the same thing with a movement from Schubert's *Wanderer Fantasy.*

[33] Gregory Rabassa's translation.

[34] Oddly, nobody seems entirely able to get the story on Detambel straight—including Detambel, whose website claims she was named a corresponding member of the Oulipo in the Languedoc region. (In an interview quoted in Peter Consenstein's *Literary Memory, Consciousness, and the Group Oulipo,* she says both that "people automatically attach me to l'Oulipo, erroneously," and that "I've only been a member for a short time!") In any case, she is not counted among the group's members in its publications, on its website, or in other official materials.

from a telephone directory. They all had good reasons for being invited, and presumably equally good reasons for saying *non merci,* be it the fear of career hijack, the ominous till-death-do-us-part clause, or something else entirely. That's all I know of the affair.

You could add one more to that list if you count Michèle Métail, a sound-poet and scholar of ancient Chinese poetry whom Le Lionnais inducted in 1975 as the group's first female member, and who amicably but staunchly parted ways with the group in the early 1990s after a disagreement about the communality of members' creations. In the early years of her involvement, she worked notably on making poetic value from uses of language that were more technical than literary ("Our next guest will be Michèle Métail, whose ability to do without verbs you have all admired," Le Lionnais wrote to the group): her *filigranes* (watermarks) and *poèmes oscillatoires* (oscillatory poems), for instance, respectively use idiom and antonymy to construct a halo of associative meaning around a given word.[35] Later, she began assembling a theoretically infinite poem from chains of genitive phrases, which today allegedly comprises more than 20,000 lines.[36]

---

[35] Her B.O. volume on the former, subtitled *Poems of Emptiness,* contains 170 poems that represent a given word solely by other words connected with it in idiomatic expressions: a *filigrane* about the word *blank* might make a poem out of *stare, slate, check, to draw, to fire,* and so on.

[36] I gave an unwitting example of such a chain in the previous chapter, when I described Duchêne and Leblanc's *Rationnel mon Q* as a "series **of** demonstrations **of** the irrationality **of** the square root **of** 2."

Métail was, along with Bénabou, an early explorer of what the Oulipo likes to call *langage cuit*—cooked language—after a term coined by the poet Robert Desnos in 1923 to designate familiar expressions that border on cliché. *Langage cuit* is to language what Duchamp's readymade is to the object: something used so often and unthinkingly as to have lost any original artistic intent, and that now belongs firmly in the realm of the third sector, waiting to be considered in new light on a gallery wall or a handsomely typeset page. Métail's *portraits-robots,* for instance, are piecemeal character descriptions made of common phrases involving body parts: Mathews, who translates the name of the form as "identikits," gives an example ending with *game cock, fatted calf,* and *crow's feet.* The Oulipo treats such language as the raw material for equally *anoulipian* and *synthoulipian* experiments, from perverbs to *sardinosaures* to anagrams of Parisian Métro stops; this is as good a way as any to demonstrate the potential not only of literary invention but also of language that, as it were, occurs in nature.

─◄○►─

The first round of recruits, beginning with Roubaud, would eventually come to be labeled the Queneau generation.

───────────────

Métail's interest in the form came from the horrifyingly agglutinating German phrase *Du schöner Donaudampfschifffahrtsgesellschaftskapitän,* which literally means "the captain **of** the company **of** trips **of** steamboats **of** the Danube."

That these Oulipians (besides Métail) were handpicked by Queneau is notable in comparison to the current democratic order of things, but also as testimony to his understanding of how the group would evolve. He recognized that the creation side of creativity was the way to sustain the collective operation; surely he was also aware of the tension between the analytical and synthetic readings of potentiality, and his presidential wisdom was to do nothing about it.

202

Bellos has argued more than once that the Oulipo was Queneau's "long-term insurance policy, with a maturity value called immortality." Now well into a second decade, the influx of new members, most of them much younger than Queneau,[37] brought the president's responsibilities into focus. Michelle Grangaud explains in a biographical article that Queneau tried to shape the functioning of the group in opposition to three cautionary models: the cult-of-personality volatility of the Surrealists, the radical iconoclasm of the Bourbaki collective, and the prescriptive stubbornness of the Académie Française. If the Oulipo was indeed to be his legacy, he was careful to err on the side of vagueness, to refuse to dictate even to his disciples what literature should be or how to make it.

Instead, Queneau was something like a distant

---

[37] Queneau was much older than some of the founders, too: Bens and Roubaud were both thirty years his junior. Only Schmidt, Le Lionnais, and Duchamp were older; Le Lionnais was the only one who used the informal *tu* form of address with him.

guru, an aloof paternal presence whose approval was hard-won but limitlessly gratifying. "For each one of us, he had a particular admiration and fondness, but never expressed it directly," Fournel wrote. "One had to detect it based on often mysterious signs, just as one also had to divine the secret advice he issued to one or another of us."[38] One of Roubaud's *moments oulipiens* recalls his coming across a mention in Queneau's journals of a meeting at which Roubaud read "an elegant Christmas tale" and feeling distressed to remember that the tale in question had nothing to do with Christmas—but consoled, thirty years later, by that *elegant*. One of Bénabou's is about Queneau beginning a meeting by asking, quite ceremoniously, why the Arabs disliked Toulouse-Lautrec; only after Bénabou nervously mumbled something about the Islamic repugnance for representation of the human form did Queneau burst into laughter and explain that Toulouse-Lautrec was *un impressionniste*—that is, *un nain pré-sioniste,* or a pre-Zionist dwarf.

203

The same presidential inscrutability comes through amply in Queneau's cryptic pronouncements, which constitute a good percentage of his airtime in Bens's published minutes. "Culture is the opposite of arithmetic," for instance, or "It is important that others think [language] doesn't exist, but we believe it does," or "Etymology is a snowy slope that leads us down into an abyss of crap." In response to an imaginary telephone directory generated

---

[38] Jean-Jacques Poucel's translation.

by the most common phonemes in French first and last names, he effuses, "What's interesting is that it's not *interesting.*"

His written example, though, especially his earliest work, leaves no doubt that these young recruits, fascinated in some way or other with the materiality of language and the ephemerality of poetic expression, had come to the right place. In his first collections of poetry, like *L'Instant fatal* (The Fatal Instant) and *Le Chien à la mandoline* (The Dog with a Mandolin), Queneau exudes a winning fixation with words—it's enough to love them, he says at one point, to write a poem—and a breezily satirical view on how much it supposedly takes to make poetry:

> Man oh man do I feel like writing a little poem
> Oh look there's one passing by now
> Here poem poem poem
> Come here and let me string you
> on the string of my necklace with all my other poems
> Come here and let me fix you
> in the firmament of my complete works
> Come here and let me empoet you
> let me enrhyme you
> let me enrhythm you
> let me enlyre you
> let me empegasus you
> let me versify you
> let me prosify you
>
> Aw nuts
> It got away

What little video footage I have seen of Queneau—
a few grainy black-and-white interviews, plus one awesome
featurette where he emerges dramatically from various
shadowy off-camera nowheres to explain the fundamentals
of arithmetic—squares well with this impression. He is neither serious nor jovial; his smile is a little bit defensive, his
voice low and crackly but somehow also squeaky, like a
drunken rubber ducky. When he reads his poems, he does
so without relish but still perfectly, dropping none of the
aural nuance or mischievous stuttering that makes them
so charming. When he answers questions—if he answers
them—he seems to make a game of being evasive, sometimes giggling without smiling, as though humor surprises
him. In response to one, he jerks his head back and to the
side, as if to deny it in disgust, then murmurs, almost inau-
dibly, *oui*. To another, about how to interpret one of his poems, he can barely seem to conceal his delight when he
mumbles, "Well, it's ambiguous."

205

—◄○►—

To Queneau's opaque paterfamilias, Le Lionnais reads like
the lucid, insightful one, whose commentaries on the nature of potentiality and on the oulipian quest are always
sensible and useful: "Our essential role is to invent procedures and set them free for poetry to take hold of them," or
"We can create instruments that are not poetic, so long as
they lead us to poetry." (See also: "We are simultaneously
founding the religion and the schism," and "LiPo does not

always aim to reach quality," and "Let's not forget that posterity is watching, gentlemen.")

I imagine Le Lionnais impish and endearing, a little absent-minded on the surface, endlessly amused by small jokes that get old to everyone but himself. (Jouet, whose last name means "toy" in French, recounts the three times he met the Frésident-Pondateur, Le Lionnais shaking his hand each time and asking, "Did you know I'm a member of the Société des Amis du Jouet?") I imagine him surfacing only sometimes from his own intellectual reveries, in a way that might be irritating were he not a sweet man who had made it unbowed through a few years of categorical hell. He also had a tortoise named Lady Godiva, which I find obscurely heartbreaking.

Despite some popular misapprehensions, most people in the know—Queneau first among them—would tell you once and for all that potential literature was the twinkle in Le Lionnais's eye, nobody else's. If Queneau provided the star power and exercised the administrative functions, Le Lionnais was the one whose imagination and devotion drove the enterprise forward, the one who was genuinely concerned when he felt the Oulipo was becoming more about lunch than about work. "Le Lionnais wanted all mathematical structures described by Bourbaki, from elementary set theory to the more difficult parts of group theory, topology, and the splendid marvels of Hilbert space, translated into literary terms and then used by members of his army, the Oulipo, to give the world new and unheard-of literary forms," Roubaud writes. "In his opinion, his 'young' disciples, the Oulipians, were much too lazy to do this work quickly enough. He often told them so. But he never lost faith in the soundness of the project."[39]

◄○►

In 1970 Le Lionnais sent a questionnaire to all members of the group, in an effort to gauge how the future should be taken on. The responses were by turns wry and curt, and in some cases both at once,[40] but on the whole positive. To the first question, *Do you want the Oulipo to continue?*, the most enthusiastically negative was Berge's "Yes but." (The most enthusiastically affirmative was Perec's "Fuck yeah!") It was agreed in rough consensus that the group should continue to recruit cautiously, and that it should revive the circulation of minutes from the meetings, a practice that had petered out since Bens moved to the south of France. Bénabou and Fournel became official secretaries, definitively provisional and provisionally definitive respectively and reverse-respectively, soon after; they also began to keep archives in earnest, which instigated the exceedingly long rounding-up of a whole lot of loose papers from the first decade.

There was no definitive sea change, but throughout the mid-1970s the spirit of the group's activities became

---

[39] Harry Mathews's translation.

[40] Berge, in response to the final question, *Any other remarks?*: "Yes."

less academic, less formal. Many of the younger members were extramural friends already, rather than professional or academic acquaintances, meaning that the ongoing oulipian discussion began to take on a life outside each month's meeting. It often left Paris as well: the Queneau generation took to hanging out at the Moulin d'Andé in Normandy, where Perec wrote his monster-palindrome and most of *La Disparition*. The spirit got younger too, maybe, moving from an environment where a bunch of gentlemen sat around discussing Literature to one where a bunch of dudes sat around talking lipogrammatically for the sport of it—believing only in the vaguest sense that their doing so would amount to anything, but still tackling the exercise with the feverish certainty of those pursuing great and important truths.

publish and perish

I N 1973 GALLIMARD PUBLISHED *La littérature potentielle,* the Oulipo's first real collective sortie. The book, which came out directly in pocket-sized paperback (unprecedented, this), bears the subtitle *Creations, Re-Creations, Recreations,* and presents the group's work since its inception. It's a strange little volume, enchanting and instructive and just about impossible to absorb in fewer than a dozen sittings: depending on the page you open to, you might find concrete poetry, scientific essays, intimidating graph theory, or what looks like perfectly normal prose. Its table of contents reads like that of a scientific journal, which is surely the point: the texts in it are findings, extrapolations from gathered data, new milestones in a field of study peopled by those who are not scared off by terms like "Lexicographic or Prosodic Synthoulipisms."

The book opens with two manifestos by Le Lionnais, which outline the group's purpose in a particularly roundabout way. The first argues that all literary work, indeed all linguistic intervention, combines inspiration with "a series of constraints and procedures that fit inside each other like Chinese boxes."[1] The second is a lot more abstruse and hard to tie to anything genuinely borne out in the Oulipo's subsequent work, beyond the idea of plagiarism by anticipation; most of it is spent dillydallying around fatuous distinctions like *structuralism* versus *structurElism*. Like any literary treatises worth their salt, the manifestos are unsatisfying; their saving grace is Le Lionnais's tongue-in-cheek attitude toward the notion of the manifesto in the first place. The first ends with an appeal to "those particularly grave people who condemn without consideration and without appeal all work wherein is manifested any propensity for pleasantry," explaining that even the jests and pratfalls of poets fall into the category of poetry, which therefore makes potential literature "the most serious thing in the world. Q.E.D." The second begins with an epigraph from Paul Féval, mid-nineteenth-century author of popular swashbuckling fiction: "I am working for people who are primarily intelligent, rather than serious."

Sure enough, even the strictly *anoulipian* explorations that follow are at least as mischievous as they are empirical. Le Lionnais inventories all the possible guilty parties in a murder mystery, concluding that the only killer we have yet to see is the reader. Duchateau's essay about the correspondence of word use to specific motifs in a mystery novel is about as frivolous as a high-school paper that con-

---

[1] Warren Motte's translation.

torts its analytical structure to account for every mention of teeth in *Anna Karenina*.[2] In his essay on lexical analysis, Bens admits to taking liberties with the direct and indirect articles in a list of nouns from a poem by Lescure, excusing himself on the grounds that the doctor who delivers the baby isn't supposed to have impregnated the patient himself, but that nobody objects to his use of forceps once the baby is inside.

The unifying point of the book, anyway, is to show off the structures explored in the workshop's first dozen years through bizarre and beautiful applications thereof. Perec offers an alphabetical drama called "Les Horreurs de la guerre" (The Horrors of War), in which the whole dialogue is meant to sound like the letters of the alphabet (with increasingly specific stage directions supplied to contextualize them),[3] and an illustrated abecedary,[4] where surrealistic descriptions boil down to one vocal exercise for each consonant: a blurb involving women gossiping about adul-

---

[2] Not that I would know anything about this.

[3] The first line is *"Abbesse! Aidez!"*—which sounds just like "A-B-C-D" in French. Another example of the perils of reading oulipian work in the wrong mindset: apropos of a discussion about homophones, I once mailed a copy of said alphabetical drama to a friend who had professed a great fondness for Perec. When next I saw her, she pressed me urgently to explain what she had done to be sent such a horribly morbid relic of wartime France. Once I explained the constraint at hand she was only partially relieved.

[4] An abecedary (or abecedarium, if you want to be Latinate about it) is a text arranged in alphabetical order, usually for instructive purposes. See, why not, Edward Gorey's *Gashlycrumb Tinies:* "A is for Amy, who fell down the stairs; B is for Basil, assaulted by bears," etc.

tery is translated, in the back of the volume, as *Caquet: qui cocu?* (*ka-ké-ki-ko-ku*)—roughly, "Harpy: who's cuckolded?" With Bénabou, he presents *littérature sémo-definitionnelle,* or LSD, a brother technique to the dictionary-larding game PALF, whose ultimate goal is to prove, by way of secondary definitions and poetically licensed replacements, that Gaston Leroux's "The presbytery has lost none of its charm nor the garden its splendor" is just a variation of Marx and Engels's "Workers of the world, unite!"

The Oulipo's earlier work is represented too, of course: there are explanations and demonstrations of the S + 7 method, Queneau's 10^{14} poems, Bens's irrational sonnets, and Roubaud's $\in$ (most of these under the heading of "perimathematical synthoulipisms"); there are samples of Arnaud's algorithmic language poems and Etienne's Möbius-strip poems and Queval's ode with internal heterosexual rhymes.[5] Le Lionnais introduces his *tentatives à la limite,* or attempts at exhaustion, which include a poem of one letter, a poem of one word, a poem consisting of only numbers and punctuation, and a lovely little sonnet, "La Rien que la toute la" (The Nothing But the All The), that has no verbs, nouns, or adjectives. He also proposes Boolean poems, based on an algebraic logic system of true-false binaries, which idea gives way to a play by Fournel mapped out as a tree diagram of narrative options, and to Queneau's

[5] A rhyme with a mute terminal E is said to be feminine; one without, masculine. Queval's poem thus "rhymes" one of each. Arnaud also offers a "Conte de Noël en rimes hétérosexuelles" (Christmas Story in Heterosexual Rhymes)—maybe the one Queneau mistakenly attributed to Roubaud?

"A Story As You Like It," probably the first choose-your-own-adventure fiction in history.[6]

The book ends with a "box of ideas," entirely by Le Lionnais, which over a dozen pages proposes things like three-dimensional poems that require you to wear 3D glasses to read them in their entirety, poems with words projected into space so that their disposition depends on the position of the reader's head, and anti-rhymes (not to be confused with ante-rhymes), which use antonymy as a rhyme generator. It ends with a note to the effect that the above ideas, if meted out at the rate of one per session, should provide the Oulipo with enough to discuss for the next hundred meetings. All that is left, he says, is to get seriously down to business.

213

◄○►

---

[6] Queneau was, in retrospect, a great anticipatory plagiarist of children's entertainments. The choose-your-own-adventure novel, which advances in short bursts to crossroads where the reader must choose from divergent narrative paths ("If you decide to join the circus, turn to page 61; if you decide to try to land a movie contract, turn to page 50"), became popular in the mid-1970s and quickly got joyously ridiculous ("Dr. Nair holds up his hand. His mouth lengthens into a smile. 'It's too late. I've already implanted you with the genes of a young gorilla, who was himself implanted with the genes of a giant bear'"). Also, although Queneau didn't invent it, the physical combinatoriality of *Cent mille milliards de poèmes* lives on in various flip-flap books containing creatures with interchangeable heads, torsos, and legs, with which you can assemble some exponential number of odd-looking people or fanciful creatures. See, for three, Sara Ball's *Crocguphant* and *Porguacan,* and Tony Meeuwissen's *Remarkable Animals: 1000 Amazing Amalgamations.*

The *Bibliothèque Oulipienne* series began, at Queneau's suggestion, the following year. The purpose of each installment, as Arnaud later explained it, was to "demonstrate the viability and reliability of a given structure, first and foremost in the eyes of its inventor."[7] In accumulation, each issue can be seen as a single chapter from a book like *La littérature potentielle,* in which an idea is introduced, theorized, demonstrated, or presented in full-fledged fashion. The first fascicle displays Perec's work on the heterogram; the second, Roubaud's *La Princesse Hoppy, ou Le Conte du Labrador,* lays the groundwork for a fable ostensibly for children, the one with sections of narration in impenetrable "superior dog" code that wasn't cracked until 2008. The third is Queneau's adaptation to language of David Hilbert's treatise on mathematics. Later on in the series, Calvino reprised Perec's abecedary experiment in Italian, Duchateau larded a Faulkner novel, and Braffort based a set of poems on Zeckendorf's theorem, which proves that any number can be expressed as the sum of one or more non-consecutive numbers from the Fibonacci sequence. The series became modestly popular in time, thanks in particular to mail-order demand for Calvino's explication of *If on a winter's night a traveler.* Each volume of the B.O. was and continues to be printed in runs of 150, for limited public consumption and eventual collector's-item eBay-quarryship.

By and large, these mini-volumes serve as a quick way to get ideas into the world before they've been devel-

---

[7] Warren Motte's translation.

oped enough to sustain a larger publication, although other uses aren't out of the question. Roubaud published the second chapter of *Hoppy* in B.O. volume 8, for instance, like the beginning of a serial novel; Noël Arnaud used it as a platform to protest literary theorist Gérard Genette's description of oulipian endeavor as "a game of chance, like roulette."[8] Some contributors have used the B.O. for faux-polemical agitation, or just to try out pseudonyms: Braffort has published as Walter Henry, Roubaud as Reine Haugure, Jouet as Mikhaïl Gorliouk. The format can even be used to propagate hoaxes; volume 30 is billed as Le Lionnais's third oulipian manifesto. There is no volume 30.

215

And the series found another use in only its fourth issue: eulogy. When Queneau died in October 1976, nearly the entire group pitched in to a collective tribute, which ranged from adaptations of the structure of *Cent mille milliards de poèmes* and spinoffs on *Exercises in Style* to Le Lionnais's recollection of Queneau's fondness for the word *antépénultième*. Perec's death in 1982 occasioned another tribute volume, containing memories of and anecdotes

---

[8] Genette spends ten pages of his 1982 book *Palimpsests: Literature in the Second Degree* on a characteristically shrewd analysis of oulipian treatments of preexisting texts (S + 7, lipogrammatic translations, and so on), but essentially ignores the workshop's other aspects. Roubaud tempers Arnaud's response a few years later in *Poetry Etcetera: Cleaning House,* describing Genette as "a (usually more inspired) literary theorist who seemed to be better informed, more thoughtful, and less credulous, and who allowed himself to write a particularly mediocre text on the subject" of the Oulipo. (Guy Bennett's translation.)

about Perec, as well as more formal tributes such as an English E-lipogram by Mathews and a double-acrostic palindrome called *Ce repère Perec* (Perec That Landmark) by Luc Etienne—who would request, on his deathbed two years later, that no such volume be dedicated to him.

◄○►

Darkness followed. Le Lionnais died in 1984, followed by Calvino in 1985. The Oulipo had innumerable guests at its meetings in the late 1970s, but without Queneau to make the final decision it didn't co-opt anyone after Métail in 1975. Nobody was willing to pull the plug on the workshop, but nobody was quite sure how to proceed. Perec took unofficial charge until he died, at which point Roubaud took over in equally unofficial capacity. After Le Lionnais died, Arnaud became president.

On the other hand, Oulipians began to get serious about publishing. Perec's *Life A User's Manual* and Calvino's *Winter's night* became landmarks not just for the workshop, but for modernist literature writ large; *Atlas de littérature potentielle,* a sequel to *La littérature potentielle* published in 1981, found the group's explorations redoubled in intensity and inventiveness, and its theoretical considerations undertaken much less flippantly. This one boasts the famous *Table Queneleieff* (a riff on Mendeleev's periodic table of the elements), which classifies the Oulipo's forms by scope and methodology, and Roubaud's oft-repeated remarks on oulipian composition: (a) that a text written according to a certain constraint may mention that constraint; (b) that a text written according to a *mathema-tizable* constraint may illustrate the consequences of the theory behind that constraint.[9]

The *Atlas* delves deeper and more systematically into the kinds of structures introduced in the previous volume—extensions, emendations, departures. There are new forms referred to as "shackles," as "constellations," as "spirals." Perec gives a lively reading of ways to apply Queneau's work on the plot device where character *x* mistakes character *y* for character *z;* Claude Berge introduces a way to transform a fourteen-line sonnet into a fifteen-line sonnet by splicing and permuting each alexandrine at the caesura. There are snowballs and palindromes and homosyntaxisms, but also new beasts like the eodermdrome, a riddle invented by a team of American linguists where a circuit between five letters (or other elements) lends itself to a word (or other succession) that links each pair of angles only once.[10]

The greatest difference between the *Atlas* and its

217

---

[9] These remarks, which take all of half a page, are often misinterpreted as a pair of prescriptions on how to write; in fact, according to their title, they simply propose "Two principles sometimes respected in oulipian works." The classic example of the first is of course *La Disparition,* which in addition to being a book without the letter E is a book about a world in which the letter E has gone missing.

[10] Try writing the letters D, E, M, O, and R in any pentagonal configuration, then connecting them using the order in which they appear in *eodermdrome.* See also *scarcer seas* and *shoes on hens.* Roubaud applies the eodermdrome at the macro-narrative level in *Parc Sauvage.*

predecessor is the increasing reality that many oulipian analyses could be done much more efficiently by computer—from calculations formalizing a set of texts to dumb gruntwork like inventorying all the adverbs in a poet's oeuvre. Braffort, the group's resident computer maven, is distinctly more present in the pages of this book, especially in the section devoted to *Oulipo et informatique,* which gets quite technical in the marrow of things before Calvino brings it back a little more broadly with an essay entitled "Prose and Anticombinatorics."

Even before the *Atlas* was published, preparations were underway for the creation of the ALAMO (*Atelier de littérature assistée par la mathématique et les ordinateurs,* or Workshop for Literature Assisted by Mathematics and Computers), which would emerge in 1982 after a couple of years of preliminaries. The group, intended as the continuation of oulipian pursuits by high-tech means, was primarily Braffort's brainchild, born of the early tinkerings that could randomly generate artificial aphorisms or spit out personalized sonnets from Queneau's hundred thousand billion on huge sheets of dot-matrix paper. With Braffort and Roubaud at the helm, the ALAMO became not so much a subcommittee of the Oulipo as a sister society, concerned initially with faster versions of typically oulipian exercises —*rimbaudelaires,* for instance, in which vocabulary culled from Baudelaire's corpus was applied to the hollowed-out syntactic structures of Rimbaud's poems—but soon enough with its own forays into automatic literary production.

To the latter end, which it referred to as the pursuit of "implicational" text-generating methods, the ALAMO developed a handful of *littéraciels* (litware, after the word *logiciel,* for software) that would, in effect, get the computer to set its own parameters. Instead of using a computer to filter and substitute elements into a given template, these programs acted as recursive and self-refining models that allowed the computer to decide, in relatively unpredictable fashion, what templates to use in generating new generators. Ultimately, despite birthing a wealth of new acronyms (LAPAL and PALAP, for starters, plus FASTL and MAOTH and TALC), Braffort and company have yet to find total traction in the implicational realm. But the search continues, leading to conferences and school workshops every few years, and now the ALAMO shares the load with international affiliates including ALAMO-USA and the Italian TEAnO, which is to the OpLePo—*Opificio di Letteratura Potenziale, est.* 1990—as the ALAMO is to the Oulipo.

219

◄○►

Still, computers were only one new avenue to explore, or another vehicle with which to explore the familiar ones. Publication of the *Atlas* boosted readerly awareness a bit, if less appreciably than *La littérature potentielle* had, and by the early 1980s the Oulipo was a real public entity, giving regular readings and running workshops and meeting people who were, as Arnaud puts it, "not merely consumers of the Oulipo but inventors of new structures or constraints."[11]

---

[11] Warren Motte's translation.

Potential literature was still nebulous as a concept, but as a brand it was bestowing on authors and works a certain dimension of familiarity—one hesitates to call it celebrity or notoriety, but cachet—in the right circles.

Jouet and Caradec, who couldn't be much less similar in background and outlook on literature (though both would become regulars, along with Le Tellier, on the radio show *Des Papous dans la tête*), joined the fold in 1983. Jouet had participated in a workshop run by Perec, Roubaud, and Fournel a few years prior, and it was agreed that the newly late Perec would have wanted him to be an Oulipian; Caradec had been around the right circles since before the Oulipo existed, and now that Latis had been dead for a decade nobody saw any reason to keep him out. In a multiday conclave that year, both were chosen over a handful of other candidates—including Pierre Rosenstiehl, who in any case would attend a number of meetings in the 1980s before his formal induction—for immediate recruitment. Both were more than ready to be subsumed into the group's activities, and the group was more than ready for a kick in the pants to both its analytical and synthetic branches.[12]

The ensuing years cemented the workshop's public standing. The deaths of Perec, Calvino, and Le Lionnais occasioned—as the deaths of artists will do—a revisiting and veneration of their bodies of work. Their less famous counterparts in the Queneau generation weathered the loss, producing more fascinating and iconic work: Rou-

---

[12] Not to mix metaphors.

baud's *Some Thing Black* and Bénabou's *Why I Have Not Written Any of My Books* came out in 1986, Mathews's *Cigarettes* the following year. The founding members didn't produce much of monumental renown during this period, but they kept working: Bens wrote a handful of novels and short stories, including the prize-winning *Nouvelles desenchantées* (Disenchanted Tales), which sportingly strip all the magic from supernatural incidents. Arnaud and Queval and Duchateau contributed to the B.O.; even the estranged Chambers came out with *Loiterature,* a series of essays about the virtues of writerly meandering, which, though not actually oulipian in any meaningful sense, does provide a new framework in which to read Bénabou's novels.

Just as importantly, the world outside—outside the workshop and outside France—was starting to pay serious, sustained attention. The Oulipo earned some illustrious fans, from Umberto Eco and Jim Jarmusch to *Scientific American* puzzlesmith Martin Gardner and cognitive-science pundit Douglas Hofstadter. Motte's *Primer* in 1986 stirred interest among English-speaking writers and academics, which laid the groundwork for the *Oulipo Compendium* and its enthusiastically weird blurbs from Paul Auster and Susan Sontag.[13] Comp-lit syllabi the world 'round started mentioning the Oulipo itself, not just its individual

---

[13] Auster, who praised the book as "a late 20th-century kabala," has more recently claimed, at least in semi-private correspondence, to find the Oulipo of little interest and to admire Perec only in spite of his association with the workshop. Sontag called the *Compendium* "a seedbed, a grimace, a carnival," and I have no idea what that means.

luminaries, and scholars began to spend quality time wrapping their heads around the implications of the project—culminating, albeit a decade or so later, in Marc Lapprand's *Poétique de l'Oulipo* (Poetics of the Oulipo) and Peter Consenstein's *Literary Memory, Consciousness, and the Group Oulipo,* plus a spate of more specific books and less comprehensive essays. These treatments, if sometimes jargonistic and occasionally hyperbolic,[14] testified to a new global audience that was earnestly engaged with the workshop's explorations and productions, as eager as the Oulipians themselves to find out where all this was going.

222

◄○►

The next round of recruitments didn't come until 1992. Le Tellier was inducted after Fournel's house published his openly oulipian *Voleur de nostalgie,* an epistolary novel whose characters are all named Giovanni D'Arezzo (plus or minus the apostrophe). The group also officially inducted Pierre Rosenstiehl, a specialist in graph and maze theory whose oulipian pedigree dated back to 1944, when, at age eleven, he would go out nightly in Burgundy and reorient road signs in order to misdirect the Wehrmacht's withdrawal. "Since then," he wrote in a 1990 essay, "I have thought of literature as an art of struggle inside a laby-

---

14 Consenstein: "The group Oulipo, in renaissance style, demonstrates that a great tradition of literature is as capable as a surgeon in avoiding death and therefore enriching life."

rinth."[15] A professor at EHESS (School for Advanced Studies in the Social Sciences), editor-in-chief of the *European Journal of Combinatorics,* and recipient of the Légion d'Honneur for his contributions to French education, he participates in the group's private activities but rarely appears in public. Besides a recent novel-essay about the Ariadne myth called *Le Labyrinthe des jours ordinaires* (The Labyrinth of Ordinary Days), his most notable contribution to date has been the optimized route he provided for Jouet's exhaustive metro poem.

The third recruit that year was the Romanian poet Oskar Pastior, whose work, with its predilection for anagrams and sestinas, is both weighty and innocent, marked by an instinctive awareness of hardship and an earnest fascination with the combinatorial possibilities of language. Pastior's biography shares much with Le Lionnais's, albeit with less of a scientific bent: he spent five years in a Soviet labor camp in Ukraine, after which he returned to Romania to finish his studies in German literature and worked in radio, then in 1969 moved to Berlin, where he lived and wrote and lectured and collaborated (with, among others, 2009 Nobel literature laureate Herta Müller) until his death in 2006—just before he was to receive the Georg-Büchner-Preis, held to be the highest honor in German literature.

Pastior was a natural Oulipian, despite not writing in French: indeed, his linguistic outsider status helped

---

15 Harry Mathews's translation.

to push the boundaries of potential literature, inspiring oblique collaborations from Mathews, who helped translate one of Pastior's books, *Many Glove Compartments,* into English, and from Forte, who later co-adapted a book of Pastior's German anagram poems to French. Pastior also contributed variations on Goethe to round out the series starting with Perec on Proust and Mathews on *Hamlet;* his affiliation also yielded a lasting tie to the poetry circuit outside France, most notably through the Literaturhaus Berlin, which has held a triannual Oulipo festival since 1991.

The linguist Bernard Cerquiglini joined the group in 1995, the same year he published *L'Accent du souvenir* (The Accent of Memory), a so-called autobiography of the circumflex accent. His role in the group is that of "language guardian," which makes sense given his résumé: amid high-profile gigs such as directorship of the Institut National de la Langue Française (National Institute for the French Language) and presidency of the Observatoire National de la Lecture (National Reading Observatory), he hasn't found much time to be more active than the occasional *jeudi* cameo and a 2008 B.O. piece about the amusing foibles of dictation software.

Cerquiglini, whose boyish curls and lively demeanor make him look like a very dignified koala bear, also has a program called *Merci professeur!* on the French network TV5, where he explicates various linguistic questions, such as the etymology of the word *cocktail,* during quick snippets in which it is for some reason impossible not to pay attention to his hands. To watch his glowing and animated defense of the outmoded word *courriel* (a clipping of *courrier éléctronique*) for "email" instead of the anglicized *mél,* in part because you can refer to spam as *pourriel* (*pourri* meaning "rotten"), is to see love for language in action.

—◦—

Michelle Grangaud, also co-opted in 1995, certainly helps to combat the misapprehension that the Oulipo is one extended episode of linguistic drollery. ("There's not much . . . *hilarity* in Michelle Grangaud's work," I recall Forte explaining to somebody in Bourges.) She was born in Algeria and grew up against a backdrop of intensifying hostility between nationalist groups and French colonizers; happily, the more immediate backdrop was a house full of books. The year before the war broke out, she discovered poetry more or less at random: "Without understanding any of it," she says of "The Drunken Boat" by Rimbaud, "I felt very intensely that it was beautiful." She discovered Proust a few years after that, and then, alighting in Normandy in 1962, still reeling from the war behind her, was ensorcelled by a copy of *Madame Bovary* she happened to find. "Later I found out that Proust's favorite author was Flaubert," she recalls, "so there was a logic to my own preferences."

Grangaud speaks of reading with an agreeably cabalistic reverence; it was the same luck, to hear her tell it, that brought her to an exposition on the German author, painter, and anagram-jockey Unica Zürn in 1983. "I was seized by the beauty of this conception—so primary, in a way, or in any case so evident that we forget it constantly— that *all* our thoughts are made with just twenty-six letters

and the game of their permutations, which is, in truth, infinite," she wrote to me once. "In that observation lies all the
beauty and all the mystery of human thought." She found
that she could play at Zürn's game with relative ease, and
began to experiment with the form. By the time she met
Harry Mathews at a poetry biennial in 1993—he told her
the Oulipo collectively admired her work, which as far
as he knew was an ingratiating exaggeration but turned
out to be the truth—she had published a handful of poetry
books, including one, *Stations,* consisting entirely of anagrams made from the names of Parisian Métro stops.

Mathews set things in motion and Grangaud became the Oulipo's second female member—second historically but first functionally, since Métail had already kissed
off the workshop. "I've been told only those who don't want
to be get recruited," Grangaud wrote to me, "which was the
case with me, for reasons I'll explain later." (This was some
years ago.) Since then, she has perfected the anagram and
the *poème fondu* (melted poem), an exercise that reduces a
poem-length (or longer) text to the dimensions of a haiku,
and a trick called the *avion*—airplane, but also an abbreviation of *abbreviation*—based on condensing words along
non-phonetic lines. She has invented light formal constraints, too, such as the syllabic bodice around the story-
fragments in the lovely *Geste* (Gesture), or the phonetic
chain connecting each line in *Souvenirs de ma vie collective* (Memories of My Collective Life). Lately she has been
working with lexicographic history: her most recent entries
in the *Bibliothèque Oulipienne* are a set of *morales élémen-*

taires that restrict themselves to words that entered the French language in a given year.

Grangaud is slim and wasplike and wears black almost all of the time; she is mild in person, but in performance exudes a tremendous nervous intensity. Being one of the rare females doesn't seem to bother her—though she compares her experience in the Oulipo to a Giraudoux play called *Juliette au pays des hommes* (Juliette in the Land of Men).[16] Instead, she can be unsettling to watch because every word she utters seems to come directly, and with great freight, from the heart. She's also simply quite bleak: at the last *jeudi* I attended, she read a multi-page list of afflictions, in the order in which the words for them appeared in French; one of the few films she contributed to Odile Fillion's series about Paris streets finds her on the rue Sigmund Freud, frankly describing a recent dream in which she strangled her grandmother. What she typically lacks in lightness, though, she makes up for with smolderingly steady talent, in both technical aptitude and unflinching poignancy. "You have the feeling that she could write *The Divine Comedy* in anagrams," Mathews once told me.

◄o►

Many of the recruits since the turn of the century, starting with Salon in 2000, could be said to constitute a Roubaud

---

16 "I haven't read it," she admits, "but the title is very evocative for me."

generation: the final judgment is collective, but the group's co-optations of Garréta, Beaudouin, and Audin all originated through contact with him. Anne Garréta, a writer and theorist, came to Roubaud's poetry seminar in 1994, then again in 2000, to present the buried structures in her work: her first novel, *Sphinx*, tells a love story between two characters whose gender is never made clear. *Ciels liquides* (Liquid Skies) narrates the surreal deterioration of a promising young law student who gradually loses the use of language; *La Décomposition* follows an assassin as he kills off various characters in Proust's *Recherche*. Her first novel post-co-optation, *Pas un jour* (Not One Day)—which won the same prize in 2002 that Perec's *Life A User's Manual* did in 1978—reflects on the women she has desired or been desired by: its epigraph is "Life is too short to resign oneself to reading poorly written books and sleeping with women one does not love."

Garréta, who was co-opted two years after Monk but narrowly beat him to the indeterminate honor of being the first Oulipian younger than the Oulipo, is an extremely talented writer in a mode that seems perpendicular to the workshop's standard values. Although her novels are heavily preoccupied with the dimensions and effects of language and literature, the approach they take to those issues is neither winking nor mischievous, but rather engaged, politicized, at times almost militant; their composition is intense and tightly controlled, but the language that comes out often reads as fluid, florid, furtively romantic. In a sense, the challenges she sets herself are authorial and not compositional: even the technically daunting suppression of sex markers in *Sphinx* feels motivated by the desire to say something political about gender, not something grammatical.

This divergence comes into sharper relief through the strong, sometimes polemical opinions Garréta leaves out of her fiction. (She invoked Michel Foucault a few years ago, in an interview with the popular gay culture magazine *Têtu,* by way of claiming that the Oulipo has in fact been a queer experiment all along.) Garréta teaches comparative literature in Rennes half the year, and at Duke in North Carolina the other half; in person she trades breezily in shorthand for complex concepts and peppers her speech with words and phrases in English ("Most of these things are not my cup of tea," she told me once in a slow, deliberate growl about the majority of oulipian forms). Her intelligence is not without self-effacement and good humor, but not without dogma either, which can jar at times with the otherwise unacademic tenor of oulipian proceedings. As a liaison to the scholarly world, though—which remains potential literature's most consistent and attentive interlocutor—she knows what she's doing, namely giving the workshop's conservative tendencies a swift, forward-thinking kick in the ass.

Valérie Beaudouin, a soft-spoken woman who, like any good Oulipian, encounters innumerable misspellings of her last name, joined the group in February 2003. This came a few years after she published a graduate thesis, under Roubaud's distant supervision, wherein she co-developed a tool called the metrometer that can analyze French verse—principally alexandrines, at least for starters—in syntactic and syllabic terms while also accounting for such stumbling blocks (and oulipian treasure-troves) as mute-E elision and diaeresis. The tool builds extensively on a theory of poetic rhythm elaborated by Roubaud with mathematician and *go* enthusiast Pierre Lusson; it was honed on all 80,000 published verses in the plays of Racine and Corneille, a direct recall to the years when the founders of the Oulipo dreamed of putting a computer to work analyzing the borders of Baudelaire or inventorying all the nouns in Hugo.

Beaudouin analyzed social-networking behaviors for the communications giant France Télécom until 2008, when she began teaching full-time. She participates actively behind the scenes in the life of the Oulipo, maintaining its website and often acting as secretary at monthly meetings, but practically never performs or publishes. She is a little reticent even to be affiliated publicly with the group; her contribution to the 2008 volume on the *morale élémentaire* is pseudonymous, and in a B.O. volume she co-authored with Garréta in 2007, which proposes a game based on Perec's *Je me souviens* exercises crossed with the compositional rules of the metro poem, a prefatory note states that she has allowed her name to appear on the cover only under duress, and that she is responsible for just one of the exercises and refuses to say which one.

So long as it's on her terms, Beaudouin's disinclination to use the Oulipo as a springboard toward much of anything is refreshing. Most Oulipians became public figures in one manner or another before even joining the group, but a few have seen fit to keep their professional, lit-

erary, and private lives separate. As the Oulipo becomes
more and more of a household name—at least in aggres-
sively overeducated households—it's the individual rather
than the collective that hangs in the balance. For a writer,
the rules of engagement are clear: Forte has a better shot at
being recognized and read than do any number of equally
talented poets, in exchange for his output's running a
greater risk of being pigeonholed. For a teacher or researcher or systems analyst, though, the reward system is
hazier. So it's pleasing to note a certain generosity in Beaudouin's devotion to the pursuit—one thinks also of Rosenstiehl drafting the route for Jouet's exhaustive metro poem,
or of Berge helping Perec to plot a path through the ten-by-
ten chessboard of *Life A User's Manual*—as a charitable, *almost* anonymous donation.

—◄○►—

This brings us up to the present: Forte in 2005, me in February of 2009, and Audin in July. We have known about the
Oulipo for the better part of our literary careers, such as
they are, and been happily influenced by the idea of it—less,
I would argue, because of its cultural importance than because of its direct appeal to our own sensibilities. Impossible to say what the workshop will look like in ten years,
much less another fifty—but in a way, that's become the
point. The more stars in the *galaxie,* the more potential
paths between them, and thus the more potentially surprising ways to behold the literary possibilities of language.

III FUTURE

packrats who build the library 2006

THIRTY YEARS TO THE DAY after the death of Raymond Queneau, I am in an ornate reading room at the Bibliothèque de l'Arsenal to commemorate the opening of the *fonds Oulipo*. Hulking on Paris's near–Left Bank behind a twisted metal sculpture that allegedly represents Arthur Rimbaud, Arsenal has been around since Henri IV's days: it held private manuscript and print collections for a few centuries, got requisitioned during the French Revolution, opened to the public in 1797—or, according to a plaque near the entrance, the 9th of Floréal in the year V—and was finally acquired by the BNF in 1934. Its present collection boasts bookbinding curiosities, medieval manuscripts, the prison records from the Bastille, and, since 2005, the Oulipo's archives, which until then had been taking up untold quantities of space in Bénabou's 9th-arrondissement apartment.

Everyone besides the two dedicated champagne-pourers in the corner is swirling around in varying states of hobnobbery: library undersecretaries, branch curators, and nearly all the living members of the Oulipo, about half of whom I am meeting for the first time. I've been in Paris for two months already, but have spent the majority of that time sparring with local functionaries in efforts to secure an apartment, a bank account, an extended-stay visa, a haircut, milk that does not turn out upon being opened to be cream, etc. Bénabou and Le Tellier are there, and the Jacqueses Roubaud and Jouet, and Salon and Braffort and Fournel and Garréta and Grangaud. Caradec is taking it easy on a bench in the corner, his arm in a sling ("I'd shake your hand, but . . . you know"). Paulette Perec, Georges's widow, is also milling about, and to my unending retrospective relief I do not know who she is while I am chatting with her.

At the moment, I know about as much as I did when I showed up in Paris: that the Oulipo has recently moved its archives to Arsenal, and that it may be in the market for a slave—its word choice, not mine—to help put them in order. I have been to one *jeudi,* where the woman seated next to me told me that she was there only for Roubaud (and, after learning that I was American, that *personne n'est parfait*—nobody's perfect) and spent the entire reading sighing audibly while doodling in a small notebook with a tiny gold pencil. I have been to two readings by individual Oulipians, at the first of which I introduced myself to Bénabou and promptly mispronounced the name of the street onto which I had moved that afternoon. The mixture of joy and terror I felt when he asked *So, when can you start work-ing for us?* is not unlike the one I will feel, a couple of years later, upon reading Fournel's email announcing that I am now an Oulipian myself.

Each real-life encounter I have had with the group so far has reminded me that there's still a great deal I don't know about it—to wit, I have already refrained more than once from introducing myself to Grangaud because I can't remember whether she is Valérie Beaudouin or Michèle Métail. At the same time, each one has reminded me that I am here because I want to be: because I am excited by the Oulipo and its ideas, and I want to understand those ideas better; because I want to make those ideas belong to every-one, not just littérateurs and academics; because I want to share my excitement with as many people as possible, and I'm sick of explaining it to them one by one. Tonight it's not immediately clear how cataloguing a few decades' worth of archives is going to help me accomplish those goals, but it's no clearer how else I might go about doing so.

237

The archives are not officially open yet this eve-ning; in fact, as I'm writing this they still aren't, except by special permission and prolonged maneuvering through the Kafkaesque labyrinth of French library bureaucracy. The reception has been organized so that members of the group can belatedly celebrate the deposition of the ar-chives, and visit the space where they may one day be view-able. Thus, after all the Oulipians (except Le Tellier, who has already dashed off to another engagement) sign a docu-ment attesting to the historic nature of the evening, we are led on a makeshift tour through various back channels of the library and down a rickety staircase to a small ground-floor room whose door says ARCHITECTES on it: this is the *fonds.* (Someone tells me later that Bénabou's first act upon arriving at Arsenal tonight was to remove a postcard bearing Latis's spindly Oulipo logo from said door, so as to avoid offending Caradec.)

The room starting to fill up with boxes of Oulipo paraphernalia is smaller and homier than one might expect; not everyone on the tour can fit into it at the same time, which forces half of us to spill into the Perec archives next door. It is a narrow, office-sized room, lit meekly by a couple of halogen lamps and enlivened by a potted plant doing a reasonably good job of staying alive. There's a table with a computer, an armoire, a file cabinet, a few feet of books, a handful of videos, and a retired Florida vanity license plate that says OULIPO. The lateral walls are lined with metal shelves that are beginning to accumulate books and spiral-bound manuscripts and archival boxes full of loosely categorized sheaves of paper waiting to be inventoried and organized. There's nothing impressive or imposing about this room or its contents, nothing that would even begin to rival the personal library of anyone on the tour. It looks exactly like what it is: a space not yet moved into, where a lot of work remains to be done.

Over the next several months, I join Camille Bloomfield, a doctoral candidate at the University of Paris at Saint-Denis (and therefore apparently ineligible for the "slave" designation), in doing that work. By the time I start helping out, she and Bénabou have already winnowed the holdings to a handful of categories, not including the books and journals owned or contributed by members or para-members. There is one dossier for press clippings about oulipian publications and public appearances, one for ephemera from writing workshops, one for posters and photographs and originals of images like the *galaxie oulipi-enne* (oddly, the cut-and-paste job is a lot more obvious up close than it is in a forty-foot projection). There is a box where we toss anything verbose and incomprehensible enough to peg as 'Pataphysics-related, and a separate *dossier inclassable,* for things to be dealt with later, to which we add regularly but whose size never appears to change.

239

In each dossier, we categorize and catalogue, sort and shuffle and inventory. We move pieces of paper be-tween folders and folders between boxes; we remove a lot of rusty paper clips and replace them with plastic ones. I wonder at one point whether the shelf of books from Le Li-onnais's private library is arranged according to some ar-cane oulipian filing system, like Sandomir's POURQI letter order, before concluding that it's just really poorly alpha-betized. Construction outside drags on in that globally indefinite way, blocking off direct access to the archive (which is itself reached through a dubious side door so far from Arsenal's main entrance that it hardly seems to belong to the same structure) for several months. Every so often Bénabou brings over a few new unsorted boxes, and slowly but surely the room fills up.

Still, the *fonds* never becomes huge or command-ing or exhaustive, something to inspire awe in someone whose awe for the Oulipo is not already articulated—cer-tainly not compared to the *fonds Perec* next door, which contains translations of *La Disparition* into languages that don't even have a letter E.[1] But my own oulipian awe is undimmed, and there's plenty for me to mull over. I learn that Jacques Bens wrote softcore erotic novels under the monovocalic pseudonym Gwen Treverec. I learn to recognize the handwritings of different Oulipians and, as the decades pass, their preferred fonts.[2] I catalogue a card on which Calvino has written his Paris phone number and committed a minor error of French grammar, which I find immeasurably comforting.

Of comparatively consistent interest is the correspondence dossier, which gathers wisp-thin carbon copies of typewritten letters—Le Lionnais to Duchamp, at each of his three known addresses: Don't be a stranger to the Oulipo, and p.s. Do you still find much time for chess?—and postcards that appear to have been sent for no other reason than to show off Latis's cactus collection. There are inter-Oulipian squabbles and gestures of diplomacy, letters of recommendation for recruitment and letters of pseudo-resignation like the one from 2001 in which Métail asks that her name be officially replaced on the oulipian roll with an ellipsis. (Request declined.) There is a letter in-

---

[1] Dedicated geeks have rendered *La Disparition* into Turkish (*Kayboluş*), Russian (*Исчезание*), and Japanese (煙滅), which makes its translators into English (*A Void*, plus the unpublished *A Vanishing* and *Vanish'd!*), German (*Anton Voyls Fortgang*), Swedish (*Försvinna*), Italian (*La Scomparsa*), Dutch (*'t Manco*), and Spanish (*El Secuestro*, which omits A instead of E) look like slackers.

[2] Comic Sans! Et tu, Salon?

viting the Oulipo to participate in a project that revolves around stochastic generation, and a diplomatically scandalized response from Bénabou on Oulipo stationery ("The Oulipo loathes randomness and leads against it a struggle which literary historians will not fail to recognize as one of the fundamental axes of the group's work"). There are articles sent by in-the-know affiliates with tongue-clucking references to the *habitual errors* therein, usually meaning someone has affiliated the Oulipo with Surrealism; there are financial statements from publishers and formal invitations from municipal cultural councils and hotel receipts confirming special requests for extra mattresses.

241

Then of course there is fan correspondence—some scholarly, some polemical, some ambitious and adoring and dripping with obscurely misplaced kindred-spirit reverence.[3] There are sheaves of like-minded offerings from all manner of oulipophiles, most of which are mundane and boringly constrained (on one hand, it's encouraging that these weren't just thrown out; on the other, it's unlikely that these people ever imagined their homophones and tautograms would elicit *phthbtt* noises, years hence, from a couple of archivists). Conversely, a few are truly inspiring and innovatively oulipian and ruined only by the sender's request to be considered for membership in the Oulipo—

---

[3] See for instance page 84 of a textbook called *Help Yourself to Essential French Grammar,* where exercise E requires the adverbs *well* and *unfortunately* to be filled into the sentences "Bénabou ran ____" and "____ Perec hurt himself." (Probably not an accident that in French the latter, *Perec s'est blessé,* is a monovocalism.)

which is, of course, the only official way to guarantee that one will never become a member.

    Some evenings I leave the *fonds* feeling defeated, by the regress of oulipian history or by the drudgery of the day's work, and go back to my apartment between the Moulin Rouge and the Sexodrome to flop down with the easiest, lightest, most *secular* book I can lay hands on. Other evenings I leave to find the outside world enchanted and encoded, whispering sweet monovocalic nothings to me from billboards and bakery windows, lobbying for the syllabic significance of every phrase I overhear on the Métro. I can feel my thought patterns changing gently, being primed along oulipian lines; I cannot tell whether this is the understanding and excitement I came to France looking for, or just a different kind of defeat. On the better days I am instinctively aware of the potential of my own thoughts; on the slow days it's all I can do to inventory and categorize them—criticisms, compositions, the *inclassable*—in the hopes that I can read some sense into them later.

―◄○►―

The pride and joy of the *fonds* is the collected minutes from every monthly meeting since the mid-1960s. Each session has an agenda, generally established during the aperitif, that dictates the structure of contributions and discussion points; there is also a narrative-ish account of the proceedings, recorded with varying degrees of lyrical digressivity by the meeting's secretary. (Oulipo meetings have been described in the *Village Voice* as "largely male gatherings, whose docket of activities suggests a Rotary Club meeting on LSD.") The first section of the agenda is *création*—texts written or forms developed since the last meeting—without at least one of which the session cannot be called to order. The second is *rumination,* which Monk describes as "a safe section for new members who often eagerly announce some brilliant idea they think they have just had only to be told that Georges Perec had already thought of it years ago." Third is *érudition,* which serves chiefly for presentation of newly discovered anticipatory plagiarists; then there are housekeeping matters of finances and what's inevitably not working on the website and why nobody's bought train tickets for the reading in Lyons in five weeks' time.

243

Any monthly dossier shows how organized Oulipo meetings are, and at the same time how disorganized: over the course of 1964, Braffort's name is spelled at least three different ways, in some cases by the same secretary. Sorting through the oldest ones in the archives is like a documentary tour through a bygone era: elaborate letterheads, illegible notes on the back of mimeographed NASA newsletters, handwriting that no longer exists except on expensive wine bottles. I find a list of "sonnets to perforate" for experimental purposes (Mallarmé, Baudelaire, Heredia, Leconte de Lisle, Queneau), and some of the big dot-matrix printouts of the first computer-automated poems from the potential hundred thousand billion. I find Mathews's preparatory sketches for a lipogram called "You Can't Take I With You" [*sic*][4] and, in a folder from 1982, shortly after Perec's death,

---

[4] For the record, and for the sake of glorification by association, these sketches look a lot like the notebook page I filled in high school while making my E-less tape.

the envelope on the back of which Luc Etienne had doodled alternate words for *Ce repère Perec,* his palindromic homage: *crêpe, cèpe, épée.* I find a sheet of pangrams fresh from Perec's typewriter, complete with handwritten addendum apologizing for a few holes where his cat attacked the page. Elsewhere I turn up some of his attempts at pangrams shorter than the status quo.[5]

As far as the actual minutes go, serious business and serious prattle appear to have remained in roughly constant equilibrium throughout the workshop's evolution. A 2001 convocation from Bénabou announces that the next meeting will broach certain issues about where the Oulipo is and where it is going:

- Where are we vis-à-vis the notion of the constraint?
- Have we become a "literary group"?
- How should we resume contact with mathematicians?

---

[5] The French equivalent of the *quick brown fox* sentence is *Portez ce vieux whisky au juge blond qui fume* ("Bring this old whiskey to the smoking blond judge"); Perec's *Plombez d'onyx vif ce whig juste quaker* ("Fill this tight Quaker Whig with brisk onyx," or something like that) bests it by five letters. In a completely different dossier, there is a clipped letter from David Hunter to the editor of the *Times Literary Supplement,* in response to an article about the Oulipo by John Sturrock: "My children's magnetic alphabet clings to the fridge door and—after hours of experiment and a statistically abnormal incidence of patella disorders—friends and family have identified at least two shorter ones, viz.: *Given mazy web of phlox, duck quits jar* (31) and *Judges vomit; few quiz pharynx block* (30)." Nobody has yet come up with an isopangram—a phrase that uses all twenty-six letters only once—that doesn't require a great deal of explanation about, say, what exactly a "fjord waltz" is.

The echoes of Bens's stocktaking in the very first set of minutes are hard to miss. Still, it feels curiously appropriate that the big questions, give or take some specifics, are no closer to being resolved than they were in 1960. This is, near as I can tell, the spirit in which the Oulipo guards its archives so preciously in the first place: not just for the obvious pleasures of self-enshrinement, but also for the instructive value of self-rereading, the security of maintaining totally literal access to its origins. Of course, every papercut I get from a decaying postcard and every wrist cramp I get from entering patently ridiculous archival data[6] on an AZERTY keyboard diminishes the abstract nobility of the endeavor a little, but I still have it good compared to Perec and Fournel, who undertook a project in the early 1970s to reorganize the library at Le Lionnais's house, where even the windows were shuttered by stacks of books. ("The assignment was simply to move the thousands of volumes in his collection and put them back in a different order," Fournel recalls: "his.")

245

—◄o►—

A library, to an Oulipian, is a matter of no small consequence. Books are mythical, sensuous things, and an entire

---

[6] Like "Lettre dactylographiée de N. Arnaud à Messieurs-dames BIDU, BIRDU, BIRBIDU, BRIDU, BRIBIDU, BIBUDU, BUDU, MANURIE, IVRERIE, KRAM, AKLIR, SÜM, NORN, NORILLE, EYTU, SUBAMUR, OTTUMUR, NIGAMUR, DIZAMUR, ARNOLD DESGRUMEAUX, et L'ENTREPRISE GENERALE DE TRAVAUX LITTERAIRES."

subcategory of oulipian thought could easily be devoted to novel approaches to their care and feeding. An essay in Perec's *Penser / Classer*—recently translated by David Bellos with the lovely title *Thoughts of Sorts*—offers some "Brief Notes on the Art and Craft of Sorting Books": by binding, format, color, date of purchase. Anne Garréta spends a delightful essay called "On Bookselves" exploring her suspicion that books are alien species who evolve and multiply by thwarting our best attempts at categorizing them; she concludes by proposing ten alternative bookshelf-organizing principles, grouping books that do or don't contain the word *book* or books that have crossed an ocean or books that contain at least one sentence you know by heart. In a B.O. volume called *Les bibliothèques invisibles,* Braffort assembles a bibliography of real books owned by fictional characters and of imaginary books cited in real works of fiction. For more of the latter, see *La bibliothèque impossible,* a mural created in 1984 by Jouet and an artist named Bertin, in which a massive bookcase looms over a lonely street in the 14th arrondissement, filled with titles ranging from Hugh Vereker's *The Right of Way* and Pierre Menard's *Quixote* to the collected memoirs of Sir Francis Haddock, distant ancestor of Tintin's boozing, blustering sidekick.

My first round of interviews with the active members of the Oulipo was as much an excuse to snoop around their personal libraries as anything else. Salon and Forte and Braffort have entire wall-dominating Oulipo-only bookshelves; Fournel has a side office and Mathews an upstairs annex just to corral everything from books I've read to books I've never even heard of but whose nonexistence I immediately find unimaginable. I found it odd, even scandalous, to see only a handful of books in Le Tellier's living room the first time he received me at his apartment down the street from Sacré-Coeur. (I found the rest in a different room on a subsequent visit.) My reveries around that period often involved spending an afternoon nosing around in Perec's library, or Calvino's, or Queneau's—or a week in Le Lionnais's, provided I was allowed to leave without doing any filing.

All of which is to say that thinking about Oulipians as writers is an incomplete enterprise without thinking about them as readers. It's not that they're better or worse readers than anyone else, or more or less attentive or perceptive, or cleaner or messier,[7] but that oulipian reading, by definition only a degree away from oulipian writing, is somehow closer to a form of worship than most other modes of reading. A book, whether it's a first edition of Coleridge or the *California Driver Handbook,* is never just a

---

[7] To borrow Anne Fadiman's dichotomy in "Never Do That to a Book," Oulipians are the conventional assortment of courtly and carnal lovers of their books. Le Lionnais, according to his secretary, Dominique Miollan, didn't care at all for books as objects; she submits as proof his habit of marking pages with metal paper clips—which, sure enough, resulted in a whole lot of nasty, rust-encrusted books in the *fonds Oulipo.* Forte lends his books out eagerly, and used to call me every few weeks to see if I had his copy of something-or-other at that moment—most of the time I didn't—while Bénabou, since I have known him, is constantly convinced that someone has stolen his copy of something-or-other. To his credit, he explains the frustration of this extremely convincingly in *Dump This Book.*

finished product: it's more like a prototype, a cipher, a blue-print for further invention. And so to be faithful to this, the *fonds Oulipo* would ideally be one of those infinite hyperli-braries like Borges's Babel, a huge labyrinthine fire hazard of shelves upon shelves sagging with the weight of ac-cumulated human knowledge and artificial intelligence, where you can't find anything because everything is there, and where room still needs to be set aside for the volumes yet to be written.

Needless to say, this is not the case. The archive doesn't even begin to suggest the contours of such a library, probably never will, and would be redundant if it did. In-stead, it's valuable in much the same way that the Oulipo is valuable as a potential novel: it's a story told by its own characters, a museum of artifacts compiled by a team of readers and the readers who read them. (Got that?) The collection's historical dimension is instructive, but the best things in it are the same bizarreries and accidents that stimulate oulipian creation before the fact: amusing typos, unexplained mailings, books whose prefaces dictate that their pages may be cut only by lobsters and people who eat dessert before the rest of the meal. I don't learn much, in my months of archival servitude, about the mechanics of literary composition, oulipian or otherwise, but I do gain insight into how these people read their world—and how it makes them want to write it, too.

Because these are, not to put too fine a point on it, people who pay close attention even to their marginalia, people who even in their incidental dips into third-sector language can't bear to be prosaic. *(Let's not forget that pos-*

terity is watching, gentlemen.) Fournel used to send out
meeting summonses with tree diagrams in the RSVP section: *IF coming THEN will dine OR will not dine.* Caradec could
always be counted on for a pun, even if there was no particular point to his missive—one note clipped to an old letter is inscribed *porc lézard chives,* which means "pig lizard
chives" but sounds like *pour les archives,* or for the archives.
Some Oulipians' sorry-can't-make-it replies are more impressive than anything else in the whole month's dossier:
Mathews once emailed from his computer in Key West, on
which he didn't know how to input accents, and so limited
his response to words without any; Métail once mailed in
thirty-three variations of the RSVP coupon, à la one-third
of Queneau's *Exercises in Style,* which led to the cumulative
conclusion that, no, she would not be in attendance.

The particular value of this archive, then, is that it
makes detailed sense of the sensibility that unites the members of the Oulipo. But it also unites them with those other
people—who are not members for some arbitrary or symbolic reason, because they don't speak French or because
they died four centuries ago—who likewise think this way
about language, who allow themselves to be seduced by its
pitfalls and pratfalls and pliable protocols. See Norberto
Gimelfarb's *Song of Songs,* poems made up of song titles;[8]
see Léonce Nadirpher's homophonic guessing games, in

---

[8] For example, a remarkably concise poem called "The Meaning of
the Blues":

> Stormy Weather
> On the Sunny Side of the Street

which a certain American folk-rock supergroup is reparsed as *grosses bises style nage indienne;* see Daniel Lehman's amazing *Oulipolitain de Paris,* a game of word golf[9] transposed onto a map of the Paris Métro system, intersections and all. (See a painting inspired by the fact that "Perec" sounds like the Korean word for "fish stomach.") The *fonds* is monumental, ultimately, in that it consolidates several decades' worth of precedent and legacy into one place, and represents it as a place for me, too, and for quite a few people besides. A finite number of them, sure, but one we're still tabulating.

---

[9] Also known as a word chain or a word ladder—start with one word and morph it into a completely different word with the same number of letters, changing one letter at a time, such that each intermediate step is also a real word. In *Pale Fire,* for instance, Nabokov goes from LASS to MALE in four: *lass, mass, mars, mare, male.*

safety in letters 2009

S O, A LITTLE CENSUS-TAKING music. Who are the people, besides the thirty-seven ordained practitioners and
one fictional functionary that constitute the workshop at
present, who embody and have embodied potential literature? Who, anticipatorily or in conjunction with the normal
laws of space and time, could justifiably be called—as one
Portuguese literature professor whose letter appears in the
correspondence file puts it—*victims of the Oulipo?*

"Without a time machine at its disposal," Mathews
writes in the *Compendium* entry for *plagiary, anticipatory,*
"the Oulipo has been unable to rescue from the limbo of the
past those writers who, lamentably unaware of the group's
existence, could not know that they were creating paleo-
oulipian texts without acknowledgement." He provides
an overview of some characters colonized at length elsewhere—Lasus of Hermione, generally agreed to be the au-

thor of the first lipogram; Arnaut Daniel, the trouba-
dour who invented the sestina; Ausonius, "master of the
cento." Mathews also gives a shoutout to Ramón Llull, the
thirteenth-century philosopher-monk who worked on a
combinatorial apologetics for all religions; Gottfried Leib-
niz, who teased out some of Llull's ideas with words and
phonemes in the 1666 *De arte combinatoria* (and who, according to an early journal entry, was the genius with whom
Queneau most sympathized); and Quirinus Kuhlmann, a
"dandy, visionary, and religious fanatic" who was burned
at the stake in 1689 for his subversive combinatorial love
poems.

Whole theses have been written enumerating the
group's forebears in certain domains, and to do so exhaus-
tively would be the undertaking of a lifetime (a worthy one,
to be sure, and one that would no doubt be more interesting
than Pierre Bayard's *Le Plagiat par anticipation,* or Anticipatory Plagiarism, which gingerly gives credit to Le Lionnais for the concept, clucks its tongue at the Oulipo for
not elaborating a serious enough theory of influence, then
veers off on a theoretical jag based mostly on challenging
accepted notions of chronology).[1] I'll limit myself here to

---

[1] Bayard, also author of the delightful treatise *How To Talk About
Books You Haven't Read*—note the Bénabaldian title—follows Gen-
ette in the tradition of French academics who are magnificently in-
ventive and shrewd as readers and probably total dicks in person.
Le Plagiat par anticipation does a pretty good job of summing up the
Oulipo in its introduction, and in establishing a useful distinction be-

some of the bigger influences in the oulipian wheelhouse, lest we both get lost in the rabbit hole and wind up dead in a dusty bookshop, buried under a stack of old issues of *Word Ways*.

—◦—

Here is the first sentence of Raymond Roussel's entry in the *Oulipo Compendium:* "Poet, novelist, playwright, gifted amateur musician, chess enthusiast, neurasthenic, homosexual, and drug addict, Raymond Roussel began life as the happy child of immensely wealthy parents connected to the Napoleonic aristocracy."

Said charmed life didn't end too happily, and, after Roussel's pathetically macabre suicide in a hotel in Palermo, his estate provided for the publication of *How I Wrote Certain of My Books*—a title since reverently hijacked by Calvino and Bénabou—which laid bare the compositional secrets of some of the novels Roussel had vanity-

---

tween works written under declared constraint and those written under "secret, even involuntary constraints," but Bayard more or less misses the point when he laments that Le Lionnais and the Oulipo in general have used the concept as little more than a cute joke because they were "incapable of elaborating a veritable theory of plagiarism by anticipation"—which gives you the impression of Bayard as the slimy new husband of the ex-wife of the put-upon hero in an action movie, who talks like this for the whole story until he ends up begging the hero's forgiveness while hanging precariously from the landing gear of a helicopter or something.

published. The vignettes that make up *Impressions of Africa,* for instance, were created by taking two sentences that were identical but for a couple of spelling differences—say, *billard* (pool table) in one and *pillard* (plunderer) in the other—writing a story that began with one sentence and ended with the other, and removing the bookend sentences to erase the evidence. A similar process, plus a method of breaking words and phrases into smaller phonetic units (such as "fausse note tibia" from *phonotypia,* leading to a character who plays shrill flute melodies on his own amputated tibia), generated the tales in *Locus Solus.* A sequel to the former work, *New Impressions of Africa,* written in alexandrine verse, experiments with the narrative equivalent of a whole bunch of nested parentheses.

Roussel's initial brush with a cult following came in the 1920s, when the Surrealists caught wind of one of his self-financed plays—which had been freaking out establishment types and causing audiences to throw small blunt objects at the actors—and hurried *en masse* to support the spectacle. The dazzling and incomprehensible elements that make regular appearances in Roussel's fiction—take the balloon-mounted apparatus in *Locus Solus* that is very slowly assembling a gigantic mosaic out of human teeth—certainly do call to mind surrealist imagery, but there's too much discipline behind them, in both the conception and the explanation, to link the two more than superficially. When early interest waned, Roussel fell out of popular favor for a few decades; by the time Michel Foucault exhumed him for a book-length critical essay in 1963, the

Oulipo was about ready to lay claim to his legacy. Caradec wrote a biography of Roussel in 1972, then another in 1997; Monk translated the latter in 2001.

Roussel's work has particular resonance in that of Mathews, who even co-founded a literary journal called *Locus Solus* in 1961 with New York School poets John Ashbery, Kenneth Koch, and James Schuyler. Mathews's early novels, *The Conversions* and *Tlooth* especially, incarnate Roussel's superhuman attention to technical detail in the service of bizarre imagery, its indulgence of almost-disembodied vignettes and arborescent detours. Sturrock, who argues that the Oulipo itself was "brought into existence in order to encourage Roussel-like experiments in the generative powers of language," suggests that this was valuable for a lot of its writers in the early days because it was ideally detached from personal revelation or disclosure —therapeutically inexpressive. Indeed, Queneau's *Children of Clay* and Perec's *Disparition* and, in a sense, *Life A User's Manual* do take the shape of extensive searches for something that may or may not exist, stories where you see an oddity and only much later discover the story behind it: a lot of tangents distracting from the central absence of a center.

A contemporary of Roussel's, and another one of Caradec's biographical subjects, was Alphonse Allais, a humorist who wrote homophonic alexandrines (also known as *holorhymes*) and eye-rhymes, in which two end-words share terminal letters but don't actually sound alike—like *liar* and *caviar*. (A peerless demonstration of this for the

255

English language is a poem called "The Chaos," by Dutch linguist Gerard Nolst Trenité, which, true to Roubaud's first principle, is a poem about English-pronunciation traps that is itself saturated with irregularly pronounced words: "This phonetic labyrinth / Gives *moss, gross, brook, brooch, ninth, plinth.*")[2] Allais was also an anticipatory plagiarist of John Cage: his funeral march for the deaf—nine blank measures —preceded Cage's famous *4'33"* of silence by more than half a century.

      Lewis Carroll enjoys frequent props as a benevolent ancestor, more for his interests—logic, wordplay, mathematical games, pseudonymity—than for any single work, although Roubaud did translate his fanciful epic poem *The Hunting of the Snark* into French in 1981. "If *Through the Looking-Glass* is based on a game of chess, it is so in a way too informal to be called oulipian," Mathews explains in the *Compendium,* but "among Carroll's minor writings several are unquestionably oulipian": tautograms, anagrams, word golf, acrostics, and so on. His *Dynamics of a Particle,* Mathews writes, "reads like an illustration of oulipian strategy in reverse: he celebrates 'the advantage of introducing the human element into the hitherto barren regions of mathematics.'" Roubaud, reflecting on the genesis of $\in$, ex-

---

[2] Also worth mentioning is the *reductio* argument, popularized by George Bernard Shaw, in favor of English spelling reform on the grounds that *ghoti* should be pronounced "fish," given the pronunciations of *gh* in "rough," of *o* in "women," and the *ti* in "nation." By the same logic, *ghoughpteighbteau* is proffered as a perfectly good way to spell "potato."

plains that the idea of staging a set of poems as a match between sides in a game of *go* came from "my master, Lewis
Carroll."

Other anticipatory plagiarists are more localized,
like Unica Zürn for the anagram and Stefan Themerson, inventor of semantic poetry, for LSD. Perec's extensive history of the lipogram in *La littérature potentielle* begins with
the inventors of *gematria,* a method of interpreting Hebrew
scriptures based on the numerical value of the letters in
each word, and ends with American sailor Ernest Vincent
Wright, who wrote the E-less *Gadsby: Champion of Youth*
in 1939 and then promptly died.

257

Anticipatory plagiarism shouldn't be confused with
influence: Kafka, for instance, was particularly important
to Perec's literary formation—Louis Begley, in *Franz Kafka:
The Tremendous World I Have Inside My Head,* brings to
mind a bleak interpretation of oulipian constraint when he
remarks that Kafka's characters "struggle in a maze that
sometimes seems to have been designed on purpose to
thwart and defeat them. More often, the opposite appears
to be true: there is no purpose; the maze simply exists"—
but nobody would accuse him of anticipating anything
properly oulipian. Ditto William Faulkner and Joseph Con-
rad and James Joyce, all of whom, according to Queneau,
were writing structurally elaborate novels before doing so
was fashionable in France; ditto Gertrude Stein and Agatha
Christie, both favorites of Roubaud's. Ditto Jonathan Swift
and Henry James, who imagined situations rife with oulipian implication but did not themselves compose that way;
ditto John Barth and Donald Barthelme and Samuel Beck-

ett and other authors whose work is plenty experimental but whose methods weren't all that *potential* when you get down to it.

—◄○►—

It's a bit easier to trace the Oulipo's influence on contemporary authors than it is to triangulate all the antecedents, even if taking a full account is just as much of a cut-open-a-down-pillow-on-a-windy-day-and-gather-all-the-feathers kind of errand. Gilbert Sorrentino, the Brooklyn writer who taught a course at Stanford on generative devices, assembled an estimable body of largely constrained work prior to his death in 2006. "Almost all of my books are written under the influence of some sort of preconceived constraint or set of rules," he told an *Alt-X* interviewer in 1994. "Some of these are loose and flexible, like the time scheme in *Steelwork,* and others are quite rigorous, like the alphabetical framework in *Misterioso.*" His groaning masterwork, *Mulligan Stew,* in which an attempt to write an avant-garde murder mystery is gradually overtaken by all the textual ballast of the novelist's everyday life, is oulipian in the way that *Pale Fire* is: a viciously funny meditation on literature as a volatile, human process, in which the formal peculiarity of the presentation mirrors the subject at hand.

Doug Nufer, a wine merchant who lives in Seattle, has written novels such as *Negativeland,* in which each sentence contains a grammatical or semantic negation, and *Never Again,* in which no word is ever repeated. (Like Sorrentino, and most Oulipo-proximate anglophone authors, Nufer enjoys a cordial colleagueship with Mathews, who allegedly once responded to a manuscript of Nufer's with a prim "How nice that you have so much time on your hands.") Mark Z. Danielewski's neo-noir tome *House of Leaves* calls to mind Calvino tweaking on crystal meth and conspiracy theories, while his *Only Revolutions,* a casual epic poem of sorts, is meant to be read for eight pages, turned upside down and read for eight pages from the other end, and so on until the twain meet. Mark Dunn's sprightly epistolary novel *Ella Minnow Pea* tells the story of a town where certain letters are outlawed one by one and uses an accordingly diminishing alphabet[3]—a technique that both exemplifies Roubaud's principle about constrained works' discussing their own constraints and lends itself nicely to arguments about the fundamental absurdity of censorship. It's also a particularly well fleshed-out update of James Thurber's equally sprightly 1957 fable *The Wonderful O,* in which a pirate named Black—who has detested the letter O ever since his mother got wedged in a porthole—sails to an island called Ooroo in his ship, the *Aieu,* and promptly banishes all things with the letter O in them:

> "Much good they'll get from these," said Black, "or any others. I haven't finished with the O's in music, in harmony and melody, that is, and compositions. They'll have no score, and what is more, no orchestra,

---

[3] The diminishing alphabet, which has never been applied on the same scale by anyone within the Oulipo, also raises an interesting version of the paradox of the heap: at what point does a lipogram become a *beau présent*—that is, when do you stop thinking about the letters you're suppressing and start thinking about the ones you have left?

or podium, or baton, and no conductor. They can't play symphonies, or rhapsodies, sonatas or concerti. I'll take away their oratorios and choirs and choruses, and all their soloists, their baritones and tenors and sopranos, their altos and contraltos and accompanists. All they'll have is the funeral march, the chant and anthem, and the dirge, and certain snatches."

"They'll still have serenades," said Littlejack.

Black made an evil and impatient gesture. "You can't serenade a lady on a balcony," he said, "if there isn't any balcony."

260

And then there are some authors who probably wouldn't call themselves oulipian in any operational or metaphysical sense of the word, but who might consent to using the adjective for one or two of their works.[4] Take *Alphabetical Africa,* a snowballing tautogram by Austrian-born writer Walter Abish:[5] the book consists of fifty-two

---

[4] An ongoing internal debate slightly less interesting than the pros and cons of revealing the constraint involves whether or not any text by an Oulipian author should be considered oulipian—much as Caradec considered pharmaceutical inserts part of Céline's bibliography. I've been told the workshop officially confirmed in the early 1970s that this was to be the case, but according to the archives the same dictum was proposed and rejected in June 2001. (At the same meeting, it was proposed and ratified that someone should nominate the Oulipo for a Nobel Prize.)

[5] . . . of whom a surprisingly efficient encapsulation comes from John Updike, reviewing Abish's autobiography, *Double Vision: A Self-Portrait,* in the *New Yorker* in 2004: "He sketches his life as a boy in Austria and as a young man in China but says little about his adult years in New York, or exactly when he arrived, or how he supported himself. He does not explain how he came to wear an eye patch."

chapters, of which the first allows only words that begin with the letter A, the second only words beginning with A and B, and so on until, after the unconstrained Chapters 26 and 27, letters begin to drop out again such that Chapter 28 has no Z words and Chapter 52 only words starting with A again. (The narrative is one of minor international intrigue, with a whole lot of decadent debauchery on the side; simple but arduous alphabetical constraints always seem to bring out the libido, for some reason.) Iegor Gran's *Les Trois vies de Lucie* (The Three Lives of Lucie) can be read in three ways—straight through, recto pages only, or verso pages only—which yield three different stories. (The realization, as with Wright's *Gadsby,* doesn't quite do justice to the grandeur of the formal stricture.) Richard Powers's *The Gold Bug Variations* tethers its narration to the chemical structure of DNA and the composition of Bach's *Goldberg Variations.* Mathias Enard's *Zone* is a single sentence of more than 500 pages; Vanessa Place's *Dies: A Sentence* clocks in at 145. Michel Thaler's *Le Train de nulle part* (The Train from Nowhere) has no verbs, Peter Carey's *True History of the Kelly Gang* no commas, Christine Brooke-Rose's *Amalgamemnon* no present or past indicative tenses. Theodor Geisel, better known as Dr. Seuss, wrote *Green Eggs and Ham* to win a bet with his editor, Bennett Cerf, that he couldn't write a children's book using only fifty different words.

There's Cortázar, of course, whose flirtations with oulipian tactics in *Hopscotch* and in "Clone" weren't enough to sell him on the workshop. The same goes for Vladimir Nabokov, who was considered in the late 1960s as a possible invitee but was passed over on the grounds that he wasn't likely to leave his Swiss solitude each month to chitchat about potential literature. Some oulipian affinity could be justifiably be posited—plus history seems to have recorded that Nabokov and Queneau met at some gala in the seventies and talked about their goddaughters—but, as with Cortázar, attitude would have interfered. In his notes to a late short story called "The Vane Sisters," Nabokov remarks: "In the story the narrator is supposed to be unaware that his last paragraph has been used acrostically by two dead girls to assert their mysterious participation in the story.[6] This particular trick can be tried only once in a thousand years of fiction. Whether it has come off is another question." In an essay called "Nabokov oulipien," Paul Braffort makes a sporting attempt to colonize Nabokov's work through various points of affinity, although he never comes up with a very convincing refutation of VN's comment, in the introduction to the screenplay version of *Lolita,* that "there is nothing in the world that I loathe more than group activity, that communal bath where the hairy and slippery mix in a multiplication of mediocrity." (Braffort seems, wisely enough, to ignore it.)

By and large, the Oulipians appreciate like-minded work from a distance. When it's good, it may be mentioned in passing, or preserved in archival history under the *érudition* heading of the next meeting's minutes; when it's great,

---

[6] That sentence, I feel compelled to note, is atypically inelegant, what with its unnecessary repetition of the phrase *in the story.* Tsk tsk, Vlad—if you were in the Oulipo, I might have given you the benefit of the doubt and assumed it was intentional!

they'll track down the author and invite him or her to dinner. When it's not worth their time, they don't bother with
it, so long as it doesn't appropriate and besmirch the workshop's good name. (This has yet to become a serious issue,
but there has been recurring discussion of trademarking
the name *Oulipo,* just in case.)[7] They are aware that potential literature and its associated techniques, public domain
and all, are no longer under the control of the Oulipo: that
the creature has grown up and out in ways they can't expect to keep up with and still get any of their own work
done.[8] They're also aware, and more so each year, that literature is not the only vocation that can lend itself to the
quest for potential.

263

—◄o►—

---

[7] The advantage of a made-up name like *Oulipo* is that it can be pro-
tected legally, as a brand, from the kind of vultures who sell Borges
olive oil and Choco-Leibniz biscuits.

[8] And this is only in books, mind you. There's Lars von Trier and
Jørgen Leth's *Five Obstructions* and the rest of the Danish Dogme 95
film movement, which applies to filmmaking a more hardcore version of the three unities of classical drama; there's Brian Eno and Peter Schmidt's *Oblique Strategies* cards, which contain instructions or
phrases intended, after their own cryptic fashion, to resolve dispute
or inertia; there's Sophie Calle's lovely, *Exercises in Style*–esque *Take
Care of Yourself,* in which she reprints a jerkishly diplomatic breakup
email and circulates it to 107 women—same number as there are
anonymous census-answerers in Jouet's *107 âmes,* mind—from various walks of life (sexologist, headhunter, clown, clairvoyant, sharp-
shooter, police commissioner, parrot) to weigh in on it. But these all
belong in another book entirely.

In October 2007, at L'Autre Canal, a swankily converted industrial-cum-cultural space on the outskirts of Nancy, the French intellipop label Ici d'ailleurs is putting on a *soirée OuMuPo*. I have shown up, more or less uninvited, to write about it for a magazine that will fold before the next issue makes it to print. (In retrospect, this might turn out for the best, since my nerdy little dictaphone and I don't get any interesting material or commentary from anyone involved, although someone does pour wine on me from a balcony while an American DJ named Rob Sonic eggs on the locals.)

All of the performers at the *soirée* have participated in the OuMuPo project, in which a DJ or electronic musician is instructed to produce a forty-two-minute mix composed under a handful of formal and procedural constraints, the most important being that it can contain anything from the Ici d'ailleurs catalogue and nothing else. The six volumes so far have included contributions from Japanese turntablist DJ Krush and trip-hop outsider artist Matt Elliott, who recorded until 2003 as the Third Eye Foundation. Each mix is then coupled with a set of constraint-based cartoon liner notes and bundled in an anonymous-looking manila package.

This isn't a particularly new idea: avant-rock gunslinger Jim O'Rourke made an extended remix of the entire catalogue of German electronic label Mille Plateaux; Oxnard producer Oh No has made a handful of blunted instrumental hip-hop albums with similarly limited source material. Gregg Gillis, better known as Girl Talk, turned the pop-song mashup into a conceptual art form by making albums that sample about five alt-rock radio or southern rap cuts per minute. If there's a difference between such exploits and the OuMuPo mixes, it's a question of preliminary organization and compositional strictness—the difference, if you like, between a novel where successive chapters have alternating male and female narrators and a novel where each chapter is exactly 4,000 words long.[9]

The *nancéen* OuMuPo, started in 2003 by Ici d'ailleurs head honcho Stéphane Grégoire, is one of a handful of *ouvroirs de musique potentielle* that have existed since Georges Perec and Luc Etienne began experimenting with phonetic palindromes and whatnot in the early 1970s. Other incarnations, most of which are dead or dormant, have included an offshoot of avant-garde composer Iannis Xenakis's CEMAMu, whose most notable OuMuPian act was to set Le Lionnais's "La Rien que la toute la" to music; a British consortium that has dutifully explored the combinatorial possibilities of both composition and performance; and a handful of dudes in Bordeaux who have, so far, left precious little trace of their work. To date, Grégoire's OuMuPo is the most prominent, the most prolific, and certainly the best exemplar of inter-*ouvroir* collaboration: each set of liner notes is outsourced to a member of the OuBaPo, or *ouvroir de bande dessinée potentielle* (a *bande dessinée* is a comic strip).

The concept of the Ou-X-Po—workshop for potential *something*—originated with Le Lionnais, who dreamed

---

[9] As is the case with Richard Beard's *X20*.

of initiating a "universal institute of potentiality" where an infinitude of sewing circles would work in concert to get at the hidden promise in all realms of human endeavor. Le Lionnais himself deputized the first Ou-X-Po, which might have been a subcommission of the Oulipo were the Oulipo not already wary of subcommissions, in 1973: the OuLiPoPo, or *ouvroir de littérature policière potentielle—*workshop for potential detective fiction.[10] Like the Oulipo, the OuLiPoPo conceived its efforts along analytical and synthetic lines, after a decree by Le Lionnais that could apply equally well to both workshops: "Analysis must precede synthesis."

So, starting where Le Lionnais had left off, that same year, with his inventory of possible murder-mystery culprits in *La littérature potentielle,* the OuLiPoPians gathered each month to identify their own anticipatory plagiarists (in particular Ellery Queen, who used a variety of formal constraints in different novels), to probe the detective-lit implications of the Cain and Abel story and Marx's *Critique of Material Economy,* to weigh the merits of Kantian versus Spinozist detectives, and to compare definitions of the phrase "the perfect crime." Soon enough they were reviewing imaginary murder mysteries, generating

---

[10] Actually, one Ou-X-Po *was* formed as a subcommission, a year earlier than the OuLiPoPo at that: the OuMathPo, whose goal was essentially to use literary structures for mathematical purposes instead of the other way around. (Among its associates was thermonuclear-weapons designer and Manhattan Project participant Stanisław Ulam.) Not much ever came of it, whence its literal and figurative relegation to a footnote in the history of the Ou-X-Po.

plot templates from a set of specialized tarot cards, and actually writing mysteries—for example, Jacques Barine tried disobeying all of Van Dine's Commandments in order to produce what he hoped would be the worst detective story ever.[11]

Next to be founded was the OuPeinPo: the *pein* stands for *peinture,* or painting, but the group's province extends farther out in the visual arts. More dogmatic and conceptually energetic than the Oulipo, the OuPeinPo has always had much stronger 'pataphysical ties, notably through founder Thieri Foulc. Foulc's introduction to the workshop says directly what the Oulipo has elaborated and reiterated over the years: it is concerned with generating techniques, not works (those it realizes are merely "feasibility experiments"); it is not an artistic movement; it has no use for chance or for notions of beauty; it is entitled to its own bizarre rules, thank you very much ("the world's most famous painting" is never to be mentioned, under penalty of a ten-franc fine). In the annex of the *Oulipo Compendium* devoted to the OuPeinPo, *symmetry* is defined as "the absolute enemy."

Officially revived in 1980 (after a dimly remembered sprint from 1964 to 1967), the workshop has assem-

---

[11] In a 1928 issue of *American Magazine,* S. S. Van Dine, born Willard Huntington Wright, published a list of twenty rules for mystery writers. Some are reasonable (do not deceive the reader outright; have no truck with mafias or secret societies or murderous butlers) and others a little more brittle (have no more than one culprit, no accidents or suicides, no love interests).

bled its *Grand Oeuvre,* a living-color answer to the Oulipo's *Table Queneleieff,* in which rows and columns are filled, meeting after meeting, with new possibilities for methodology, source material, and abstract elements such as "feeling." There is *lamellisection,* in which a preexisting image is cut up into strips and reassembled methodically; *lipopict,* which forbids some element, be it a color or part of the viewer's field of vision; *onomometry,* in which the spatial proportions of a portrait are determined by the letters in the subject's name; *plaiting,* which combines two canvases cut into respectively vertical and horizontal strips to attain separate variations on a master image; *déculottage,* the process of applying paint to a wooden panel in such a way as to reveal a certain desired image beneath, once the wood and undercoating have been planed away. All of which is to leave out more technical manipulations, like the *puzzlomorphic trammel-net,* the *taquinoidal painting,* the *zoopictural classification,* and Jack Vanarsky's proposal for straightening the course of the Seine through metropolitan Paris.

The OuBaPo is the OuPeinPo's younger, cooler cousin—indeed, probably the hippest Ou-X-Po to exist in any functional, non-imaginary form. Conceived in 1987, also at Cerisy-la-Salle, and started in 1992 through the French comics publisher L'Association, the workshop underscores the size of the overlap between literature and cartooning[12]—right down to the strong personalities and in-

---

[12] A point on which I have personally held a startling number of arguments with elderly women.

ternal drama. (Recent years have revealed some fissures in the group's unity, due largely to its official ties to a single publisher, something the Oulipo has prudently avoided.)

There's no particular analytical side to OuBaPian work, but the distinction between new "texts" and manipulations of preexisting ones—what the OuBaPians term "generative" and "transformative" constraints, respectively —is just as acute as it was in the Oulipo's early days. The former can lead to delightful graphic applications of literary fixed forms, such as Etienne Lecroart's sonnets, palindromes, and even an alphabetical drama à la Perec, or to more purely visual limitations like François Ayroles's partial iconographic restrictions, in which the same pose displayed in different contexts could mean the difference between enjoying an ice cream cone and making a deeply impolite gesture. The transformative model is represented, for instance, by Gilles Ciment's reduction of a sixty-two-page Tintin adventure into six eloquent, wordless panels.

Through L'Association, the OuBaPo has also distributed some next-level cartoon products, including a set of three dice on which each face shows a permutable situation, meaning the thrower can create 216 possible three-panel stories. A more sophisticated variant is the board game ScrOUBAbble, a version of Scrabble in which letters are replaced by cartoon panels and words thus replaced by stories (to be judged and scored, if you're into that sort of thing, by consensus). OuBaPo-America, established in 2001 and run by the group's official foreign correspondent, Matt Madden—best known for reinterpreting Queneau's *Exercises in Style* with an equally mundane anecdote represented in ninety-nine different visual idioms—numbers four members to the French OuBaPo's nine.

Then there's the OuTraPo, the workshop for potential tragicomedy, founded in 1991 by Stanley Chapman, a British eccentric who, although one of the Oulipo's first foreign correspondents, never had much to do with the group after translating Queneau's *Hundred Thousand Billion Poems.* The OuTraPo, whose official patron saint is the British playwright Tom Stoppard, investigates theatrical constraints, in text and in performance, imposed on either end of the script: it takes as its foundational influence the three unities of classical drama (whereby a play takes place over a one-day interval, in the same physical location, and with as few subplots or digressions as possible). More militant constraints, such as the prohibition of female actors in Elizabethan performance or that of male actors in medieval Japan, are approached actively and seldom analytically; the OuTraPians put on plays and spectacles in some cases just to prove it can be done—as with Milie von Bariter's staging of *Le Bétrou* by Julien Torma, a supposedly unperformable play by a probably imaginary playwright. When Chapman died, in the summer of 2009, he was allegedly preparing a production of *A Hundred Thousand Billion Dramatic Pieces.*

—◦—

Since Noël Arnaud's death in 2003, von Bariter has been the Collège de 'Pataphysique's official *provéditeur coadjuteur du potentiel,* which means he not only keeps track of activity among Ou-X-Pos but also has the power to bestow a formal blessing on new ones, which, he estimates, have come into being at the rate of at least one a year since the early 1990s.[13] Workshops with said blessing belong to the Collège's network of subcommittees, the Cymbalum Pataphysicum, which is more recognition than they get from the Oulipo itself; indeed, most latter-day Ou-X-Pos have much more in common with Jarry's science of imaginary solutions than with oulipian notions of potential. The more stable and prolific ones manage to dovetail both traditions (the OuLiPoPo, the OuPeinPo, and the OuBaPo all publish or used to publish small-run equivalents of the *Bibliothèque Oulipienne*), but the increasing majority align themselves with the Collège. "The 'potential' at stake in each workshop," von Bariter writes, "corresponds to one type of imaginary solution."[14]

271

Most of what I know about the scrappier Ou-X-Pos I learned one afternoon from Paul Edwards, a British professor at the University of Paris–VII and founder of the OuPhoPo, which seeks, to hear him tell it, that which is 'pataphysical in the realm of photography. Since 1995, the OuPhoPo has held exhibitions and circulated limited-edition publications sharing studies on the potential of photographs and the instruments that make them: photos bearing contradictory meanings, experiments with photo-sensitive clay, one member's progress in transforming the

---

[13] It also means he gets to use oulipian in-jokes: he explains, in a 2006 interview for *Drunken Boat,* that "the key to inter-*ouvroir* organization" is laid out on page 17 of Le Lionnais's third manifesto.

[14] Jean-Jacques Poucel's translation.

universe into a giant pinhole camera. One series of publications has come out with its successive editions numbered 18, 18.5, 18.75, 18.875 and so on, entirely for the purpose of thwarting the BNF's filing system.

Edwards lives in one of those small Parisian apartments that is stacked from floor to ceiling with books and literary ephemera but somehow is not dusty, and he seems to have a mind to match. The day I called on him, he deftly filled me in on all the relevant Ou-X-Pos and at least half of the irrelevant ones, including some that exist in name only (like Noël Arnaud's OuMonBeauChaPo, or "Now where's my hat?"). Sharing of personnel between the smaller *ouvroirs* is extensive, so it doesn't shock anyone to find a high-ranking Collège member involved in the OuCarPo (cartography) or the OuHistPo (history), nor an Oulipian in the OuPolPot (politics—note the extra T) or the OuMaPo (marionettes). Just as present is the contentious spirit of the Collège, as evidenced in the often hilariously volatile escapades that ensue any time two or more Ou-X-Pos come together in public. There is even a three-person workshop for potential catastrophe, the OuCataPo, which exists solely to predict what disasters will occur in/at such an event.

The Collège does as good a job as it can of keeping the legit X-Pos from the fake ones, given that the whole enterprise is rooted in a fake-serious approach to everything. In 2005, the trimesterly journal of 'Pataphysics published an appraisal of current Ou-X-Pism that included all of the abovementioned workshops (Oulipo included), plus the OuArchiPo (architecture) and the OuCiPo (cinematography), but that left out plenty of quasi-official counterparts. Consider the OuCuiPo, the workshop for potential cooking, which Mathews and Arnaud founded in 1990, seemingly for the purpose of publishing two volumes about food and then moving on with their lives.[15] There are two OuGraPos, one for graphic design, founded in 2001 by three German art students, and one for grammar, co-founded in 2002 by Alain Zalmanski; there are two OuJaPos, one for gardening (*jardinage*) and another for Japanese studies. There is an OuTyPo (typography), an OuMyPo (MySpace), an OuWiPo (Wikipedia), an OuPyPo (pygology, which I think means the study of butts), and, at least theoretically, an OuPornPo ("the *Kama Sutra* being an anticipatory plagiarism of combinatorial pornography").

273

Are they serious? Sometimes. There are certainly oulipian or 'pataphysical constraints to be applied in the search for new approaches to, say, radio and sound art (OuRaPo) or search engine–generated poetry (OuFlarfPo), but it gets dicier when you try to fathom what constraint-based politics would be, or what the 'pataphysical elements

---

[15] For new OuCuiPian work, see Alain Zalmanski's A-monovocalic menu in the 2006 *Drunken Boat* dossier on potential literature; needless to say, the menu's gastronomic consistency should be regarded with the utmost suspicion. The reality of potential cooking is probably best illustrated by a chapter in Mathews's *Sinking of the Odradek Stadium* that describes an evening of shitfacedly inebriated and ultimately disastrous conceptual cooking, recounted with such authenticity and detail that it makes the very workshop seem a lot less far-fetched. I will also submit here, for want of a better place to do so, that the Jewish holiday of Passover, in which the story of the Israelites' liberation from Egypt is told (and eaten) over the course of a meal, is extremely rich in OuCuiPian potential.

of MySpace are.[16] Not that it can't be done—the OuHistPo, for an inter-*ouvroir* gathering in May 1999, assembled a reasonably convincing "historical lipogram" examining what might happen to history if an event were removed: a tongue-in-cheek gesture that could have real analytical weight if presented to and by other people than, well, Ou-X-Pians.

But then this is me thinking about it as someone with a grounding not just in literature but in potential literature. Edwards, who isn't particularly interested in the Oulipo's explorations, sees it differently. The Ou-X-Po enterprise, he explained to me, is predicated on understanding Le Lionnais's approach to knowledge through Jarry's synesthetic sense of the human comedy. The OuPhoPo is dedicated to uncovering the same things, self-evident once you know what to look for, that made the early 'Pataphysicians declare that everyone was living (')pataphysics whether or not he or she acknowledged it. ("Need we wish for there to be 'Pataphysics in Buenos Aires?" Latis wrote in one of I. L. Sandomir's treatises. "It was there, as everywhere, before we existed. It will always be. It need not even be: it does not even need to be to be.") What are the things common to every photograph, the things we take for granted in our visual interaction with the world, and how can we isolate and exploit them? What is it that we can pull out from underneath cinematography or cartography, to expose the weird and troubling and inspiring parts of life itself?

---

[16] Verily, the mind reels.

The underlying belief shared by the Oulipo and the legion of Ou-X-Pos, serious and non-, is essentially that any enterprise or discipline can be treated as solid and particulate, as an experiment we can tweak and tinker with until we get results that interest or comfort or provoke or unsettle us. In the familiar cases, the approach is to mathematize; in something like photography, where calculation is already inherent, why not try adding literature? It's a matter of inviting a contrary perspective and trying to make a productively unstable peace—of challenging the endeavor in the faith that the answer is already present in the question, the way the sculpture is already present in the stone. "It's all there," Edwards says about the lascivious parts of a story by the nineteenth-century writer R. D. Blackmore called *Frida,* which he doctored to produce an altogether dirtier book called *Id.* "You just have to find it."

275

Edwards, for his part, is fascinated by the figure of Jarry's Ubu—represented in the original woodcut as a pointy-hooded *bonhomme* with the spiral *gidouille* on his huge paunch—and sees versions of it everywhere, collecting those that aren't bolted down. Before I left his apartment, he showed me a pebble that he said looked like Ubu. He was not wrong.

◄o►

Each summer since 2005, Alain Zalmanski has held a picnic for *oulipotes* and *philoulipiens* in Le Vésinet, a small town southwest of Paris, to celebrate ("joyously and without constraint") the beginning of the summer and the end of the year's *jeudi* series. It's an occasion for members of *la famille* to get to know one another better and to welcome timid newcomers into the fold. I've never made it to the *Oulympiades,* as they call it, but I don't have much problem imagining how joyously stilted the conversation must sound to an uninitiated observer.

Zalmanski, a retired chemist, runs an extensive and informative[17] website called Fatrazie, which aggregates artifacts from the various comings and goings of the Oulipo, the Ou-X-Pos, the Collège de 'Pataphysique, anticipatory plagiarists and contemporary contemporaries, word gamers and math puzzlers, and so on. He is also a de facto moderator of the Liste Oulipo, a listserv started in the late 1990s by Philippe Bruhat and Estelle Souche and the single most consistent arena for chatter related to the Oulipo, inspired by the Oulipo, or apt to be interesting to the kinds of people who deem the Oulipo worth their time. It's more or less the online equivalent of the workshop itself, where someone may propose an idea (How could one represent poetically the properties of an isosceles triangle?) or a query (What's the longest word in French whose letters are in alphabetical order?) or a challenge (How many anagrams can you make from "Pamela Anderson"?) for a handful of likeminded individuals to mull over.[18] The functional advan-

276

---

[17] . . . albeit inattentively fact-checked: I'm still listed thereon as "Eric Levin Becker."

[18] The answers are, respectively, to write a sonnet where each line has one fewer syllable than the last; *aegilops,* a kind of grain; and several, some of them quite ribald.

tage of the email medium over the monthly dinner medium is self-evident—in terms of experimental demonstrations, the Liste has probably generated more content already than the Oulipo has in nearly four times as long—and the anonymity is mitigated by moments like Bourges and *jeudis* and the *Oulympiades,* which offer an occasion to put names with faces. As a matter of unspoken policy, the constraint used in a contribution to the Liste is typically explained immediately following the text, so that others may riff, repair, and compete.

277

How much of it is good? Depends, to paraphrase Caradec, on the post. Some contributors take the Liste seriously—for instance, Gilles Esposito-Farèse, a clean-cut theoretical astrophysicist who just happens to be ridiculously skilled at creating oulipian texts (everything from the usual forms to a "Poem of 14 lines of 14 syllables of which the right margin depicts the profile of [Jacques] Roubaud," which, like some of the more concrete-poetic contributions to the Liste, requires viewing in a font where each character is of equal width). Others use the Liste more casually, reacting to others' efforts with polite astonishment or the occasional you-missed-a-syllable, or pitching in aptonyms, real-life convergences of name and profession—former U.S. secretary of education Margaret Spellings, vasectomy-reversal specialist Dr. Alden Cockburn,[19] and so on.

Apart from the occasional researcher with a fac-

---

[19] A cursory Web search turns up a directory listing for Dr. Cockburn, complete with photo that finds him looking very much in on the joke.

tual question bound to be answered in less than ten minutes, most additions to the Liste are from the same dozen or so contributors, which lends it a further character not unlike that of the Oulipo itself, or any other collective of writers: there are the polished and prolific ones, the peevish prankster, the quiet patron saint, the refined female minority, the boorish but funny wild card who types in all caps. There is an annual-ish digital chapbook series called the B.L.O. (which stands for *Bibliothèque Liste-Oulipienne,* and which is no better an acronym, to Anglophone sensibilities, than that of the *Bibliothèque Oulipienne*); seven of the mainstays even published a set of 101 constraint-based reinterpretations of Gérard de Nerval's sonnet "El Desdichado" under a collective pseudonym in 2002.

There's also *Zazie mode d'emploi,* or Zazipo, run in Lille by a French teacher and carpenter named Robert Rapilly: a program that organizes annual Oulipo readings and that sponsors constrained-writing workshops year-round. Each year, Rapilly also selects a passage by an Oulipian that gets contorted, translated, asphyxiated, transduced, upside-downed, essplussevened, and more by the *Listoulipiens,* until hundreds of texticules have been published on the Zazipo website. (Annie Hupé, a retired math teacher who is now a regular on the listserv, told me she joined in 2005, during the frenzy of variations on a Roubaud poem, and didn't understand a word for about a month.)

The *Oulipotes* keep up a fairly robust dialogue, often inspired by utterances of interest in the news—like the scandalous text message from Nicolas Sarkozy to his ex-wife on the eve of his marriage to Carla Bruni, *Si tu reviens j'annule tout* ("Come back and I'll cancel everything"), which triggered a multi-week stream of six-word stories.[20] They draw the collective attention to notable piecelets of oulipistic information: that until recently the human genome was a lipogram in Z; that Sarkozy's famous toadying remark, *Je veux reconquérir le coeur de l'Amérique* ("I want to recapture the heart of the U.S."), is a perfect alexandrine. They've even midwifed new Ou-X-Pos, such as the OuBiPo, which tracks instances of involuntary constraint in the Bible. Anything is fair game: when I was announced as a new Oulipian, someone promptly made a few anagrams out of my name, then urged others to follow suit to see if they couldn't make better use of my K.[21] ("Ian Monk" is a devil of a name to anagrammatize in French, which I'm sure displeases Monk not at all.)

For all their creative and collaborative energy, though, many of the contributors have no great interest in the Oulipo itself, or in literature as a trade. (Most of them, contrary to the way it often seems, have jobs.) The Liste is a forum for diversion, a small digital community that pro-

---

[20] The standard, of course, being "For sale: baby shoes. Never worn," attributed probably apocryphally to Ernest Hemingway. But while you're down here, you'd probably also appreciate Alan Moore's "machine. Unexpectedly, I'd invented a time" (which, admittedly potentially problematically, treats *I'd* as a single word).

[21] My favorite, courtesy of non-*Listoulipien* Luke Woods, is *revel: I can bleed ink.*

vides verbal baubles of any origin to think about and toy with. It's nice, really, to have a group of generally talented people who don't have any aspirations to take the parlor game out of the parlor—especially in a city like Paris, I often think, where the literary hustle is so active. The Oulipo itself is involved, but mostly as a pretext; the Liste is its own entity that serves to illustrate and accommodate the oulipian temperament, not to generate things of literary value.

"These enthusiasts are contemporary heteroclites —the kind that may well have figured in Raymond Queneau's *Encyclopédie de fous littéraires,* were it to be written one hundred years from now," Jean-Jacques Poucel writes in his introduction to the Oulipo dossier in *Drunken Boat,* "and, consequently, their contribution to the oulipian enterprise is difficult to fathom." For my money, that contribution is made neither in the capacity of an audience nor even in that of an experimental annex for new forms: rather, their gift to potential literature is their effort, conscious or not, to make its value less literary.

Why that's a good thing depends on whom you ask. My take on it, as someone who came to comprehend the academic significance of the Oulipo only belatedly, and even then mostly out of a sense of duty, is that potential literature should be simple and accessible and first-degree, and that the best thing one can do for it is to prove how gratifying it can be for those of us who don't even know what it is—to prove the 'pataphysical nature of it, if you like, except with no patsy. The Liste does this by being basically democratic: about membership, about contributions, about the value of everyone's texts and the potential of pretty much anything that passes through linguistic channels. As Fournel says of the Oulipo's writing workshops, the essential thing is the text. If the ongoing buzz of the Liste inclines some people toward promiscuous and impossible notions of what literature is, so much the better.

—◦—

At present, Tom La Farge, a Brooklyn-based teacher who runs a writing group called the Writhing Society, is two volumes into a thirteen-part chapbook series explaining in greater detail how to get inside the headspace of various techniques and constraints. Although he dedicates his pamphlets enthusiastically to "the great and generous Oulipo," he makes it clear that these are not proprietary forms, going so far as to end the first volume, *Administrative Assemblages,* with a list of okay-now-*you*-try exercises for time lines, catalogues, maps, classificatory portraits, and the like. The spirit is similar to the draw-on-your-life and write-what-you-know shtick of any creative-writing instructor, but the depth is much greater, the stakes much more imaginative. *Administrative Assemblages* contains detailed instructions on how to create a travelogue based on the same combinatorial principles as Queneau's *Cent mille milliards de poèmes.*

This is an excellent public service, and La Farge provides it with great aplomb and evident love for the devices and their practitioners. Its implication—and arguably more so here than in Oulipo workshops, if only because those are necessarily limited by the number of Oulipians and constraints of space and time—is that part of creativity is having at your immediate disposal a range of forms that can accommodate, or if need be shape, the idea in your head. If the sun setting over a church at the end of happy hour is seventeen syllables' worth of interesting to you, you may compose a haiku, or if you need fourteen more you can trade it in for a tanka; if you meet someone and consider him or her ever so slightly more eligible as a lover because of an unusually spelled name,[22] you may find yourself taking stock of the words you could use in a *beau présent*. There is something unromantically actuarial about this, sure, but that's how potential literature becomes actualized literature. Options are weighed, choices made. Writing is, after all—here's the dirty little secret leaked by the modern era—work.

Which is all well and good, except that it presupposes that you're already thinking in a few different ways. It presupposes your wanting to express your feelings about the sight of that sunset in some written medium, and in one more formally elaborate than the usual one-word-after-another; it presupposes that you even learn how to spell the names of your friends. Oulipian pedagogy, such as it is, presupposes that you want to convey something artfully, that you care just enough. Without that, there's not much point in its tugging your sleeve until you realize that every mis-

---

[22] Not that I would know anything about this.

spelling is a potential parlor game, and every parlor game a potential novel.

Back to that in a moment.

—◁○▷—

A very different side of the same coin is *n*oulipo, the umbrella term for an aggregate of North American writers who work in a consciously experimental poetic mode and who came together, in Los Angeles in 2005, for a conference of that name to wax academic on their collective relationship to the workshop, its canon, and its dogma (or lack thereof). *n*oulipo isn't itself a collective the way the Oulipo is, but it's arguably an adjective the way *oulipian* is: give or take individual inclinations and various degrees of polemical intent, *n*oulipian literature is generated by something more calculated than inspiration. It can be formalistic, aleatory, satirical, techno-millenarian, or whatever, but there's a method to it.

It would be wrong to peg the authors assembled at the *n*oulipo conference as descendants of the oulipian model; by and large, the common denominator among the associated names—including Christian Bök, author of *Eunoia*,[23] and Nufer, one of the few who writes fiction as well as poetry—is an intimate but somewhat passive-aggressive relationship to the workshop. It's less what the Oulipo

---

[23] ... of which a review in the *Times of London* grants charitably that "it is done well but I do not see how one could read it, as one reads books with more vowels."

would look like had it been founded in the U.S. a decade or two later, more a way of gauging its effect on a handful of people whose poetic sensibilities have had no choice but to develop in a world where the Oulipo exists. *n*oulipian writers, if you like, are those for whom the existence of the Oulipo is an involuntary constraint.

The 2005 conference is documented in a bright-pink tome called *The* n*oulipian Analects,* which is organized in the same dubiously navigable glossary format as the *Oulipo Compendium.*[24] It gathers most of the papers and performances given in Los Angeles, as well as some older work by the participants, who included Monk and Fournel, and overall offers a handy introduction to many of the splintered cliques and clubs and listservs that might collectively constitute the *n*oulipo: UbuWeb, an avant-garde site for visual and sound poetry, started by the poet Kenneth Goldsmith;[25] IN.S.OMNIA, one of the Internet's first bulletin

---

[24] That is, the primary organizing principle in both is alphabetical order. In the *Compendium,* Roubaud's introduction comes before anything else, but the *Analects* takes the jig to an extreme, filing the copyright page under C (page 53) and the editors' introduction under I (page 103) and plunging the reader into a rather dense throat-clearing ("the interest in voluntarily adopted restrictions is clearly motivated by an attempt to avoid the romantic narcissism of much traditional bourgeois literary production") on the very first page. Weirdly, privileging the alphabet to such a degree gives both volumes the intended sense of egalitarianism, but also one of arbitrariness, making the alphabetical device seem a little bit weak and ineffectual—which one assumes was not the intent.

[25] Goldsmith, whose avowed medium is "uncreativity as creative practice" and whose conceptual exploits include transcribing a year's

boards for poetic mischief; LuciPo, or Lucifer Poetics, a North Carolina–based collective present by association; and, present by antagonism, Flarf, which also shrugs off the romantic idea of inspiration but replaces constraints with Internet search engines as its generative devices.

Some of the essays compiled in the *Analects* investigate new readings of and uses for oulipian practices in a fairly open-minded spirit (invoking, for instance, the bad-ass concept, generally attributed to N. Katherine Hayles, of the "posthuman condition"), but the underlying agenda among many participants stems from disappointment with the Oulipo's lack of political engagement—this despite their recognition that the workshop is "political only in the way that anything has a politics, but otehwise, no."[26] Juliana Spahr and Stephanie Young speak of their discomfort at the "masculinist tendencies of much constraint-based writing"; Johanna Drucker questions the effectiveness of an

---

worth of weather reports and inventorying his every movement for thirteen hours, is not represented directly in the *Analects*. But Bök, himself an UbuWeb denizen, alludes to an interview with Erik Belgum in *Read Me* where Goldsmith explains, "One of the greatest problems I have with Oulipo is the lack of interesting production that resulted from it . . . judging by the works that have been realized, they might be better left as ideas."

[26] [*sic*]. The essay that makes this concession, Juliana Spahr and Stephanie Young's "'& and' and *foulipo*" (don't try formatting that at home), was delivered and is reproduced in the *Analects* stripped of most instances of the letter R, for reasons that are both kind of clever and kind of abstruse. It was also delivered partially via recording, while Spahr and Young took their clothes off and put them back on in front of the audience a couple of times.

avant-garde movement once it becomes too popular, and notes later that the *n*oulipo conference's "attempts to police the use and definition of what passes as 'oulipian' sometimes have an unpleasantly shrill edge of authority anxiety." Bök is particularly active in taking the group to task, under a slender veneer of admiration, for offering "solutions to aesthetic, rather than political, problems" and for being, unlike Breton's pseudo-Marxist vision of Surrealism, "impressive in its formal technique, but inadequate in its social rationale":

> Oulipo may argue that surreal revolutions represent unaware enslavement to unknown constraints, but Oulipo does not account for the fact that, despite this problem, Surrealism nevertheless promotes forthrightly a mandate for social change, whereas Oulipo does not, despite its self-conscious, self-liberated algorithms for creativity. If *willful ignorance* about such rules can result in covert obedience to their poetic dominance, yet still entail a social critique (as is the case for Surrealism)—how might *willful obedience* to such rules result in a poetic critique, yet still entail a covert ignorance about their social potential?

. . . which indictment is artful and shrewd, except that these were never the terms the Oulipo set for itself. Part of Bök's slippage, as La Farge points out in a review of the *Analects* for the blog *Exploring Fictions*, comes from an overblown reading of the group as fundamentally prescriptive. (In an otherwise apt enumeration of six axioms of oulipian creation, for instance, Bök uses the word *must;* recall that Roubaud, after whom some of the same guidelines

are named, describes them merely as "principles sometimes observed by oulipian works.") Just as the group is
pointedly non-doctrinal for the writer—"We say that you
can write like this if you *want*," Monk stresses in the *Analects;* "there is no *obligation* to be Oulipian"—it's pointedly
non-doctrinal for the member as well. The alternative to
Breton's mandatory commingling of literature and class
struggle—that which caused Queneau to imply in the 1930s
that Surrealist rhetoric had more than nothing in common with Nazism—is the voluntary withdrawal that makes
the Oulipo, by design, collectively disengaged. As Fournel
pointed out at the *n*oulipo conference, this doesn't preclude
individual engagement or individual realization of Bök's
"social potential"—look, for starters, at Jouet's communi-
tarian poetry and ongoing "Republic novel"—it just avoids
the pitfalls of the party line. The point is not for the workshop to be anti-bourgeois or anti-colonialist or anti-feminist
or even anti-bigot: the point, insofar as there is one, is for it
to be anti-demagogue.

◄○►

The n*oulipian Analects,* in any case, evinces more than just a
political beef, and more than just a collective expression of
insecurity or influence anxiety. It gets at something about
how the Oulipo's terms *do* work, what they *do* allow for; it
says a lot about the reality of the workshop as a presence,
half figurative and half practical, viewed from the outside.
The participants in the *n*oulipo conference are all writers,
creative or academic, and consequently obligated to care
enough, maybe to care too much, about how the Oulipo

affects their work. No wonder the tenor is fraught with reservation and revisionism: when you're dwelling in the shadow of this group, its methodologies and inclinations (speculative grammatology and whatnot) and disinclinations (surrealist randomness) are bound to seem like received wisdom, an ideology to be picked at or railed against. The question nobody asked is: why dwell in the shadow of this group?

In his final radio interview with Georges Charbonnier in 1962, Queneau spoke openly for the Oulipo when he claimed that its project had nothing to do with modifying the way literature was created, with imposing anything other than possibility on anyone other than the dozen of them. "If you like, a new literary school could emerge and use the things we've clarified and experimented, in a more or less gauche way," he allowed, but insisted that this was not the final intent. "The meaning of the Oulipo is to give empty structures, to propose empty structures," he said.

"Well then, I'll ask this," said Charbonnier: "Is that possible?"

"Probably," Queneau murmured, after a pause.

Compared to the Surrealists' with-us-or-against-us rhetoric, that refusal to dictate the conditions or applications of literary creation is an appealing stance. From the standpoint of any old doctrineless writer, though, especially half a century into the oulipotopian experiment, it's a bit naïve to assume that emptying a structure of its particulars after it's been used to successful effect is enough to restore its full potential. Consider something as elementary as the E-less novel: there was Wright's *Gadsby* in 1939, there was Perec's *Disparition* in 1969, and there is *Casimir ou l'imitation,* a novel that Jacques Jouet has been working on for decades now. *Gadsby* is a curio that nobody pays much mind; *La Disparition,* through some combination of luck and skill, became a landmark gesture in the history of über-modern literature. So no matter how good *Casimir* is—and judging by the first chapter, which Jouet has read out in public a few times in recent years, it's shaping up to be excellent—is anyone ever going to read it without recalling *La Disparition?*[27] And now imagine that you're not even a member of Perec's immediate in-group but, say, a modern-day Swedish author who has no oulipian affiliation or inclination—who's never even *heard* of *La Disparition*[28]—but for whom it is urgently and independently desirable to write an E-less novel. How well do you think that's going to work out for you in the long run?

Nobody denies that the forms and constraints in which the Oulipo trades belong in the public domain, but at the end of the day the people who invent or find or resurrect them are the ones who get to use them first, and thus the ones most likely to reap their rewards. The situation is not particularly generous for any writer whose ultimate desire is to create works rather than posit possibilities, and

---

[27] Of course, Jouet is perfectly aware of this; indeed, whether or not another E-less novel can be written is the very question that drives the experiment. Still, not for nothing is this the one project that I've ever known to give Jouet, who produces and publishes literature at a greater rate than most of the writers in the world, any trouble worth mentioning.

[28] Even though you could presumably go check out a copy of *Försvinna* from your local library.

I suspect this is what made Queneau's answer to Charbonnier's question so unsatisfying. But a lot happens between an empty structure and an actual text, and the distinction is a crucial one to understand. "The Oulipo is not about written works," Mathews told an interviewer in 1989. "It's about procedures. The books are our own business as individual writers."

The Oulipo's generosity, then, is something like a conceptual generosity: it lies more in suggesting that literature might have a cookbook than in furnishing any actual recipes, more in framing an idea as the center of a labyrinth, and the finished work as the outside, than in offering any tips on how to navigate out. That's plenty inspiring to writers of a certain sensibility, and evidently frustrating to writers of a slightly different one—but what this kerfuffle finally demonstrates, to my mind, is that it's shortsighted to peg the oulipian endeavor as an experiment intended exclusively for writers. (Scientists publish their findings to the attention of other scientists, but science is *for* the rest of us, too.) What makes the Liste Oulipo so successful where the *n*oulipo can be volatile is that it creates a gathering-ground where nothing is at stake, for the benefit of people who *don't* want or need to be writers. This is something I want very dearly to be true of the Oulipo, whether or not reality bears it out: I want it to be of as great a value, if not a greater and more genuinely generous one, to people who are not in it for the sake of literature—their own or anyone else's—but who simply wish to indulge and explore their curiosity about the way they see the world.

potential weaving 2009

W HAT ELSE, THEN, AND whom else, is all this really for? How can it be for you, whoever you are, re-gardless of your intent and orientation and inclination or disinclination, as the case may be, to associate yourself with the writerly act? How can you use all of these ideas for pur-poses other than producing the next roller-towel *Finnegans Wake* or epic poem about industrial plastic manufacture?

Let's start with the almost insultingly obvious ba-sics: reading oulipian texts makes you a better reader of oulipian texts. Getting to know the workshop's collective output is an undertaking of great variety and pleasure and some degree of sacrifice: even while there's not that much content, when you compare oulipian writing with most similarly groupable thingums in literary history, there's such a high concentration of approaches to and applica-tions of the same few core ideas that reading a new work is almost always like fitting a new piece into a puzzle. That simile is doubly useful in that it also captures the commitment and excitement—or frustration and pointlessness, depending on your attitude—of sitting down to do the same puzzle over the course of a day or a week or a year or your lifetime.

To read the oulipian corpus even a little bit attentively is to absorb some of those connections that make the *galaxie oulipienne* such an enticing symbol of possibility. The most casual oulipian tourist might spend a moment pondering which came first, Jouet's chronopoem structure or Le Tellier's quip in *A Thousand Pearls* about timing the boiling of an egg by reciting Rimbaud's "Le Dormeur du val" three times (four for a harder boil). She might compare the strictly regulated word count in Monk's *Plouk Town* with the strictly regulated syllable count in Roubaud's early poetry collection *Trente et un au cube* (Thirty-One Cubed); she might compare the gender ambiguity in Garréta's *Sphinx* with the gender ambiguity in Mathews's *Tlooth,* or compare Audin's textbook on the algebraic geometry of spinning tops with Sartre's definition of literature, almost a quarter of a century earlier, as a "strange spinning top" that exists only in motion.[1] Even the newest hot-off-the-presses form harks back to older counterparts: Forte's ninety-nine

---

[1] She might also consider, if for no other reason than its bizarre hilarity, a certain photograph in which Tom and Ray Magliozzi—better known as Click and Clack, the Tappet Brothers, hosts of the NPR show *Car Talk*—bear an eerie resemblance to Perec and Fournel, respectively.

pseudo-random observations share their piecemeal narration style with Grangaud's *Geste,* which shares its roundabout catalogue approach to the otherwise indescribable with Perec's attempts to "exhaust" the spot where he was sitting or to record every piece of food he ingested for an entire year.

Inevitably, these affinities and variations draw new lines between discrete points that might have gone estranged for years, for centuries. Each line, in turn, suggests a new perspective on the whole phenomenon—one that's totally, imperiously conclusive until you read something else and triangulate a new understanding of how it all works. This is what the Surrealists were after, in their own arrogant way, and the only idea that I've ever really found compelling in Breton's manifestos: the greater the figurative and symbolic and associative discord between two images, the more interesting their combination. The oulipian mini-canon, elaborated in the opposite of a vacuum, is rewarding as much for the perpetual recalibration it demands as for the novels and poems themselves. Perec said of his own reading habits, in *W or the Memory of Childhood,* that they were

> virtually part of history: an inexhaustible fount of memory, of material for rumination and a kind of certainty: the words were where they should be, and the books told a story you could follow; you could re-read, and, on re-reading, re-encounter, enhanced by the certainty that you would encounter those words again, the impression you had felt the first time. This pleasure has never ceased for me; I do not read much,

but I have never stopped re-reading [. . .] I re-read the books I love and I love the books I re-read, and each time it is the same enjoyment, whether I re-read twenty pages, three chapters, or the whole book: an enjoyment of complicity, of collusion, or more especially, and in addition, of having in the end found kin again.[2]

Complicity is fundamental to every reader-author relationship, but the oulipian covenant also implies a radically modern equilibrium of readerly freedom and readerly burden. It's been so ever since Queneau deputized the reader of his hundred trillion poems—where "the 'author' is at best a collaborator, and where the text demands a collaboration of me," as Tom La Farge puts it—as an active participant in the composition process. "The oulipian reader must, in a sense, not only simply receive the work but also accept it, extend it his hospitality," Le Tellier explains in *Esthétique de l'Oulipo.* "This concentration is of the same nature, though not the same order, as that which presided over the creation of the text. It is the same path, only walked (or considered) in reverse. There is creation, re-creation, and also recreation."

The ideal oulipian reader, then, is one who enjoys that game of triangulation for its very endlessness, one who would be content to work on a puzzle she has no hope of ever solving. She's the one who, finally, geeked on the rush of unraveling secret oulipian snarls, begins to look reflex-

---

[2] David Bellos's translation.

ively at any old text with an eye out for buried constraints, hidden indices, serendipities of which not even the author was aware. She's the one who has already taken to heart Caradec's warning, in his biography of Alphonse Allais, that Allais "does not write for you, but against you."

Nowhere is this better expressed than in Bénabou's *Dump This Book While You Still Can!*—an extended allegory for the tumultuous experience of interacting with a world that, due to some clerical error or other, is not organized according to oulipian protocols. The narrator, a thinly veiled Bénabou, encounters a book that opens with a cautionary stay-the-hell-out (whence the title) and immediately sets about trying to sort out what it means. In a protracted séance that ultimately takes up the whole story,[3] the narrator submits the mystery volume to all kinds of examinations, most of which the seasoned reader will recognize as oulipian techniques: breaking sentences down into their syllabic components and looking for embedded acronyms, taking each noun and counting back seven entries in a dictionary, investigating anomalies in punctuation and comparing ink densities among words on the page. He changes positions, tries new lighting, copies out passages, forgoes sleep—all for the sake of teasing out the crazy secrets he has con-

295

---

[3] I confess to a feeling of perplexity, the first time I read *Dump This Book*, once I realized that the entire novel was going to be about this one situation, akin to my feeling of perplexity when I realized, about forty-five minutes into the movie *Booty Call*, that the entire movie was going to be about that one night and its agonizing search for a condom.

vinced himself reside just under his nose, in this book that for some reason simply *does not want* to be read.

The story moves forward in Bénabou's customary lyrical reverie, but with enough momentum to convince you that you might one day find yourself in the same situation, that such a predicament could frankly happen to anyone. At one point, accounting for his ruinous certainty that there is more to the book than meets the eye, Bénabou alludes to all the meanings that are *potentiellement tissés*—potentially woven—into the text. That is, even if they weren't there before, there's still the possibility for them to be there now. And you see, just then, that the story is proposing to you a definition of potential literature: it's what you get when you go looking in language for meanings that aren't there, and find them anyway.

◄○►

Jacques Jouet asked me, one evening a few years ago, why Snowy the dog is persistently scratching himself throughout the first few pages of the Tintin adventure *The Secret of the Unicorn*. The story begins with the boy reporter and his dog strolling through a maze of antique stalls, where Tintin purchases a miniature ship and is instantly beset by strangers offering to buy it from him at any price. (Derring-do ensues.) The answer to the riddle, which I found a few days later with some light coaching, is beautifully simple: Snowy is scratching because he's at a flea market.

The play on words is a little too good to be accidental, but whether or not Hergé intended it as a wink to attentive Tintinophiles is precisely the immaterial part:

what matters is that it's there now. Jouet has also invoked, at various times, the one street in Paris named after a work of literature (rue Lucien-Leuwen, from an unfinished novel by Stendhal), the fragment of a *morale élémentaire* hidden in Act II of *Hamlet* (Lucianus: "Thoughts black, hands apt, drugs fit, and time agreeing"), and the momentary appearance of a book called *Morale élémentaire* in Jean Renoir's *La Grande Illusion.*[4] Jouet is, in short, an expert noticer of these little felicities, these meanings potentially woven into all the sectors of language and sometimes beyond. The beauty of potential, if not of the human mind, is that just the noticing suffices to make them real.

Queneau's most quoted remark is probably his declaration, in the 1937 novel *Odile,* that the true artist is never inspired—he is *always* inspired. As a counterpoint, recall his dictum from an early Oulipo meeting that there is no literature but voluntary literature, and this begins to come into focus: meaning, such as it is, doesn't exist on its own. Someone has to find it, midwife it, present it to the world as more than just a coincidence. The real artist is always inspired not because he creates things that are unmistakably intentional, but because he is sensitive to the sorts of things that at first seem like accidents. He replicates them on his own terms, as an expression of his own preoccupations or sensibilities or desires, or he just sticks them on a gallery

---

[4] It can be glimpsed about an hour into the film, during a scene where someone delivers a crate expected to contain caviar but which turns out to be full of books. (Would you believe me if I told you the man in the foreground shortly thereafter, who rushes to keep the angry Cossacks from setting fire to the czarina's books, bears a curious likeness to Jouet?)

wall and calls them art; even when he's wrong, he's right. (This is where Marcel Duchamp earns his keep as the most famous Oulipian nobody knows was an Oulipian: the implicit derision of the gesture aside, he showed that we can make even a urinal into a work of art, simply by saying it is so.) Take a poem Queneau published in 1967:

> On the bathroom wall
> in the Palais-Royal metro station
> you can read this statement
> to me it seems monumental
>
> *utilization of this stall*
> *is strictly reserved for the*
> *financially underprivileged*
> *and for the infamous poor*
>
> Eight feet seven feet
> Eight feet seven feet
> it's a quatrain
> very Verlaine[5]

To be oulipian is, in essence, to be complicit with these unexpectedly, unintentionally monumental statements wherever you may find them. If potential literature is not exactly the dialogue it is possible to carry on with them at all times, it comes from a fundamentally similar place: both make living in the supposedly nonliterary world into an ongoing game where numbers and letters and words and phrases are combined and split and reconfigured and exchanged, and where it's always only a matter of time before you win.

---

[5] Rachel Galvin's translation.

And, more than you might think, the day-to-day history of the Oulipo is just a lot of men and women being tickled by such victories. Mathews, the minutes from one monthly meeting read, was "pleased and proud to have immediately recognized that a comment from his granddaughter, *j'ai tellement de trucs dans le fond de mon sac—* 'I've got so much stuff in the bottom of my bag'—was an alexandrine. He is congratulated." (The following comment recorded is Monk's: "So the Oulipo is good for something after all!") After a non-Oulipo dinner one evening in Paris, Forte read aloud to me a lewd text message from his girlfriend, who was several bottles into a champagne tasting in Reims, and noted—not sheepishly, not to compensate for the lustiness, not for any other reason than that it added to the excitement of the message—that it was an alexandrine, too.

This sort of happy accident is not where oulipian creation always begins; far from it. But I want to stress that it's as good a starting point as any, that no generator is too small if you're willing to put in the effort. Look at Raymond Roussel, who took two sentences that differed by a couple of letters, bore down and used them to create entire hallucinatory worlds, and thereby demonstrated very clearly the only difference between a pun and a novel: work.[6]

Bear with me for a moment longer. It sounds paradoxical, but what I have in mind when I talk about "oulipian creation" refers not just to members of the Oulipo, nor just to writers at large, nor just to people who create any kind of appraisable art as a livelihood. It refers to anyone

---

[6] Also: opium.

who does anything creatively, even if it's nothing more active or tangible or performative than watching life go by. That is, even if you're not the sort of person who happens to know a lot of words that don't contain the letter E, even if you can't be bothered to spend the time that this one freaking *astrophysicist* finds to spend making perfect palindromes and transductions and syllabic sestinas, you can still pay enough attention to be a creative reader—of literature and of the world, in accordance with the hypothesis that the two are secretly the same thing. My point about the teachings of the Oulipo, the takeaway here for the blessed non-writers of the world, is that creative reading is no less noble, no less rewarding, no less potentially spectacular, than creative writing. To do either one well is simply to leave things more interesting than you found them.

300

◄◘►

Very well, then. Suppose that now you're empowered to read the world as though it were a book, perhaps even as a book in whose very authorship you are an active collaborator: does that mean you . . . *should?* Surely there are risks. For instance, can you get potential literature to stop shaping and formatting your thoughts once you've let it start?[7]

---

[7] See psychologist Abraham Maslow's law of the instrument: "It is tempting, if the only tool you have is a hammer, to treat everything as if it were a nail." The narrator of Donald Barthelme's 1964 story "Me and Miss Mandible," a former insurance claims adjuster, puts it more grimly: "After ten years of this one has a tendency to see the world

Does formal peculiarity eventually come to take precedence over the event or statement that hosts it? Is it dangerous to find greater consequence in Sarkozy's unintended prosodies than in his desire to redeem Franco-American relations? Might Mathews have been so hypnotized by the number of syllables in his granddaughter's remark that her bag was full of crap that he neglected to help her empty it? Can the paradox of liberation through constraint actually just wind up imprisoning you in a more pragmatic, mental, non-artistic way? Does my interest in the Oulipo bear out what is fascinating to me, or does it dictate it? Is potential literature, in practice, descriptive or prescriptive? Is a dictionary the record of a language or its rulebook? Is hell endothermic or exothermic?

I see no reason that the Oulipo shouldn't simultaneously be the expression of and the rationale behind what I find interesting and appealing and worthy of my time: that's what liking something enough to engage with it continually is all about. But then why, beyond the assurance of interpersonal harmony and the avoidance of acrimony, does the group insist that once an Oulipian means always an Oulipian? If in twenty years, after several works of patient, patent oulipian construction, I write a novel devoid of all structure or calculation, will you believe me when I tell you I composed it completely freehand? Will it matter?

This question affects the reader as well as the au-

---

as a vast junkyard, looking at a man and seeing only his (potentially) mangled parts, entering a house only to trace the path of the inevitable fire."

thor, be she an official member of the Oulipo or someone who dabbled in constrained writing in her callow youth and now has sudden difficulty dissociating herself from it. "When the constraint is perceptible, it puts a stamp of rationality on the resulting text, however eccentric or oracular the content," Australian scholar Chris Andrews writes. And "written by an Oulipian" is a perceptible constraint indeed—one over which the author has no control (short of resorting to pseudonymity, which the Oulipians clearly have no compunction about doing, although it's not as if any of them ever took on a pseudonym in order to write stuff that was *less* weird). If I write my constraint-free novel to convey what I feel is an important message, but you don't register it because you're distracted by the search for clues to my compositional secrets, aren't you cheating me? And if my unconstrained novel also just kind of blows, but you give me the benefit of the doubt because you assume it's built on structures that you'd like or at least respect if you just understood them, aren't I cheating you?

Think back to Albérès, the hapless critic who read all the way through *La Disparition* without noticing that the most common letter in the alphabet was missing. In calling Perec's effort a stilted and hazily political pseudonovel, he obviously missed the point, but he wasn't *wrong*. The book *is* stilted and hazily political, inconsistent even compared with other stilted and hazily political novels like Bulgakov's *Master and Margarita,* for the simple reason that it has an enormous handicap. In that episode, who cheated whom? In this game—especially once the stakes involve publishers and advances and readers and reviews,

rather than just you and the typo in your brunch menu—
who ever really wins?

—◄○►—

The Oulipo has no official answer beyond a pantomimed
shrug. It does not take itself so seriously, after all; it's a
group of more or less ordinary people who read and write
because it's what they like doing, who limit their compositional practices superficially because they believe it lib-
erates them creatively, and who are curious to see if the
results are worth telling anyone else about. If they're not,
what is lost?

    I ask that last question rhetorically, but I can still
think of a few ways to answer it: time, purpose, contact
with reality. To read the world as a book, whether or not
you intend to take notes in the margins, is to court a certain mania;[8] once you get entrenched in conspiracy-theorist
reader mode, it's hard to accept that a text is not constrained but just poorly written, that a shelf of books was
alphabetized not mischievously but neglectfully, that the
figure in the carpet is not a text at all. When you have a de-
coder ring, to paraphrase Maslow's adage, everything starts
to look encrypted. "And above all, I couldn't get rid of this

303

---

[8] Such as "referential mania," as Nabokov describes it in his wonderful 1946 story "Signs and Symbols": "Pebbles or stains or sun flecks
form patterns representing in some awful way messages which he
must intercept. Everything is a cipher and of everything he is the
theme. [. . .] He must always be on his guard and devote every minute
and module of life to the decoding of the undulation of things."

formula, which went round and round in my head like a stubborn refrain," Bénabou's narrator in *Dump This Book* says at one point: "*co-ded-thus-de-code-able-co-ded-thus-de-code-able-co-ded-thus-de-code-able . . .*"[9]

It would be dishonest for me to argue that the Oulipo doesn't attract and enable personalities with pattern-seeking neuroses; I can't deny that my own interest in potential literature originates in a place that, had things turned out differently, could well have made my life much unhappier. But things having turned out as they did, my neuroses having been attracted and ensnared and encouraged, I find it hard to be anything other than grateful for my affliction. My experience is not entirely like Mathews's, in that I did not suddenly feel welcomed into a fold that celebrated practices I had theretofore thought shameful. It's more accurate to say I discovered the Oulipo with an overwhelming sense of relief, welcomed the idea that literary language, instead of anything and everything else around me, could be the surface onto which I projected my obsessive-compulsive mental fidgetings. If I had been someone else, it might have been painting or history, puppetry or pornography, some other X to solve for; if I'd been lucky, it would have been one that already had an *ouvroir* on the case. As it turned out, I *was* lucky—not to find what I didn't know I was looking for, exactly, but to find the questions I didn't know I was asking.

---

[9] Steven Rendall's translation, although I have taken the liberty of changing to *de-code-able* what he left as *de-co-able,* presumably because writing the middle syllable as it is spelled normally would insinuate, misleadingly, that the story has something to do with cod.

questions and answers 2009

I n 1934, Marcel Duchamp gave his friend François Le Lionnais an inscribed copy of his *boîte verte*, a green felt-covered box filled with ninety-four elaborately printed pages of notes and studies toward the creepily iconic sculpture nicknamed *Le Grand Verre*, or *The Large Glass*. (The full title, Duchampian in its verbosity and a little bit Calvinian in its syntactic jaggedness, is *The Bride Stripped Bare by Her Bachelors, Even*.) When Le Lionnais was deported by the SS ten years later, the piece was confiscated along with most of the rest of his books and papers.[1] And then in 1966, strolling through the Moderna Museet in Stockholm while

---

[1] Which, when you think about it, means you have to give this guy even more credit for his gigantic library than you'd give to someone whose efforts at amassing books hadn't been disrupted by Nazi machinations.

there on UNESCO business, he spotted it again, dedication and all. He wrote to the curator, hoping to reclaim his personal copy in exchange for the replacement he had bought after the war. No response. Eventually Le Lionnais's original copy was auctioned off; when Bénabou traveled to Stockholm in 2007 to pursue the matter, accompanied by an official from the French embassy, the green box had disappeared and left no trace of its purchaser or present whereabouts.

It was only a matter of time before this little quagmire showed up in oulipian lore. I first heard about it from Olivier Salon, who mentioned it after visiting the *Grand Verre* in Philadelphia, and then someone alluded to it at a *jeudi* later that year; there is an elliptical mention of the affair in *Un certain disparate,* and a footnote about it in a letter on Braffort's website. But the affair didn't gain real momentum until Jacques Jouet decided—and why not—to bring Duchamp and his green box into the swirling snowglobe of the Hugo Vernier mystery, anchoring it forever after in the Oulipo's open-source creation saga.

―◄○►―

When we left our story, Roubaud had blown the Vernier myth wide open and made it clear that, er, nothing was really clear at all. In *Le Voyage d'hier,* he had set the oulipian train of thought on a slow track toward the conclusion that Vernier was at once Perec and Queneau and the Oulipo as a whole. It took about seven years, but finally, in 1999, a rash of sequels delved much further into the intrigue. A précis:

Le Tellier's *Voyage d'Hitler* proposes an explanation for the disappearance of the Vernier book, by way of a young German literature professor who discovers that Hitler had dispatched an entire "Hugo Gruppe" to recover it and expose the plagiarism behind the "universal pretension of French thought"—but that the uncannily literate Führer discovered, to his horror, that the German greats had ripped off Vernier's verses, too. Jouet's *Hinterreise* picks up where Le Tellier leaves off, in Hitler's bunker, and follows a young Russian literature professor as he traces the path of the Red Army soldiers who made off with the book. By the end of his volume, Jouet has implicated Mozart, Bach, and Schubert in an ongoing chain of plagiarism. Monk's *Voyage d'Hoover* introduces us to a young British literature professor who, over a few days in the United States with Dennis Borrade, manages to uncover some sordid details indeed about Shakespeare and, rather less surprisingly, J. Edgar Hoover.

The next few installments scatter the breadcrumbs farther afield: in *Le Voyage d'Arvers* (Arvers's Journey), Jacques Bens reveals that the famous nineteenth-century sonneteer Félix Arvers stole his masterpiece from a forgotten poet named Hugues Auvernier. (There is also a hot nun.) Michelle Grangaud's *Un Voyage divergent* (A Divergent Journey) consists of a correspondence between the narrator and a cousin who is off on an archaeological dig and has just discovered traces of a forgotten scribe named Eugopherniés. François Caradec's *Voyage du ver* (The Worm's Journey)—each B.O. copy of which has a tiny hole punched through the pages—is narrated by a worm living in the bookshelf at the Borrades' villa who, busily chewing his way through a library full of oulipian titles, meets the female worm of his dreams and learns that all this mystery boils down to a mere filing error: Hugo Vernier's name was actually Vernier Hugo. Later, in *Le Voyage des verres* (literally The Glasses' Journey; translated as "A Journey Amidst Glasses"), Mathews is approached by an operative named Parsifal III Bartlstand, who reveals that the CIA has been watching the Oulipo for some time. He offers to reveal some choice Vernier-related information, too, but Mathews declines, having long since tired of the whole business.

Meanwhile, one Reine Haugure, *soi-disant* secretary of the Association des Amis d'Hugo Vernier, summarizes the story to date and augments it with a whole lot of new-information-that-has-just-come-to-light; Mikhaïl Gorliouk, the protagonist of Jouet's *Hinterreise,* writes an impassioned letter to Jouet that brings Calvino into the mix. Then Forte—who was not even an Oulipian when he wrote *Le Voyage des rêves* (The Dream Journey)—finds a man who recalls an evening in New York where Mathews and Perec tried fruitlessly to co-opt Julio Cortázar for a collective novel project. After a lull in the series, *Le Voyage du Grand Verre* (The Large Glass's Journey) has Jouet learn from a friend in Burkina Faso that Mathews, growing up on the same New York street where Duchamp once lived, came into possession of the sole surviving copy of *Le Voyage d'hiver,* which had inspired his fellow Oulipian to produce one readymade we never saw: a vernier.[2] A response

---

[2] A vernier is, in English as in French, a small graduated scale used to subdivide measurements on sextants and barometers and such.

from Haugure called *Le Voyage d'H . . . Ver . . .* concludes
that none other than Henry James was influenced by Hugo
Vernier when he created the tight-lipped and enigmatic author in "The Figure in the Carpet," right down to the name:
HUGH VEREKER.

The story ends there for the moment, but you can
be sure we haven't heard the last of it. If the narrative
thread has gotten dispersed and unfocused, like a lazily
played game of exquisite corpse, the series serves a loftier
purpose in that it allows the Oulipo to imagine its own origins, its own relevance, on a fictional basis. You could call
the cycle a mythical counterpart to the *moments oulipiens,*
ongoing attempts by the members not only to tell themselves stories but to tell themselves *as* stories—only this
time they're doing it with their idols, their influences, the
ancestors they never knew. These tales are filled with young
literary types who have some privileged link to the intrigue
—a recently deceased uncle, a cousin on an archaeological
dig, a fortuitous visit from a CIA agent or a sexy she-worm
—that allows them to take hold of the whole story and explain what it means. The whole story being, in a more or
less literal sense, the workshop itself.

In college I argued that the cycle of stories was the
group's collective effort to work out the kinks in its relationship to Perec, both by redefining him to fit better into
its history and by redefining itself to better reflect the impact and legacy of his genius. At the time—Forte's was the
last installment—this might have been true; a few years
down the line, however, it reads as much more than that. It
is about Perec, for sure, what with all the half-buried references to his bibliography and background, the search for

309

answers disrupted by war, the endlessly embroiled implications about literal and artistic parentage—but it's also about what the workshop itself is, in the past, present, and future tenses. It's about anticipatory plagiarism as it really manifests itself in collaborative creation—the theory of influence, if you like, that Bayard faults the Oulipo for never elaborating. As Perec said of his ancestors, whose collective biography he always planned to write one day, "If I write their story, they will be my descendants."

The idea that Hugo Vernier is more than rhetorically the Oulipo's true founding father—an idea laid bare in large bold print in Roubaud's last *Voyage,* and also dramatized in weirdly cheesy fashion during a 2008 reading where, after Le Tellier read out Perec's story,[3] Vernier himself[4] made a cameo to read a short text—is convenient above all because, like Nicolas Bourbaki and Jean-Baptiste Botul and QB, Hugo Vernier never actually existed. If he's not real, nothing that can be surmised about him is authentically right or wrong. To tweak or overthrow what's already known, you have only to invent a revelation, a typo, a draft long lost but recently unearthed by a young literature professor or a handsome American archivist. History is infinitely malleable, so long as you can make your case be-

---

[3] The part about Degraël's dying thirty years later in a mental hospital got a big laugh from the audience, which was the first time it ever occurred to me that that image might be humorous.

[4] Vernier bears an uncanny resemblance to what Beaudouin would look like if she wore a three-piece suit, bushy mustache, and powdered white periwig.

lievable; in this way, Hugo Vernier is a lot like potential literature itself.

—◄○►—

The reason I've come back to Hugo Vernier is that the saga of his perpetually misplaced book of anticiplagiatory verse illustrates the importance of quest to the Oulipo. A good solid search, especially for something you'll probably never find, drives the plot forward both on and off the page. The less you know, the more you want to know. Hitchcock knew it as well as Homer did: get the audience invested in the pursuit of a puzzle piece, be it the key or the antidote or the identity of the dead man, and they'll follow you for as long as it remains missing. That's why it's so hard to write a satisfying ending: "solutions," Mathews says, "are nearly always disappointing."

311

To wit, the best oulipian stories—even more so than the best stories elsewhere—are about people looking hard for things that turn out not to be particularly significant after all. The content of the original book in Calvino's *Winter's night* is quickly forgotten, even as the fact of its existence keeps the plot going; the unifying peculiarity of the mysterious volume in Bénabou's *Dump This Book* has nothing, by the end, to do with the real story. So it goes for the philosopher's stone in Le Tellier's *Voleur de nostalgie,* the mysterious malady in Jouet's *Fins,* the phantom computer file in Roubaud and Garréta's *Eros mélancolique,* the treasure or inheritance or vengeance that motivates the characters of Mathews's novels to do the bizarre stuff they do.

So it goes for just about every dramatic incentive that moves Perec's fiction or pseudo-fiction along, from the crisis of the missing symbol in *La Disparition* to the elaborately self-effacing art project in *Life A User's Manual* to the meaning of truth in recollections about the past in *W or the Memory of Childhood.*

It is neither an accident nor a deficiency that none of these things are ever found, in a conventionally conclusive or rewarding sense, and that in some cases they may as well not even exist. Quest is another kind of scaffolding to the oulipian work, a less sturdy but more human kind than in the lipogram or the sonnet. Quest is what remains when the McGuffin turns out to be in another city or in a different book or on some other plane of existence—and so in the Oulipo, as in these stories, it is the act of seeking that defines the characters. They become who they are in searching for a solution, through the optimism and momentum of working toward it on their own terms, with the creative tools and interpretive resources at their disposal. The bigger the haystack, the better it is not to have a particular needle in mind. Think of the Oulipo, if you like, as a search party for those of us who don't know what we're looking for.

Like most others, that idea has already passed through the lens of Perec, who, in an essay called "Notes on What I'm Looking For," tries to answer the question of why he writes. He ends up mostly dodging it, dwelling instead on *how* he writes and what he wants to accomplish— to avoid ever writing the same kind of book twice, to fill a shelf at the BNF, to cross the entire field of literary possibility without ever meeting his own footsteps—but he concludes, in a touchingly helpless way, that the very question is one he can answer only by writing. Perec wrote to make sense of the world, and his insistent exploration of form and subject depended heavily on the idea that there was something obscure but crucially important to be found. His fascination with puzzles bespoke the same need: at the end of the day, even if you don't find the solution, even if there *is* no solution, believing in the possibility of one goes a very long way.

313

What appeal could puzzles possibly have to people who have lived through the most serious things the world can offer? Perhaps it's no safer to take for granted that a puzzle can be solved, in one way or in several, than it is to take for granted the simpler things about the world: that man is fundamentally good, that your way of life is stable and secure, that your interests will at some point dovetail with those of an invisible creator. The important difference is that a puzzle is still what you make of it, how you choose to handle and combine its pieces, no matter what you expect them to depict when they all come together. If death is the only way out of the maze, as Roubaud says one of the first Oulipians said, true liberation lies not in finding an impossible escape but in simply looking for it, because to seek is to be alive. The cleverest rats build themselves labyrinths of inexhaustible complexity, channel after subtle channel.

The question of why the Oulipo exists, I think, has to be answered twice. The men who founded it—most of whom took an active part in the Resistance to the Nazi invasion of Europe, and some of whom were profoundly, irreversibly marked by its consequences—came to their literary pursuits with a deeper sense of both the importance and the frivolity of what they were doing. Most of them were also 'Pataphysicians, meaning they were steeped in a sort of defensive glibness in the face of the world's cruelty, fully aware of the stakes of literature in such a context. (Duchamp's genius, vis-à-vis Adorno's oft-misquoted comment on the possibilities of art after Auschwitz, was to show that even if "after Auschwitz" couldn't be changed, "art" could.) There was an etched-in wariness to those early days, a disenchantment with the old certainties—a shadow of truth to Le Lionnais's claim, in the first Oulipo manifesto, that potential literature was "the most serious thing in the world. Q.E.D."

That subtext of coping shifted and diminished over time, but it took more than a generation. Perec's entire body of work can be (and usually is) read as an elaborate series of comings-to-terms with the loss of his parents in the war; Calvino's early writing, which bled through to his French period, was just as intimately familiar with the wages of Fascism, the idiocies of power. Their voices are more earnest and more innocent than those of the founders, but the search for the missing letter or the defective book continues to symbolize a much greater search: for a sense of meaning in a vacuum, for a sense of control in a world that reminds you every now and again that control is beyond your reach. For them in particular, the Oulipo was a way of finding power in what little they could hold on to: you can't change history *avec sa grande hache*[5]—all you can change is the way you put its pieces together.

The oulipian relationship to tragedy looks a lot different now. Even if much of Pastior's and Grangaud's writing originates in the same violence and dislocation that inspired Latis's *Organiste athée* or Le Lionnais's *Peinture à Dora,* it comes across as more personal, less generational, historically defanged—in large part because it now falls on ears much deafer to what that kind of hardship is like. It is easy to be moved, as I am, by *Some Thing Black,* written after the death of Roubaud's wife, or by the second movement of *Opéras-Minute,* written after the death of Forte's father; but the scope is smaller, more intimate, than it is in what Perec wrote about the loss of his parents. Even "Twin Towers," Monk's affecting three-dimensional memoriam to the attacks on New York in September 2001, is a response to an event rather than to a whole zeitgeist. The purpose of self-expression, the stability of history, the meaning of meaning itself—these are not questions the Oulipo asks much today.

And that's a good thing, of course, not least because it means there is less systematic brutality in the world, relatively speaking, that compels us to ask them. But in the place of those interrogations, what is at stake? What, besides the fundamentally self-reflexive research of how its own forms and ideals have evolved, does the Oulipo really accomplish and stand for? Seriously—with the accumulated

315

---

5 In *W,* Perec plays on the homophony between *hache* and the pronunciation of the letter H in French; that phrase thus means both "history with a capital H" and "history with its great axe."

weight of all the blank stares I have ever met while trying to explain this phenomenon and my interest therein—*why?*

(a) *No particular reason*
And clearly the joke's on you if you've read this far.

(b) *Because*
Potential literature is an affirmation of a very simple, very modern, terrifyingly crucial kind of certainty: that all questions can be answered if you search long enough. Somewhere deep down, a little deeper down now than it was fifty years ago, the Oulipo is nothing but an erudite little battery of tests designed to prove a few people's collective trust, hard-wired or hard-won, that all of our everyday meanings, our most profound truths, are parts of a puzzle that will not leave us with one piece shaped like a W and one hole shaped like an X.

That the Oulipo tests this hypothesis on literature, or, more precisely, on its constituent linguistic parts, is a strength rather than a weakness. Language is just as artificial as literature, probably more so—a diffuse and shape-shifting and ideally unstable system we invented a long time ago—but then the same can be said of most of the means we routinely and unthinkingly use to describe and deal with our surroundings. Queneau was not being silly when, in 1933, he praised Raymond Roussel for uniting the rationality of the poet with the madness of the mathematician: for anyone who takes comfort in a successful Ou-X-Pian experiment, all the questions worth asking about the universe are going to be phrased in the same way.

You can read the Oulipo's application of scientific

precision to aesthetic endeavors as a cynical gesture, as the distillation of absurdity, or you can admire the infradisciplinary cleverness behind the idea of joining two mutually exclusive puzzle-solving strategies and seeing what pans out. "Let us see what my psychological reaction is when I learn that writing is purely and simply a process of combination among given elements," Calvino wrote once. "Well, then, what I instinctively feel is a sense of relief, of security. The same sort of relief and sense of security that I feel every time I discover that a mess of vague and indeterminate lines turns out to be a precise geometric form."[6]

The key to the oulipian project, I think, lies in that inattention to disciplinary boundaries: the ability to take comfort in the certainty that every non-literary language act simply isn't literary *yet,* and moreover to find in it the same comfort that you do in the certainty that ten dimes make a dollar, that blue and yellow make green. The scary part, but the liberating part too, is that there's no greater truth, or at least none worth invoking, that isn't just as artificial as literature, just as mutable and self-justified and tautological as language. Science can explain the flood of light in a darkened room, but not why it matters, not why it feels like a miracle. Potential, in the Ou-X-Pian sense of the word, is just a way of chasing down and expressing that thing, whatever it is, that you're sure makes the world make sense.

For me, and for most of the people in this book, that thing is language. Potential literature is what we might

---

[6] William Weaver's translation.

call language in the hands of a crafty reader, the way potential music is sound to a crafty listener. Reading, no matter what you're reading, presupposes a belief in the potential of the text—to speak to you, enlighten you, stir your imagination or temporarily distract you—just as living, if it is to have any sense, presupposes a belief in the potential of your life. If that sounds corny, remember that the man who first articulated this idea this way made it through a concentration camp by reconstructing the world's most marvelous paintings in his mind. To live your life craftily, whether you read it as a labyrinth or a puzzle or simply a long combinatorial succession of evenings and mornings, is to move through it with the purpose and the security that come from knowing you hold the tools to give it shape and meaning.

ACKNOWLEDGMENTS

The research project that culminated in this book was possible first and foremost through the support of the Fulbright Commission, particularly Amy Tondu and Arnaud Roujou de Boubée. In turn, the Fulbright grant was possible thanks to the help of Thomas McDow, Linda De Laurentis, Marie-Hélène Girard, and Alyson Waters. The indulgences of Sabine Coron, Camille Bloomfield, and Abigail Lang were invaluable in facilitating my research and in legitimizing my very being in the eyes of the French government.

Thanks are evidently due to anyone and everyone who spoke with me for this project—not least the Oulipians themselves—but some sources of information, perspective, and good cheer who have not made it by name into the text merit mention: Frédéric Terrier and France Lebro, Benoît Richter, Coraline Soulier, Mireille Cardot, Claire Lesage, and Jean-Luc Joly.

I am grateful to those people who had little to do with the research itself but who offered me a steady lifeline to the world beyond it: Nina Holbrook, Nathaniel Motte, Annaïg Combe, Margery Arent Safir, Michelle Noteboom, the Sieglers, the not particularly aptonymous Hubert Silly, and KC Gleason. And I am conversely but equally grateful to everyone who has ever sent me a relevant (i.e., esoteric) book, link, or clipping on the grounds that they couldn't see how anyone besides me would appreciate it.

Thanks to Rami Levin, Warren Motte, Gabe Smedresman, Martin Glazier, Nate Preus, Jacqueline Ko, Abigail Baim-Lance, and Andi Mudd, who were willing to do constructive battle with the manuscript (or portions of it) back when it had twice as many footnotes. Thanks to Anna Stein for guiding said manuscript through the publishing jungle to its home at Harvard; thanks to John Kulka for making the manuscript into a book once it arrived, and to Maria Ascher and Kathryn Blatt for weeding out all its mistakes and inconsistencies so I wouldn't have to try convincing you they were intentional.

Thanks—lest it go unsaid—to the Levins, the Beckers, the Baims, the Maciels, and all combinations and variants thereof.

Finally, my enduring gratitude goes to Jean-Jacques Poucel and Anne Fadiman, without whose guidance, example, and friendship this book would forever have remained potential.

Dunn, Mark, 259
Durantaye, Leland de la, 83, 185

Eco, Umberto, 143, 194–195, 221
Edwards, Paul, 271–272, 274–275
Ɛ. *See under* Roubaud, Jacques
Eliot, Thomas Stearns, 46, 94–95
Enard, Mathias, 261
Eros mélancolique (Melancholy
    Eros). *See under* Garréta,
    Anne; Roubaud, Jacques
Esposito-Farèse, Gilles, 277, 300
Esthétique de l'Oulipo (Aesthetic
    of the Oulipo). *See under* Le
    Tellier, Hervé
Ethique simpliste (simplistic eth-
    ics), 61–62, 64, 66
Etienne, Luc, 56, 184–185, 212,
    216, 244, 265
Exercises in Style. See under Que-
    neau, Raymond

Facial hair, 4, 25, 27, 40, 87, 93, 99,
    111, 186, 310
Faulkner, William, 135, 214, 257
"Figure in the Carpet, The." *See
    under* James, Henry
Fillion, Odile. *See Oulipo dans les
    rues, L'*
Fins (Ends). *See under* Jouet,
    Jacques
Flarf, 141, 273, 285
Flaubert, Gustave, 184, 225
Form: evolution, 45–46, 57–62,

109–110; proprietary nature,
    54–55, 200, 288–290
Forte, Frédéric, 25, 37, 48, 53–55,
    68, 88, 94, 108, 197, 224, 225,
    299, 308; as formal experi-
    mentalist, 27, 45–47, 60, 99,
    104–105, 108–109, 111, 292–
    293; as libertine book-
    lender, 247; biographical
    details, 44–46; Faustian
    pigeonholeability, 231; not
    to be confused with basket-
    ball coach of same name,
    43; *Opéras-Minute*, 46, 315;
    Toulousain accent, 44, 53,
    65
Foucault, Michel, 174, 229, 254
Foulc, Thieri, 150, 267
Fournel, Paul, 26, 38, 63–64, 77,
    101–104, 109–110, 154–155,
    185–188, 203, 284; bio-
    graphical details, 186–187;
    duties discharged as presi-
    dent of the Oulipo, 16–17, 18,
    188, 237; duties discharged
    as secretary and/or slave of
    the Oulipo, 185, 207, 245,
    249; writings, 109–110, 187–
    188
Fourth-wall, breakings of, 10, 20,
    166, 194

Gallimard, 116, 117, 125, 145, 188,
    209

327

329

334